Up
Another
Notch

Institution Building at Mead

Books by William H. A. Carr

Up Another Notch
The Du Ponts of Delaware
The Emergence of Red China
JFK: A Complete Biography
The Basic Book of the Cat
The New Basic Book of the Cat
Perils: Named and Unnamed
From Three Cents a Week . . . .
Hollywood Tragedy
Beauty in the White House
Diplomatic Immunity
Those Fabulous Kennedy Women
Medical Examiner
Savage Scalpel
Black Gold
What Is Jack Parr Really Like?

This book was printed on the following papers:

TEXT: Mead Publishers Matte®, 55 lb., manufactured at Mead's
Publishing Paper mill, Escanaba, Michigan.

PHOTOGRAPHIC SECTION: Mead Offset® Enamel, 80 lb., manufactured
at Mead's Chillicothe, Ohio mill.

Up
Another
Notch

Institution Building at Mead

William H. A. Carr

McGraw-Hill Publishing Company
New York   St. Louis   San Francisco   Auckland   Bogotá
Caracas   Hamburg   Lisbon   London   Madrid
Mexico   Milan   Montreal   New Delhi   Oklahoma City
Paris   San Juan   São Paulo   Singapore
Sydney   Tokyo   Toronto

Library of Congress Cataloging-in-Publication Data

Carr, William H. A.
    Up another notch : institution building at Mead / William H. A.
Carr.
        p.   cm.
    Includes index.
    ISBN 0-07-010159-0
    1. Mead Corporation—Management.   2. Paper industry—United
States—Management.   3. Forest products industry—United States
—Management.   4. McSwiney, James W.   I. Title.
HD9829.M4C37   1989
338.7'6762'0973—dc19   89-30783
                                                        CIP

1234567890   DOC/DOC   8954321098

ISBN 0-07-010159-0

*The editors for this book were William A. Sabin and Barbara B.
Toniolo, the designer was Naomi Auerbach, and the production
supervisor was Suzanne Babeuf. It was set in ITC Garamond Light.
This book was composed by the McGraw-Hill Book Company
Professional and Reference Division composition unit.*

Printed and bound by R. R. Donnelley & Sons Company.

For more information about other McGraw-Hill materials,
call 1-800-2-MCGRAW in the United States. In other
countries, call your nearest McGraw-Hill office.

Contents

Preface

This is a book about corporate leadership—specifically the leadership of the Mead Corporation during the years from 1968 to 1982, when James W. McSwiney was head of the company.

It is a story of risk-taking, of building two massive new plants (at Escanaba, Michigan, and at Prince George, British Columbia) at a time when it seemed the Mead Corporation did not have the money for such costly—but ultimately profitable—ventures.

It is a story of willingness to fight for what was believed to be right, to defend the company against a hostile takeover attempt that became the "battle of the year" in American business—a battle that ended in victory for the Mead Corporation.

It is a story of a man who had the self-confidence to build what *Business Week* called "a prototype of the corporate board of the future"—a strong and independent outside board that represented the shareholder's interest with a steadfastness and determination that is more uncommon than it should be.

It is a story of a leader who felt himself responsible not only to his shareholders, but also to his employees, a man who tried new and unorthodox ways to enable the workers to participate more fully in the internal life of the company.

True leadership has always been difficult to define and frequently as difficult to find. There is nothing easy about leadership. As Peter F. Drucker once wrote in a brief essay in *The Wall Street Journal*, "The foundation of effective leadership is thinking through the organization's mission, defining it and establishing it, clearly and visibly." In Drucker's view, "Whether the compromise [the leader] makes with the constraints of reality—which may involve political, economic, financial, or people problems—is compatible with his mission and goals or leads away from them determines whether he is an effective leader."

Drucker said that the second measure of a leader is that he or she sees the leader's role as one of "responsiblity rather than as rank and privilege." As the person who is ultimately responsible, a true leader selects aides who are strong and able; the leader does not feel threatened by the excellence of others. He or she realizes that able people often are ambitious, but the risks that arise out of ambition are not as great as the damage that mediocrity can do.

Finally, Drucker wrote, an effective leader is able to earn the trust of his or her followers.

By all those criteria, McSwiney was a leader of the first rank.

Bergen Evans has said, "There is no necessary connection between the desire to lead and the ability to lead, and even less to the ability to lead somewhere that will be to the advantage of the led." McSwiney had the ability, as well as the desire, to lead, and those who followed his leadership benefited from it.

He was not without flaws. He made mistakes from time to time. But he provided strong leadership to the Mead Corporation that enabled it to expand on a vast scale, to become a major factor in the forest products industry and the information industry.

The story of McSwiney, and especially of his years at the helm of the Mead Corporation, contains many lessons for anyone interested in business management. During his years, Mead had to cope with the problems of acquisitions, antitrust issues, corporate governance, inflation, recession, and human relations.

It is a story that is not likely to be repeated. McSwiney was probably the last of the self-made corporate leaders. There will be others who, lacking a college education, still make their fortunes in business, but they will have to do so by starting their own companies, not by rising through the ranks of an established organization as McSwiney did. Although it was not his intent, by bringing professional management to Mead, he blocked the way for young men and women to gain positions and advancement in the corporation unless they had earned the educational credentials that he himself did not possess when he went to work for Mead over half a century ago.

But such a change was inevitable given the enormous transformation of American society in the last half of the twentieth century. In a sense, the McSwiney story is in microcosm the story of American industry as it came of age.

As our society is challenged by changing economic and social conditions, some of the lessons to be drawn from this tale may find new applications

Acknowledgments

To a significant degree, this book is based on materials gathered by William J. Ahlfeld and Carl Rieser, augmented by interviews and other research by the present author.

An earlier book about the Mead Corporation, *In Quiet Ways*, privately published in 1970, also proved helpful in providing information on earlier years of the company.

Alan Wiseman, of the Washington law firm of Howrey & Simon, provided a manuscript that served as the basis for much of Chapter 13, "Antitrust: The Fight for Fairness." Wiseman himself played an important part in that fight.

The resources of Nexis, Mead Data Central's computer-assisted research for news, business, and other fields of activity, were drawn upon for some of the research.

Kristin Vonnegut and Betsy Crowell were extremely helpful in the research and the preparation of the manuscript for publication.

Brooks Boeke Carr, the wife of the author, played a major role in helping to bring this book into being.

Nevertheless, the author alone is responsible for the text, which, he hopes, gives a fair representation of what life was like in a major U.S. corporation during a particularly eventful period of its existence.

Up
Another
Notch

Institution Building at Mead

JAMES W. McSWINEY

One

The Boy in the Mill

In 1978 an executive of the Mead Corporation, one of the largest U.S. companies, was talking to a Harvard Business School research assistant about James W. McSwiney, then the company's chairman of the board of directors. "He's a powerful man," the executive said, "magnetic, very difficult to say no to, even when you know you should say no."

It was an attitude that many people had toward McSwiney during the half century that he was part of Mead. But others found they could debate issues with him, disagree with him, stand up to him, without suffering any harm to their careers—indeed, there were a good many who owed their advancement in the company to McSwiney's respect for their independence.

Nevertheless, both attitudes were correct. Like most people, McSwiney was full of contradictions. Although he had only a high school education—perhaps because of it—it was he who put professional management concepts to work in his company. Two of the most notable of his characteristics were his insatiable hunger for knowledge and the breadth of his interests. In many ways he was the epitome of the organization man, but he felt very strongly that "organizations tend to blur reality and stifle originality." In some ways he was a bit old fashioned and quite conventional, but he warned "we must be willing to be a little nontraditional and a little unconventional if we are to build and maintain an organization that can deal with dynamic issues and processes."

He was a workaholic who often spent 16 hours a day at his work, but he was given to saying that "one problem of workaholics is that they don't take time to reflect." Nevertheless he reflected a great deal on himself, his company, the people around him, and the world in which he did business.

In a society that sets a premium on certainty and precision, McSwiney said things like this: "One of the greatest gifts a chief executive officer can have is a tolerance for ambiguity and a willingness to build an organization that accepts ambiguity. Otherwise, you'll have an organization that only does things it can be certain about."

He played an important role in helping to develop new concepts in management, including employee participation, the separation of powers of the chair and chief executive officer, and the function, scope, and duties of the board of directors and its committees, thus furthering professional management, but he himself worked best on an intuitive basis. As chief executive officer, he was larger than life, a figure of towering strength and energy, but he was wholly dedicated to the concept of the "leader as servant" and he practiced what he preached, giving leadership and vision to his organization. A clearly ambitious man, he nevertheless rejected the office of president when it was first offered to him, asking that it be given to another person. He took on unions in several prolonged strikes, but he said that under other circumstances he probably would have joined a union. Comfortable in the exercise of authority, he nevertheless shared it willingly with his directors and, through a successful experiment in limited self-management, with his employees. When environmentalists first criticized the paper industry for polluting the atmosphere, he instinctively rejected their protests, but he soon reversed himself and played a significant part, through a team led by Peter E. Wrist, in helping to improve conditions. He was driven to compete, but his ultimate competition was with himself. Work was his life, and he admired hard work probably more than any other trait among his associates, but he had empathy and compassion for the people he worked with. He was stubborn to a fault, but he loved to hear about new ideas, and he was willing to be persuaded. He made mistakes in his leadership of Mead, but he also led it into dramatically new and ultimately profitable fields. An eminently practical person, he gave the people of his company a sense of mission and purpose, as a true leader can. He was thoughtful, but he could act quickly and decisively. He had a good sense of humor and was fun to be with. He was the kind of man that both men and women like.

He had a theory about how to gauge how others felt about anyone. "If I want to know what A thinks about B," he said, "I say something good about B, and then I wait and start counting mentally. If it takes A 15 seconds to react by saying something about B, I know A has reservations about B."

When McSwiney went to work for Mead in 1934, sales totaled $12,277,923 and profits amounted to $31,436 after taxes. In 1968, the first year that McSwiney was president and chief executive officer of Mead, the company reported net earnings of $31,572,000 on net sales of $897,591,000. In 1981, the last full year of his tenure as chairman of the board, Mead reported net earnings of $106,900,000 on net sales of $2,899,700,000. In 1981 the return on net assets was 7.2 percent and the return on equity was 12.0 percent, which compares with 12.2 percent and 17.0 percent, respectively, for 1978, a year in which Mead was No. 1 among the top ten in the forest products industry. Neither RONA nor ROE had been reported 13 years earlier. During 1981 Mead's total assets surpassed $2 billion for the first time, having doubled in seven years. The company was in the midst of a five-year, $1.5 billion capital program "to build a new and higher earnings base."

When he retired from Mead, he had been working for the company for 50 years. He was honored as an industry leader, a civic leader, a builder, a creator. He had been successful as very few are successful. He had worked his way to the top, and he had done so largely on his terms.

It is not likely that anyone in McEwen, Tennessee, would have expected such good fortune.

McEwen is a town of less than 1300 in Humphreys County, about 57 miles west of Nashville. It was largely settled by Irish railroad workers who helped to build the Nashville, Chattanooga & St. Louis Railway—later bought by the Louisville & Nashville Railroad.

There, James Wilmer McSwiney—who was always, inevitably, to be called "Mac" by his friends—was born on November 13, 1915. The McSwiney family goes back a long way in Irish history, and apparently Scottish, too. The "Mc" meant "son of." The Gaelic of the surname proper is said to be "Suibhne," meaning "well followed." It is believed that the McSwineys were "battle-ax chieftains" in County Donegal, but by the time Mac's forebears came to America in the 1840s, the family had been living for many years in County Cork. Mac's grandfather told him that Terence MacSwiney was a first cousin. Terence MacSwiney, a leader of the 1916 Easter Uprising in Dublin and onetime lord mayor of Cork, became a cause celebre in 1920 when he died during a hunger strike after being imprisoned by the British in London. Mac's grandfather visited Terence's sister, Mary, when she visited the United States.

Mac's great-grandfather left Ireland because his family was determined that he should enter the priesthood, and he was even more determined that he would not become a cleric. He settled in Pennsylvania, where he went to work for a railroad. His son moved to Tennessee to become a railroad bridge superintendent. "A fine-looking man," as his grandson remembered him, Grandfather McSwiney used to let the little boy sit on his lap and play with his gold watch and the gold coins in his pockets. McSwiney's father, James Speedy McSwiney, a carpenter for the railroad, later became supervisor of a construction crew. He married a local girl, Delia Margaret Conroy. James McSwiney was their first child. When the baby was six months old, the family moved to Nashville, Tennessee. Two other boys, Eugene and Benjamin, were born to the couple.

In Ireland the McSwineys had been Roman Catholics. Delia McSwiney's family, the Conroys, had settled in McEwen by 1857 and they were Roman Catholics too. Although the Conroy family remained Catholic, James McSwiney's mother converted to Protestantism when she married, and the boys were raised as Methodists. Every Sunday their mother took them to church and to Sunday School. There was a regular Wednesday prayer meeting, too, but as he grew older Wednesday night "was a time to increase one's awareness of the opposite sex," Mac recalled many years later.

When McSwiney was about 12, his mother died of pneumonia. Her death was a staggering blow. His father was a stern and distant man who would lock his eldest son out for the night if he were not home for the 10 p.m. curfew. The father had difficulty demonstrating affection to his family. In later years McSwiney said he had the same problem, except for his grandchildren. "Somehow it is easy and natural to display my feelings for my grandchildren," he said. "Otherwise I have to rely to a great extent on my belief that my family knows I care for them deeply. My actions and care have always been better than my words. Outside my family I seem to do better." As a business leader, Mac often would put his arm around the shoulder of an associate because he felt that, "by touching, you can communicate more than in any other way."

His relationship with his father may have been a factor in forming another McSwiney characteristic: "It is difficult for me to accept a compliment or a gift. I wonder if I am deserving. It's much easier for me to give than to receive."

The elder McSwiney tended to see things in black and white simplicity. He not only advocated basic principles, but also practiced them. "No way in the world would he take advantage of anyone," his son remembered years later.

"My father always underestimated his own ability," Mac once said. "He was educated in a one-room schoolhouse, but he could do trigonometry and calculus. He refused several promotions, but when he was 65 — he worked until he was 72 — he did accept a promotion. He said then, 'It's too late to worry about a mistake now.'

"He always gave me the feeling that I wasn't all that he would have me be. 'You're not the brightest kid on the block, but you have average or better intelligence,' he told me. 'Success depends on applying yourself. Work 10 percent harder or 10 percent longer than those around you, and the odds are that you'll be able to match or exceed them.'"

Even as a child, McSwiney took his father's counsel to heart. He was highly competitive; even in the second or third grade he wanted to beat everyone else in class. Like most highly competitive people, he only competed in activities at which he knew he was good.

One of the things he was clearly good at was learning. He did so well in school that he was permitted to skip the fifth grade.

As a small boy, he did all the things that most of the other kids were doing, like saving string, making it into a ball, and wrapping it in "tire tape" to make a baseball, with which he and his friends played "one-eyed cat." Despite his friends, he often felt lonely. On the way to high school, it was not unusual for him to stop at a poolroom nearby. In the world of the 1980s, that sounds racier than it was in a Southern city in the 1920s, when pool rooms were a relatively innocuous center of masculine recreation. Mac was always more comfortable with older people than with his own age group.

There were favorite adults in young McSwiney's life—his father's housekeeper, his Aunt Nellie, an uncle who loved to read and was so good at solving *The New York Times* crossword puzzles that he began making up his own puzzles between runs in the mail car between Louisville and Nashville.

After his mother died, Mac attended summer school each year because "It was better to keep busy that way than to stay around the house." As a result of the summer classes, young McSwiney was able to graduate from high school at the age of 15, in 1931.

College was not even a consideration. In those days, a relatively small proportion of high school graduates went on to college, compared with today's graduates. In 1932, for example, a total of 138,063 Bachelor's degrees were granted in the entire country, compared with nearly 1 million in 1981–1982. Moreover, college was not part of the world in which the elder McSwiney lived. "I was not conditioned at home with the expectation of going to college," Mac has said. He added that his father felt he had carried out his responsibilities by seeing his son through high school.

It was an understandable attitude, given the times, for the McSwineys were managing to get along when many other people weren't. "We were never hungry," Mac said, "and Dad had a few dollars put aside—a lot of people didn't in those days. But it wasn't a lot of money, and there were no extras around."

It was, in fact, close to the depth of the Depression. Some 2300 banks collapsed that year and people were so hard up that even bootleg liquor sales fell off. (Prohibition was still in force.) One of the hit songs of the day was "Smile, Darn Ya, Smile," but few Americans had much to smile about. In 1931 the U.S. population was 90,710,000, the labor force was 50,680,000, and the unemployed numbered more than 10 million, or some 20 percent of the labor force. Unemployment for them and the fear of losing jobs for millions of others created a general demoralization. Millions of businesses, large and small, failed and banks and insurance companies were foreclosing on farms in every state.

As Peter F. Drucker once wrote, "Depression shows man as a senseless cog in a senselessly whirling machine which is beyond human understanding and has ceased to serve any purpose but its own." Many people felt themselves at the mercy of forces with which they could not cope, and they turned to socialism or fascism or mysticism or any of the thousands of other movements that seemed to offer an anchor against the tidal waves sweeping the economy.

As soon as he was out of high school, young McSwiney left home and went to live with his Aunt Nellie. His father took the move badly. Feeling rejected, he sometimes wouldn't speak to his eldest son or let his brothers accept Mac's gifts at Christmas. For his part, Mac never rejected his father and later established a good rapport with him that continued until the father's death.

Given the times, Mac was lucky to get a job in a drug store, making deliveries on the store's bicycle and working behind the soda fountain. After a while he became friendly with the branch manager of a bank where he hoped to get a job. He also met some men who lived in a boarding house next to his aunt's house. They worked at a Mead mill but told him they thought there were no jobs to be had there. Nevertheless, he borrowed a bike—probably from the drug store—and pedalled to the mill. There he was told that there were no openings at the moment, but to come back in two or three months when they might need someone for a new laboratory.

Shortly before the first of July, 1934, the neighborhood bank manager knocked on his door and said he knew of two job opportunities for Mac, if he was interested. One job opening was at the bank branch, the other was as an assistant in a laboratory that was being organized at the Nashville plant of Mead. Overwhelmed and baffled, McSwiney asked the bank manager what he should do.

"Talk to Mead," the bank manager said, "and then we can talk if you want to."

When Mac talked to Mead, he concluded he could earn around $18 to $20 per week. The bank job paid about $12 a week, with a promise of $15 to $18 in several years. That settled it: McSwiney went to work for Mead on July 1, 1934.

The mill, which manufactured .009 corrugated medium (as this form of paperboard is called in the paper business), had been owned by the Teas family of Nashville, Tennessee, who had recently sold it to Mead. The new owners installed a small control laboratory run by Eldred Tweed, a young chemical engineer. Under the new management, the mill became successful and remained so for many years, largely because chestnut leached chips purchased from the Teas's extract plant provided cellulose fiber at something around $2 or less per ton of finished product. In the mid-1950s the mill was finally closed and the property sold. To Mac it was a sad but sound decision.

In 1934, however, it was a busy place, especially for the new lab assistant. It was Mac's duty to go through the mill, picking up random samples from the cooking, refining, screening, paper formation, and drying stages. He also collected samples of water fed to the coal-fired boilers. In the course of his work, he became fascinated with the mill's operation and the relationship of the tests he was making to the ultimate quality and production of paperboard. An important phase of the testing was the separation of pulp fibers from the water and the subsequent examination of the residue. The residue was then dried to a predetermined level to help identify potential strength characteristics of the finished sheet.

It was interesting work for young McSwiney and it helped shape his lifelong interest in the technical details of papermaking. But a wholly different kind of activity laid the groundwork for his later rise through the ranks. That was his election as treasurer of a newly formed federal credit union at the mill. In later years he came to feel that luck—exemplified by that event and by others in his career—plays a major role in the lives of all people. "The world is full of talented people unfavored by chance," he once said. He was talented, but he was also lucky.

It could not have seemed good luck at first. When he filled out the appropriate forms and mailed them to Washington, he got a letter back that said, in effect, "Do you know anything about accounting?" He didn't, so he enrolled in an accounting correspondence course.

Over the next two or three years he became quite proficient in accounting, and the knowledge served him increasingly well throughout his entire career.

In the 1937 Mead annual report, there is a discussion of credit unions and other employee benefits, including group life insurance and health and accident insurance, provided by the company. Although commonplace today, such benefits were rare in the 1930s. The 1937 annual report, the first to discuss employee relations, emphasizes the hourly wage rates that the company paid, which it said "compare favorably with those paid by other employers for similar classes of work." That year the federal Wage and Hours Act, championed by Mead's chief executive officer, George H. Mead, had been passed by Congress and signed by President Franklin D. Roosevelt.

Mead did pay well for those days, but the recession of 1937, just as the nation seemed to be starting to pull out of the Depression, hurt the paper business as well as the rest of the economy and Mead workers suffered too. For a time, McSwiney worked only every other week, and in later years he remembered averaging about $11.32 every two weeks during that period.

There were times when the bank job that he had turned down must have looked very inviting. But after a half year of only part-time work, Mac was told to begin reporting for work on a full-time basis again.

After a time he was promoted to shipping clerk, at $20 a week, but two months later business again sagged and everyone had to take a 10 percent pay cut. McSwiney was back to $18 a week.

Young McSwiney's ability with numbers and his inexhaustible energy now caught the attention of the plant manager, Thomas W. Fernald, a New Englander and a graduate of the Massachusetts Institute of Technology. Tough and demanding, Fernald became one of four major influences in Mac's adult life. From an affluent background, well educated, Fernald had the compassion, the insight, and the empathy to see how much potential there was in the young Tennessean. "He took a liking to me," McSwiney said in later years. "He became like a father to me."

Fernald brought Mac into the business office and put him to work, first on the payroll and later on the plant accounts. But the numbers were not real to McSwiney unless they were related to the mill activities, so he spent a lot of time getting to know every part of the mill.

"I'd go out into the mill every day to learn more about the operations and do the books later," he said. "I learned a great deal about the operations. I knew the nuts and bolts and how they related to cost accounting, a technique that was just coming into vogue."

His efforts did not always make him popular with management. At one point, the weight of .009 semi-chemical corrugating dropped from 32 pounds per thousand square feet to 26 pounds, with no change in the price per ton. McSwiney noted that the production cost did not alter proportionally per square foot because it took longer to process a ton of the lighter-weight product. The young accountant ran up some formulas to reflect the increased cost per ton. "I took my results over to management and tried to sell them on my idea," he recalled. "They were nice but I think they really thought I was just a brash kid."

But Fernald was increasingly impressed with the young man. When a problem arose at the company's Harriman, Tennessee, mill — the office manager had been kiting checks — Fernald, who was now in charge of the .009 corrugated paperboard division, gave Mac a $2 raise, the title of "assistant office manager," and the job of straightening out the mess.

With his career now showing some promise, McSwiney talked Jewell Bellar into marrying him. She was literally the girl next door; her father had built a house next to the home of the Mashburns, a family who agreed to let Mac live with them and their four children when it was time for him to leave Aunt Nellie's home. Jewell was very pretty and Mac was a handsome man — six feet tall, 126 pounds, with blue eyes and blond hair. They made a charming couple. On December 14, 1940, they were married in Nashville.

McSwiney, then 25, told his bride, "I am going to work hard enough to be a vice president of Mead by the time I'm 35, and I expect to make it."

When he finally was promoted to vice president, at the age of 45, she told him, "You only missed it by 10 years."

Two

George Mead
and His Company

To understand McSwiney, it is necessary to have a feel for the kind of company of which he hoped to become vice president, for the Mead company was not an ordinary business enterprise. It had a well-established reputation as a highly ethical company that manufactured the finest products and cared deeply about its responsibilities to its employees and the community as a whole.

The Mead company dated back to 1846, when Daniel E. Mead joined some friends in establishing Ellis, Chafflin & Company in Dayton, Ohio. Mead came from an old New England family that had moved west, first to Cooperstown, New York, and then to Meadville, Pennsylvania. Daniel Mead continued west until he got to Dayton, Ohio, in 1841, and there he settled down for good, working at first as a bookkeeper, and later a partner, in a hardware store. There were two paper mills in Dayton, which then had a population upward of 7000. The two paper mills had some machinery, but they used old hand presses to transform pulp into paper. More up to date, Ellis, Chafflin & Company's mill used machinery to make paper.

In 1856 Mead bought out his partners and, with a friend from Philadelphia, organized a new company—Weston and Mead. Four years later the names were reversed to Mead and Weston for reasons one can only speculate about after all these years. Six years after that the firm became Mead and Nixon. The business side of the company was handled by Mead, the paper-making by Nixon. In the depression that followed the Panic of 1873, the company was hit harder than it should have been, or so Daniel Mead is said to have believed. Apparently he laid the blame on Nixon's conservatism in refusing to adapt to more modern methods of paper-making, including the use of wood pulp to replace or supplement rag pulp. At any rate, in 1881 Mead bought out Nixon and reorganized the firm as the Mead Paper Company, with an initial capital of $150,000 and total assets of $393,882.09. Mead rebuilt the mill and the company enjoyed continuing profitability—so much so that in 1890 Mead was able to buy a second paper company in Chillicothe, the first step in an expansion program that has continued to the present.

A year later Daniel Mead died. His eldest son, Charles A. Mead, who was executor of his estate, was also his successor as president of the company. According to Herrymon Maurer Hodgson, a family chronicler, Charles Mead "was in effect an absentee owner," even though he lived in Dayton. It is not surprising, therefore, that the fortunes of the Mead company began to decline rapidly. By 1904 matters had reached such a state that a bank went to court and forced the company to accept a trusteeship. "Thus a company created and nourished over a 45-year period by one generation of capable men of business collapsed and came close to bankruptcy after little more than a decade of second-generation mismanagement," Maurer pointed out.

But a new generation, in the form of George Houk Mead, a nephew of Charles, now came to the rescue. George Mead was only 27 years old in 1905, but a bankers' committee asked him to take over the management of a reorganized firm, which would now be called the Mead Pulp and Paper Company. Favoritism played no part in the bankers' decision. George Mead had already shown that he was a rather remarkable person.

Having completed high school in two years, George Mead had entered Hobart College, at Geneva, New York, at the age of 15. It took him just three years to earn his Bachelor of Law degree with high honors, which he received in 1897.

"I then came back to Dayton," he subsequently recalled, "and started to work as a draftsman in the machine shop of W.P. Callahan &

Company on the first day of July, thinking I was going into either engineering or architecture. During the summer the Mead Paper Company was rebuilding its mill on Front Street between Second and First Streets. I usually carried my lunch, and during the noon hour after eating lunch in the drafting room where I was working, I would walk up there and watch this construction. By the end of the summer, I had determined I was going to follow engineering rather than architecture, and I thought I would like to get a job and try working with my hands. So, without saying anything to my father, with whom I was living and who was vice president of the paper company (there were only my father and myself; I was an only child and my mother had died in my senior year in college), I asked the superintendent for a job in starting this paper machine which had just been installed....The superintendent gave me a job on the paper machine as a roll boy on the night shift the first week in September. Some of the other male members of the family had taken similar jobs and lasted just one week, and the superintendent, who was very definite in his thinking, thought that was the quickest way to get rid of the new applicant, but to his great surprise I appeared on the morning of the second week for work and continued through the next 12 months, working 13-hour nights and 11-hour days. On Saturday nights, we worked from 4:30 in the afternoon until 10:30 Sunday morning, which made for a pretty lengthy work week."

To make matters worse, for three months the other workers would not speak with him because he was a Mead. Eventually he won acceptance and came to know everyone who worked in the mill. The experience affected him permanently; for the rest of his life he showed an understanding of the problems of blue-collar people and a concern for their welfare that was unusual for a business leader of his generation. During that year George Mead decided he wanted to spend his life in the paper business. He went to the Massachusetts Institute of Technology, and after two years, at the age of 22, received his Bachelor of Science degree in Chemical Engineering, having taken 35 hours of instruction in his first year and 36 the second.

After graduation, Mead took a job with a new company in Boston, the Cellulose Products Company, where one of his assignments was to develop a process for manufacturing "artificial silk"—rayon. After a year, the company was liquidated, but its founder organized a second company, this time in Philadelphia, called the General Artificial Silk Company. While the new company was being set up, back in Ohio the bankers' committee asked him to take over operation of the Mead company. He declined, but he did, at the committee's request, spend several months in Chillicothe setting up a laboratory and improving the pulp mill operation. Then he got word from Philadelphia that developments there were going much more slowly than had been expected. In the end he spent 12 months in Chillicothe as chemist and pulp mill floor manager. In six months he turned a pulp mill loss of $9000 into a profit of more than $4000.

Finally Mead went to Philadelphia, where he spent two years as general manager of the rayon company. In 1905, when the president and the largest stockholder quarreled and decided to liquidate General Artificial Silk and set up two new, competing companies, Mead decided he had had enough. He was now ready to listen to the Ohio bankers, who were again asking him to come back and run the Mead company. If he didn't, they said, it would be sold.

"I was finally persuaded to undertake the reorganization of the Mead Paper Company," Mead said, "first because of the desire to protect the Mead name in the communities of Chillicothe and Dayton, and secondly, because my grandfather in a codicil to his will had stated that his estate, which included several equally important investments in addition to the paper company, should consider the paper company first in the protection of its business. The trustees of the estate were, therefore, to use the credit of the entire holding for the benefit of the paper company."

When he took over its management, the company was falling apart, and its dilapidated buildings and equipment were too. For two years Mead worked in Chillicothe, taking time out only for food and sleep. He was chemist, floor manager, policymaker, chief financial officer, and almost everything else. Somehow he managed. Somehow things got done. More than that: Somehow things improved. By 1908 production was in good shape, but sales were not.

"I found," he said, "that in our Mead company we had spent six months' time trying to save 50 cents a ton in the manufacture of paper, and our sales manager would sit at the telephone and give away a dollar a ton in order to get an order. I couldn't quite understand the economics of that....So I decided to learn merchandising."

The Mead company had sold its Dayton mill, but it still maintained a small office there, which constituted its headquarters. In 1907 George Mead moved back to Dayton from Chillicothe and began operating out of the Dayton office. He made a study of the merchandising methods of other paper companies. Then he began making the rounds of customers and prospective customers, selling not price but quality. And his emphasis was on volume sales. Mead turned out to be a natural salesperson. One of his biggest triumphs was getting the Crowell Publishing Company, a major magazine house, to sign a Mead contract.

In 1910 George Mead's success was recognized formally when he was elected president of the company. A year later the United States government worked out a tariff agreement with Canada under which pulp and newsprint could be imported to the United States duty-free. As a result, less than a year later many new paper companies with Canadian operations had been established. An uncle, Harry Talbott, who had connections with Canadian and British interests, told Mead that his associates had acquired two pulp mills. They wanted the Mead company to run the mills. Mead and his uncle both felt the undertaking might jeopardize the Mead company, so, with the approval of Mead's board of directors, Mead and Harry Talbott undertook the project as a separate venture under the name of the Lake Superior Paper Company.

Mead had already been selling white paper; now he was selling newsprint, too. A few years later the British backers of the Lake Superior company merged it with two other mills to form a new organization, the Spanish River Company, and he ran that as well, as president. He took over the sales of the Abitibi Company, which had built a mill near the Spanish River properties. By 1916, George Mead represented a powerful group of newsprint producers. He formed a U.S. sales organization for Canadian newsprint and called it the G. H. Mead Company. It had headquarters in Dayton, but was separate from the Mead paper company, as well as from the Canadian companies. In its first year of business, the G. H. Mead Company sold one-fourth of all the Canadian newsprint marketed in the U.S. By agreement with his Canadian partners, George Mead spent half his working time on his Canadian interests and half on Mead.

For some time, a considerable part of his free time had been spent with a first cousin, Elsie Louise Talbott. On November 22, 1914, they were married in the chapel of the Westover School in Connecticut, which she had attended. Their marriage, which was, by all accounts, very happy—she became her husband's closest friend and confidante—produced, among other things, six children: Elsie Louise, born September 6, 1915; George, Jr., August 3, 1917; Harry Talbott, October 16, 1918; Nelson Strobridge, October 28, 1921; Katherine T., October 12, 1924; and Marianna H., March 28, 1930.

As George and Elsie's family grew, so did his business interests. He moved into the southern U.S. paper industry, in 1916, by taking a partnership position in the Kingsport Pulp Corporation, in Kingsport, Tennessee. The Kingsport company was trying to use the soda pulping process to convert waste chestnut fiber into white paper. The virtue of this process was that the raw material was available at very low cost. The process ultimately proved profitless and the mill switched over to hardwoods indigenous to the region.

The war then being fought in Europe had opened new markets to American business interests, including the paper industry, and production boomed. But after the United States entered the war in 1917, Mead, like other paper producers, found it difficult to obtain fuel, raw materials, and labor for its mills.

In 1916 labor throughout the nation was demanding that the work day be shortened from the 10 or more hours that was common to 8 hours. Mead was one of the first companies in its industry to go to a three-shift day. Mead also introduced other employee benefits, including a bonus plan based on the company's earnings and an employee stock-purchase plan.

There were vigorous attempts by unions to organize the paper industry at the end of World War I. George Mead wasn't happy about his employees joining a union. To be sure, he was used to dealing with unions because some of his Canadian operations were unionized.

"When I went to Canada," he once said, "we found unions existing and we had no inclination to make a change. It never occurred to me to say that I thought the situation was all wrong, and that we were opposed to unionism, and that we would have to eliminate them immediately or that I would not have anything to do with the operation of the newsprint business." In fact, he felt his experiences with the Canadian unions had been "very satisfactory."

But those unions didn't represent employees of the Mead company, of whom he took a very paternalistic view. In later years, he told the floor managers' club of the Chillicothe plant, "I have always thought that it was proper for people to form an organization to combat … the grasping hand of the capitalist who is trying to crush Labor. When people can come together as we do, and have our own cooperative spirit, our own union of thought, and our own shoulder-to-shoulder idea of discussing matters, there is no necessity to pay out money to a group of people in New York, Chicago, or Cleveland to keep them engaged throughout the year to come down and negotiate with us for our own welfare. We can do that ourselves and save that money."

It was not mere rhetoric. In 1919 George Mead went to work improving working conditions in his company. He had set up an informal shop council in 1905. This now became a formal structure within the company, consisting of a 16-person committee, of which 8 were chosen by management and 8 were elected by employees. It was empowered to handle grievances and set working conditions. A pension plan was established; employees were given paid vacations; and accident and health insurance were provided—all highly unusual employee benefits until after World War II. The company helped to build a hospital in Chillicothe and also installed food and recreational facilities, which in time were turned over to the employees to operate.

The postwar depression of 1921 hit Mead just as it had launched the largest expansion in its history. "In perhaps 50 years of industrial life in America, perhaps in the entire history of the country," George Mead said in 1922, "there has never been a year quite so severe in industrial and financial affairs as the year past.…The unfortunate executive of a company is called upon to do many things that do not ordinarily come his way. I have been compelled to spend many nights and many days traveling in an effort to do my part toward keeping the wheels turning." Keep them turning he did: In 1921 Mead was the only paper company to show a profit.

Nevertheless, there had been a time, during that financial crisis, when the company seemed on the point of running out of cash. George Mead turned to two friends for help. Each made a $25,000 loan to help tide the company over. One was Colonel Edward A. Deeds, who had been head of National Cash Register and then helped found Delco (which stood for Dayton Engineering Laboratories Company). The other was Deeds's co-founder of Delco, Charles F. Kettering, always called "Boss" Kettering, an inventor and genius of world renown. Both men were close personal friends of George Mead. Deeds joined the Mead board of directors in 1925 and two years later Kettering also became a director.

By the early 1920s paperboard accounted for nearly a third of all paper production in the United States and was growing in sales faster than all other types of paper. Much of this production was used for packaging and containers. Beginning in 1911 a new process employing sulfate instead of sulfite had made it possible to make paperboard of exceptional strength (its name, kraft, means strong in German). As an initial step in getting into the Southern kraft paperboard business, Mead formed a working relationship with the Southern Extract Company in Knoxville, Tennessee. Southern Extract produced tannic acid from chestnut chips which was used principally for tanning leather. This plant became the center for the research and development efforts of the partnership. To handle the R&D work, Mead set up another entity, the Mead Research Company, which worked in cooperation with the U.S. Department of Agriculture facility at Madison, Wisconsin.

The Knoxville venture began to bear fruit in 1925, when a new semi-chemical pulp process was put into production as a corrugating medium for packaging material. There were short-term losses of about $1 million on the project, but for the long term Mead had developed a low-cost sheet that was both uniform and competitive in price. This was the base on which Mead would build its Southern paperboard business. Mead set up another organization, the Mead Paperboard Corporation, whose strategy would be to establish pulp and paper mills next to tannic extract plants throughout Tennessee and the Carolinas. These plants had access to an extremely low-cost raw material in the form of spent chestnut chips for the pulping process. The strategy resulted in the development of four more .009 semi-chemical paperboard plants, in addition to the Knoxville operation.

By the end of the decade Mead had also grown substantially in the white paper field. The Chillicothe mill was producing very sizable quantities of book-grade white paper, and had added *Time* magazine and the McCall Corporation's periodicals to the Crowell publications to create an impressive customer list. Technological improvements resulting from Mead research also enhanced the company's reputation for quality products.

In the context of the times, Mead was now a very large company. The central operation, Mead Pulp & Paper, had trebled in size between 1922 and 1929, and related but independent companies had also proliferated. At the end of 1929 all the U.S. operating facilities were put together in a new corporate entity: the Mead Corporation. It was based in Ohio and had assets of $30 million, 2300 employees, and a productive capacity totalling some 240,000 tons annually. Common stock held by George Mead and other members of the family came to about 30 percent. George Mead, now 52 years old, had indeed saved the enterprise for itself and for the family.

Despite the Depression that began with the stock market collapse of Black Thursday, October 24, 1929, the reorganized Mead Corporation managed fairly well in 1930. Earnings were up slightly.

But George Mead's separate Canadian investments were in serious trouble. A price war broke newsprint prices in half, mills began closing all over Canada, and in September 1932 the Canadian companies in which he was most heavily invested went into receivership. His personal losses amounted to about $8 million.

The Mead company remained financially sound throughout the Depression of the 1930s, although there were times when dividends, salaries, hourly wages, and hours had to be cut. But there were no layoffs.

For George Mead there was more work than ever. A member of the Business Advisory Council, which had been formed to advise the Roosevelt Administration on ways of "stimulating and reviving" the economy, he served as a representative of the paper industry helping to draft the code for that industry required by the National Recovery Administration (NRA). Among other things, NRA codes controlled prices and production for each industry. In March 1934, precisely one year after the New Deal had come into being, George Mead went to

Washington for a three-month stint on the NRA's Industrial Advisory Board (IAB). In May Mead was elected to head the IAB, which was by then embroiled in controversy. Many union leaders thought the business leaders were trying to get government to help them circumvent antitrust laws. Many business leaders thought the NRA was opening up plants to union-organizing drives and they were determined to put the NRA out of business and to defeat the New Deal at the next elections.

George Mead was in a hot seat. But he had a gift for conciliation and compromise. When the people in Mead's Chillicothe mill voted to join a national union, he expressed disappointment, but reminded his employees that he "was in no way opposed to unionism" and that he had the "highest regard" for the labor leaders he had met in Washington.

This attitude of reasonableness did not sit well with chief executives of some other paper companies. At a trade association meeting in Washington, one of them said to Mead bitterly, "You and your NRA—you got us organized."

But Mead, a Republican still, was nevertheless also a New Deal loyalist. After the NRA was declared unconstitutional by the Supreme Court in May 1935, he remained in Washington to do what he could to help the Roosevelt Administration's efforts to end the continuing Depression. When the National Labor Relations Act, upholding labor's right to organize, was passed in 1935, Mead called it "a good piece of legislation."

He worked for passage of a number of major New Deal measures, including the Social Security Act and the Fair Labor Standards Act.

In the Presidential election year of 1936, Mead, who had publicly said he thought Roosevelt was doing "a grand job," found himself the chief supporter of the Administration within the Business Advisory Council. At a meeting of that group, Mead talked quietly, calmly, and factually in his defense of the Administration. But to those who threatened to resign from the Council because of its continuing work with the New Deal, Mead kept repeating, "We will all resign or we will all stay." After a secret vote of the members was tallied, it was found that the "stays" had won by 2 votes out of 40 cast. Not long afterward, the Council elected Mead as its next chairperson.

During the year he served in that position, Mead met, often weekly, with President Roosevelt and Secretary of Commerce Daniel C. Roper. In later years, Mead had only one critical comment to make about Roosevelt: When it came to political maneuvering, Mead said, Franklin Roosevelt had a "heart of stone."

With the outbreak of war in Europe in 1939, the American economy began to surge ahead. In 1941 George Mead was appointed to the National Defense Mediation Board, which became the War Labor Board after Pearl Harbor. In the months before the United States was drawn into the war, the country was bitterly divided between those who thought America had a stake in the European war (the "interventionists"), and those who believed it was none of our business (the "isolationists"). George Mead was emphatically an interventionist. "Democracy as a way of life," he said, "is being challenged in a manner that it has never been challenged before. There is no question, regardless of what Mr. [Charles] Lindbergh or anyone else may say, but that we are fighting for our freedom and our way of life."

During 1940—when 25-year-old James McSwiney was getting married and dreaming about becoming a Mead vice president—the Administration in Washington was working with leaders in business and labor to speed up the mobilization of the economy in order to turn the United States into what Roosevelt called "the arsenal of democracy." The Defense Mediation Board, aimed at preventing or settling strikes in companies vital to the defense effort, was a part of that Administration drive. Later in the war Mead served as an industry member of the advisory board of the Office of War Mobilization and Reconversion and also as a member of the Economic Stabilization Board. In 1946 he chaired the Price Decontrol Board. In fact, it was not until 1952 that he was free of any duties in Washington.

Always a person of strong feelings about the responsibilities of citizenship, Mead undoubtedly felt a special personal stake in the war effort after he received word of the loss of his son, George H. Mead, Jr. The young man, who had been expected eventually to succeed his father as head of the corporation, had entered the Marine Corps immediately after graduating from Yale in 1941. He was killed on Guadalcanal on August 19, 1942. His parents grieved deeply, but somehow went on living, as millions of other parents would before the war was over.

George and Elsie Mead had two other sons who later served the company well and long: H. Talbott Mead and Nelson S. Mead. The former died in 1986 at the age of 67. Nelson Mead retired as an officer of the corporation in April 1986 but continued to serve as a director.

Three

Brunswick: Growth and Development

In 1940, while George Mead was tackling affairs of national importance in Washington, one of his most junior employees, James McSwiney, was getting a new assignment. Having straightened out the books at Harriman, he was sent by Fernald to Rockport, Indiana, to reopen a small mill that made .009 semi-chemical corrugated medium from straw. With the war in Europe creating shortages in paper and paperboard, Mead was increasing capacity wherever it could.

McSwiney was accompanied to Rockport by his bride. She had been a private secretary to the president of a large overall manufacturer before their marriage. Now she was employed to keep the books at Rockport. She earned about $15 a week, compared with her new husband's $25 salary. "Mac used to do everything—he lived in the mill, bought straw from the farmers, oversaw the operation, and what have you," she said. "I was the office, and he was everything else."

Jewell became an excellent cost accountant. Mac never had to worry about the accuracy or the timeliness of reports.

She was a major influence on the life of McSwiney and the children they later had—and, indirectly, on the lives of his associates. "She is a quiet woman," he said in later years, "and the soul of integrity. She has been better than a good wife and mother."

With Mac frequently away on business trips during his long career, her strong relationship with the children became especially important.

Looking back, he said, "It is easy now to see the very meaningful impact she has had on all of us."

When McSwiney recalled his Rockport experience in later years, he still had satisfaction remembering how he overcame an unreasonable bureaucratic decision of his superiors. He needed a car to go around to the farmers on his straw-buying trips, but the company refused to buy him one. So McSwiney bought a used car for $450 and sent the bill to Mead. They paid it.

One of the men in the mill quit because Mac was trying to get the paper machine to produce 200 feet per minute. The man felt that was impossible. "You are not going to kill me," he said. But Mac went to the man's home and persuaded him that the goal could be achieved — without putting unbearable stress on the operators. The man returned to work, and they did succeed in upping the output to 200 feet per minute.

With military service now confronting McSwiney and the demand for .009 semi-chemical media from straw on the wane, Mead ordered him to close down the Rockport mill again and report to the company's much larger white paper operation at Kingsport, Tennessee, as assistant office manager. The Kingsport mill was run by George Mead's cousin, Charles, in an autocratic manner. When Mac reported for work, Charles Mead said to him, "I understand you have an independent mind. Remember this: I run this mill, not George Mead. Any time you think Chillicothe calls the shots here, come to me and pick up your check."

It was now 1941 and the draft was in full swing. Because of his lack of college or technical training, McSwiney realized he would be start-ing at the very bottom in the armed forces unless he could figure something out. After checking available programs, he found that the Army Air Corps — the Air Force was still part of the Army at the time — would train him to become an instructor in pilot training. He volunteered and in 1942 he was ordered to start his training at Johnson City, Tennessee.

There he took college-level courses with the other aviation cadets and found that he did very well at them. The lack of formal higher education had given him a feeling of insecurity, although it became less and less apparent over the years as an increasing number of important people recognized the force of his intellect. McSwiney liked the courses, but he was bored by the flying.

"After the war was over," he said, "I was so fed up with airplanes that I didn't even want to see one. We'd have to take the plane up and spin it by the hour. Look this way, spin it, come out on the mark. Look that way, spin it two or three times, come out on the mark."

It may have been necessary for the training of pilots, but it was routine. It didn't occupy McSwiney's active mind.

When his training was completed, it was 1943. He was ready for assignment, but the Army Air Corps didn't have a slot for him.

"That's when I knew we were winning the war," he said. "I knew it before most of my friends and relatives. I figured if they didn't need more instructors to train more pilots, it must be because the Allies were winning, and we had enough pilots to bring the war to an end."

For lack of another assignment, the Army Air Corps sent him to an electronics school in Wisconsin to become an instructor. That didn't appeal to McSwiney, so he asked for a release from the service. He got it in 1944. (Nevertheless, that assignment may have borne fruit later in McSwiney's subsequent interest in digital technology.)

Mac returned to Nashville, where his wife was living with her mother and the couple's first child, Charles Ronald McSwiney, who had been born April 25, 1943. He had only been there two days when Fernald called. He wanted Mac to go to Brunswick, Georgia, to be chief accountant of the Brunswick Pulp & Paper Company. McSwiney was 29 then. He and his wife were expecting another child (born November 15, 1944 and named Margaret Ann after Mac's mother). McSwiney's new salary was $55 a week—pretty good pay for those days.

The Brunswick company was a joint venture of the Scott Paper Company and Mead. Edward Gayner III was general manager of the operation. Before long, Gayner was able to report to the owners that McSwiney was "probably the most promising young man we've ever had in the company."

The Brunswick mill was the first commercial facility to produce bleached pulp from southern pine. This new process created problems involving both people and equipment—problems that were difficult to isolate. As McSwiney later said, "Any time you incorporate a new technology on a commercial basis there are always a lot of bugs to be worked out in the equipment and a lot of misconceptions about what you can do, both at the operating and consuming level."

Mead white paper mills had traditionally used northern pulps made from Scandinavian and U.S. and Canadian fibers. Pulp from southern pine had a fiber of very different characteristics—"more like a stick or a match as compared with the willowy fiber of northern spruce," in McSwiney's words.

As usual, McSwiney was learning.

"I was still sensitive to my lack of a formal education," he has since said, "and a number of people I came in contact with had a Master's degree or a Ph.D. in engineering or chemistry. To be able to deal with them, I had to learn—by going in the mill and talking with them, reading literature, and so forth."

Brunswick's pioneering southern pine process, its mixture of Mead and Scott personnel, and its bootstrap financing made it a stimulating place to be. As McSwiney said, "Who knows how much you can stretch your mind and how much you can learn in such an environment?"

The plant's production manager was Gordon K. Singletary, a veteran papermaker who became a friend of McSwiney's. Singletary recalled, "Mac came to me and said, 'I want to learn the business. I know your ability, and you can help me. What can I do to help you? We'll work as a team—we can be a help to each other.'"

As he had at Nashville, in the very beginning Mac spent as much time as he could in the plant. One of the Brunswick office secretaries recalled, "Every morning he would make a swing through the mill. If a pump failed, he knew it as fast as Mr. Singletary and also knew how it would affect costs."

Mac said, "I didn't use my role to usurp his power or authority. I never went into the mill to learn things that I didn't come back and share with him."

Singletary knew that was true. He learned to trust McSwiney. He also had fun working with him.

"I enjoyed my work when he was there more than anything I've ever done," Singletary said. "We'd argue for hours."

Mac liked to argue, too, but there was another reason why he enjoyed working with the man. "When I came up with a screwy idea he didn't say, 'We tried that once and it didn't work.' He was a nontraditionalist."

They were both people-oriented, but in different ways. In later years, Mac said, "I've always cared about things and persons with whom I am involved. I'm uncomfortable if I feel that you can butter me up and get what you want. On the other hand, I guess I have suffered more personal anguish over the thought that someone didn't perceive that I cared."

He recognized that there were those who thought him "direct and abrasive," but Mac always thought of himself as candid and action-oriented. In later years he liked to say that in his entire life he had borne hostility to only one person, "and that was a long time ago."

Singletary put it somewhat differently. He said, "Mac didn't always take the time to sell a person. But without his ability to get things done, I'd have dragged my feet for days."

But Singletary had a special talent for human relations.

"He grew up in a mill town," McSwiney said, "and he had a perception of how to get along with people. He had a great loyalty and a following in the mill."

The example of Singletary did make an impression on McSwiney. Although he demanded excellence, McSwiney was liked and respected by the people who worked in the Brunswick mill. "He could get people to produce for him—they wanted to do it," said one of the people who was employed there at the time. "One of the things that he did for us was to get us enrolled in a Dale Carnegie course. There were 30 or 40 supervisors in it. We learned to get up on our feet and talk without dying of stage fright." That meant a great deal to them, and it was obvious that McSwiney knew it. The supervisors regarded it as a sign that McSwiney wanted to give people a chance to develop and grow.

McSwiney himself was developing and growing, as he would for the rest of his life. Years later, he told students at a business school seminar, "Whatever you are engaged in, learn as much about it as you possibly can so that you never make the mistake of defining it too narrowly. Don't be content to take only the accountant's view, or the inventor's view."

At Brunswick, he was the chief accountant, but the knowledge he kept acquiring about the mill and paper-making in general helped him avoid the tunnel vision of the specialist. It was clear to McSwiney after a while that Brunswick needed to spend about $1 million to replace a recovery unit in order to make operations more economical and efficient. He wrote a report with what he later described as the "grandiloquent" title, "The Economics, Feasibility, and Desirability of Bringing in an Additional Recovery Unit at Brunswick." One million dollars was a lot of money for such an operation at that time, but the board of directors of Brunswick, after reading his report twice, voted the money. Perhaps they were stunned by the report. "No accountant before that time," McSwiney said, "had given Scott or Mead anything with words like economics, feasibility, or desirability, but all of those aspects needed addressing."

The new recovery unit made it possible for the Brunswick mill to expand. The 1951 expansion more than doubled the original capacity of the mill. John Stiles, who succeeded McSwiney as chief accountant, said, "McSwiney was actively involved in the 1951 expansion. Brunswick was growing and McSwiney was the one who stimulated it."

Because Scott was at the time financially the stronger company of the two, the arrangement for the Brunswick joint venture was that a Scott executive would be the manager, working with a Mead employee. Gayner was the Scott person, and McSwiney was Mead. The other posts were filled by people from outside both companies. It was an arrangement that could have resulted in friction, but it didn't. The absence of conflict was probably a tribute to both Gayner and McSwiney. Each man was careful not to try to get an advantage for his company.

Mac's approach to the joint venture aspect of the operation grew out of his own temperament.

"People, being what they are, will say, 'Oh, that ought not to be done this way or that way because it is going to mean 50 cents more for one partner, 50 cents less for the other,'" he explained. "I used to say, 'Don't count the pennies every day. Let's look at all these things at the end of the year or at the end of, say, three years. Then, if there is disparity of any significance, all we have to do is to go to the other fellow and ask for it.' "

Paul Baldwin, chief operating officer and later vice chairman of Scott, was of the same mind—one of the reasons why he and McSwiney enjoyed a warm relationship for many years.

Because McSwiney tried scrupulously to live by that code, he felt he tended in the early days to be "more appreciated by the Scott people than the Mead people."

Gayner was a strong-willed man, but he clearly had the self-confidence to give Mac his head.

"Gayner would give you responsibility and get out of the way," McSwiney has said.

Another man who was at Brunswick at the time recalled, "If he wanted something, Mac did it. He was the spark plug."

"I didn't have the title," McSwiney said, "but I knew in my mind that Gayner would support me."

In fact, Gayner supported him to the point of recommending a new title for McSwiney: assistant secretary and treasurer, and chief financial officer.

At Brunswick McSwiney learned about "bootstrapping"—using the financial leverage that partnership through joint ventures can create. This was a technique that George Mead had used successfully many times; indeed, it was an essential part of his strategy for Mead's growth. McSwiney said, "I learned in the Brunswick situation that you could do a lot in an affiliated company that you couldn't do in a small company that was long on technology and short on capital. You could get a dollar or a dollar and a half of debt to equity in a joint venture contrasted to 50 cents of debt for one dollar of equity in one parent company."

Something else happened to McSwiney at Brunswick: He met Bill Jones.

Bill Jones—Alfred William Jones—and George Mead had married sisters. The son of a prosperous Dayton banker, Jones had gone to the Wharton School at the University of Pennsylvania but contracted tuberculosis and had to drop out. A cousin, Howard E. Coffin, who owned an estate near Brunswick, suggested that Jones take a rest cure there. Coffin, who had made a fortune as one of the founders of the Hudson Motor Company, invested most of his fortune in real estate development in Detroit and Georgia. When Bill Jones recovered from his illness he became associated with Coffin in those ventures.

In the 1920s Coffin decided to develop Sea Island and other parts of the Golden Isles, near Brunswick. He bought up land and built golf courses, causeways, and other facilities. Addison Mizener, the architect who had designed many a Palm Beach mansion, was engaged to design the Cloisters on Sea Island; the Cloisters opened in 1928 with a spate of publicity. In the early days of Sea Island, Calvin Coolidge, Charles Lindbergh, and Mayor Jimmy Walker of New York City were among the celebrities who stayed there.

When the stock market crashed and the Depression ensued, Coffin was ruined. He had lost enormous sums of money and now was faced with mounting debts. His wife died and Coffin was completely demoralized. He turned over the Sea Island Company to Bill Jones and Jones's wife, Kit, debts and all, and became a recluse. In 1937 he died.

Through a combination of imagination, hard work, a bit of legerdemain, and perhaps some luck, Bill and Kit Jones were able to make a major success of the Sea Island Company, paying off its debts, putting it on a sound footing, and creating an environment of warmth, hospitality, and gracious service.

At one point in the late 1920s, while Coffin was still in command, the two suggested to George Mead that a pulp mill might be profitably placed on a 60,000-tract called Cabin Bluff, which Coffin owned, because there was an operation on part of the land that used pine trees for the production of turpentine, rosin, pitch, and related materials. They thought the tree stumps left over from the operation could be used by a pulp mill. But it turned out that the technology to use the stumps was not advanced to a degree that made the idea workable, so it was shelved.

But in the mid-1930s, when George Mead was working to get into the kraft business, he remembered his brother-in-law's idea, and wondered if the Brunswick location might not be just right for what he had in mind. Through Charles R. Van de Carr, a vice president and a director of Mead, who was also a member of the board of directors of the Scott Paper Company, headed by George Mead's good friend, Thomas B. McCabe, Mead learned that Scott might be amenable to a joint venture. And so the Brunswick venture was undertaken. Jones was chairman of the board of directors and became increasingly knowledgeable about the Brunswick company, the Mead company, and the paper industry in general.

"Frankly, I didn't know much about the paper business," Jones once said, speaking of the 1930s, "but I did know something about forestry."

With Jones's encouragement, Brunswick bought the Cabin Bluff tract and kept adding other units until it had acquired some 593,000 acres of commercial forest land, of which approximately 91,000 acres were held under long-term leases.

In 1940 Jones joined the Mead board of directors, and later was elected to other major corporate boards, such as Westinghouse Electric's. A colleague once called him a "director's director." He used to say that he owed his wide understanding of boards and their diverse ways to his early experience on the Mead board.

"I did what Mr. Mead told me to do," he once said. "For the first 10 years, we never even saw the annual report. When you look back on it, it was, well, amazing. George ran the company—it was his."

Some time after McSwiney began working at Brunswick, he questioned the long-term viability of a plywood plant owned by a relative of Bill Jones. (In later years, Mac, looking back, would say, "I never felt intimidated to the point of not saying what I believed.") Instead of resenting the advice, Jones clearly respected McSwiney for his integrity and courage. From that sprang a friendship that deepened over a period of 30 years.

It was Jones who began to talk to his brother-in-law, George Mead, about that talented fellow, McSwiney. But the people at Scott had been hearing about him, too. For some time they had been sending Scott people they thought to have high potential to attend the Advanced Management Program (AMP) at the Harvard Graduate School of Business. Mead had never sent anyone. In 1953 Mac let it be known to Scott that he would also like to attend, and Scott agreed to arrange it. In February 1954 McSwiney left to begin the 13-week course in Cambridge, Massachusetts.

There can be little doubt about the qualms he felt when he arrived there. He had always wondered if college graduates had been able to learn skills and acquire information that he lacked. He wondered if he could compete with them intellectually.

"I suppose anyone that had not experienced a formal college program would have some misgivings about his ability to compete with those that had," he said many years later. "I knew about the program at Harvard, and I knew that it was composed of about 180 people from all walks of life with all kinds of degrees—M.B.A.s, B.S.s, B.A.s, and Ph.D.s. So I just kind of rationalized: if I went, I would find out. So I went. I didn't have any trouble, and that was very rewarding."

What happened initially didn't make things any easier for him. Although it was comforting to learn that 30 percent of the group did not have Bachelor's degrees (one wonders what the percentage would be now), at first those who had completed college didn't invite the others to parties. But those initial caste barriers soon broke down. McSwiney found the experience fun, even the horseplay. When one loquacious classmate finally gave his two-hundredth talk, the others fired a small cannon and walked around the room waving Confederate flags.

Later in life, Mac said of Harvard's AMP, "When people get back from Harvard, they often become distracting and disruptive. Any time you put the limelight on anyone, you create uncertainty among that person's peers."

When he got back from Harvard, he felt he probably had the choice of going with either Mead or Scott at their executive offices. At that point he received an invitation from Howard E. Whitaker, who was then president of Mead (Sydney Ferguson was chairman of the board; George Mead was honorary chairman, but in Mac's view he still ran the company), to go to Dayton and meet with Whitaker. He knew that Whitaker was planning to offer him a job as Whitaker's executive assistant.

"I was torn," Mac said. "Scott had the reputation for excellent management. Mead was looking for new talent. I guess, in the end, my being a Mead man made the decision."

As expected, Whitaker offered McSwiney the job. The younger man's reply apparently was not quite what the president expected.

"Mr. Whitaker," Mac said, "will you tell me honestly whether you have any feeling of limitations as to how far I can go?"

Whitaker looked at him for a long time, then said, "No, I don't think I do."

"Well," said McSwiney, "if you have any second thoughts, let me know, because if you do, I don't think it would work. I don't want to take an assignment where I am already pegged as to where I am likely to come out."

"I don't think I have to give it more thought," Whitaker responded.

"Fine," said Mac, standing up, "let me go home and see if I can talk my wife into it."

It was a hard decision for Jewell. She loved Brunswick and its people.

"But she did what most good spouses do," Mac said. "She agreed to do her part and move to Dayton.

"But when it came time for the movers, she left me at home to oversee the loading and she played golf. I don't think she could stand seeing things being moved from a place she so enjoyed."

In time, Jewell came to love Dayton. She often spoke of having two homes: the Brunswick–Sea Island area and Dayton.

Four

George Mead Finds His Man

"Great things" were expected of the white paper business in 1955, said Mead's annual report for 1954, the year in which James McSwiney went to Dayton. But the reality of Mead's overall performance was troubling. Between 1950 and 1954, white paper sales had declined from 350,000 tons to 329,000 tons, although the company was helped by a concurrent increase in paperboard sales from 324,000 tons to 360,000 tons. Total sales for the company rose from $93 million to $121 million, but net profits slipped from $6.4 million to $5.8 million.

Twenty-five years later McSwiney told a trade journal that the problems resulted in part from George Mead's admiration for the franchising system that General Motors had introduced. "The GM distribution system proved successful for Mead, too," the trade journal reported, "but, as McSwiney notes, it then seemed logical to Mr. Mead to say, 'I've got to give them Pontiacs and Chevrolets and Cadillacs—everything they want.' As a result, McSwiney says, 'We could literally make—and did make—every grade of paper you could imagine. And we made it 'good,' because Mr. Mead wouldn't tolerate inferior products.' When McSwiney became president in 1968, he said, 'We were making good paper, our customers were happy, but we weren't making money in white papers.'"

The times were changing. Mass circulation general magazines were finding it difficult or impossible to compete with television for the advertising dollars of business. *Liberty* magazine was first to disappear from the newsstands, but it would be followed by many more over the next decade or so — *Collier's, The Saturday Evening Post, Life,* and others. The Crowell-Collier publishing empire, with which Mead had been doing business for 75 years, collapsed in 1956, and it took Mead nearly a year and a half to recover the volume of white paper business lost when the Crowell-Collier magazines stopped printing.

Now settled in Dayton, McSwiney liked working as the president's executive assistant, even though he had only received a $2000 raise, bringing his salary to $17,000, when he accepted the job. He found Whitaker always kind and considerate. Apparently he shared one of McSwiney's attitudes about such circumstances: "When you bring someone new into a company," McSwiney has said, "you don't let the dogs at him until he's had a fair chance."

It may have been a little more complicated than that. According to Walker Lewis, who knew them both very well, Whitaker brought McSwiney to Dayton only because of the counsel of Bill Jones.

McSwiney was making friends of other people, too. One was George Mead's oldest son, Harry Talbott (Tally) Mead, who served on the Brunswick board. Another was Walker Lewis — Welbourne Walker Lewis, Jr., who was never called by his first name. McSwiney had first met Lewis in Brunswick, after Lewis asked Mead if he could go there to help formulate a pension plan. Lewis and Mac worked closely on that project and became good friends.

Three years younger than McSwiney, Tally Mead was a director and a vice president of Mead. In the next few years the company's stock rose from the $10–$14 range to the $26–$36 range, and Tally was largely responsible for the rise. True, the company had been improving in sales and earnings over those years, but the company's stock was selling at or below book value, a circumstance that had occurred before. But Tally had been working hard with security analysts and others to make the company's virtues better known in the investment community.

Walker Lewis was a Tennessean of the same age as McSwiney, but he had lived most of his life in the Dayton area. He had earned his undergraduate degree at Dartmouth and his law degree at Harvard. In

1939 he came back to Dayton to join the law firm of Smith, Schnacke, and Compton, which later dropped Compton from its name. The firm had provided legal counsel both to George Mead personally and to the corporation for many years. (Today Smith & Schnacke continues to provide important legal services to Mead and occupies several floors in the Mead headquarters building in Dayton. McSwiney's son, C. Ronald McSwiney, is president of the firm.) It was customary in those days for a senior partner of Smith & Schnacke to serve as legal counsel and secretary of the Mead company, and Lewis filled that position. He became a member of the Mead board of directors in 1959.

McSwiney made another friend about that time: George H. Mead himself.

The way it came about resembled a scene in a satirical book, later made into a Broadway musical comedy and then a movie, *How to Succeed in Business Without Really Trying*, in which an ambitious young man gets to the office early on a Saturday morning because he knows the head of the company is going to drop by. He assumes the president will be impressed by his diligence, and he is.

In McSwiney's case, he had always worked long hours—12- or 14-hour days were common—and he usually worked at least until noon on Saturdays. So it was routine for him to be in the office one Saturday morning when George Mead happened to come through and saw him.

"Who are you?" Mead asked.

"Of course, he knew who I was," McSwiney said later. "I had met him on a few occasions before."

Bill Jones had been praising McSwiney to George Mead for several years, and Mead had also been hearing good things about McSwiney from Walker Lewis, who was a close friend.

Lewis and McSwiney were "very blunt" with each other, according to Lewis. That's probably why they ended up getting along so well.

After McSwiney moved to Dayton, "he was thought by many to be abrasive," Lewis said. "He angered those who didn't want to change."

McSwiney realized it.

"I was critical of the way the company was being run," he said. "That didn't make me very popular among the old Mead people. They would have gotten rid of me except that Mr. Mead wouldn't let them."

"He was so energetic, so sharp, and he was into everything," Lewis remembered. "He moved with lightning speed. He had terrific drive. He didn't know what 'quit' meant. He was one of the quickest learners I've ever known. He was intuitive and restless."

As for McSwiney's "abrasiveness," Lewis felt that "it covered up a big heart." He gave an illustration: "When I retired, he was tearful. He said, 'Anything I have is yours,' and I knew he meant it literally."

Lewis and Mac enjoyed needling each other. One day, on a train to New York, Mac told Lewis, tongue in cheek, that Mead would have to start thinking about new legal counsel because Smith & Schnacke might not be big enough to handle all the corporation's business. Lewis retorted that the law firm could handle anything that Mead was able to throw at it. He was right; in later years Mac would express amazement that a firm of three or four lawyers was able to grow to one of some 175 lawyers, all the while building an increasingly solid reputation for sound, ethical, and innovative work.

One of Smith & Schnacke's attorneys who particularly impressed McSwiney was Albert Sealy, "the most persistent, hard-working, and probably one of the ablest corporate lawyers that I have ever known." Sealy and William A. Enouen, then of the accounting firm of Touche Ross and later senior vice president and chief financial officer of Mead, were the basic team to dig out information on acquisitions, find methods to pursue them, and present the proposals for acquisitions to the board of directors.

For many years Touche Ross and its predecessor companies in Dayton (Touche Ross Nevin Bailey & Smart, and still earlier, Allen R. Smart & Co.) had handled Mead's accounting needs, but its work for Mead had gone far beyond what one customarily expects an accounting firm to do these days. Besides preparing Mead's audits and tax returns, Touche Ross had supervised Mead's bookkeepers almost on a day-to-day basis. Alan Parker, a Touche Ross partner, and Herman Olt, the firm's tax specialist, were the CPAs primarily involved with Mead. After Charles Gebhardt joined Mead, in the later years of George Mead's long reign as de facto head of the company, Mead brought its accounting operations in-house, although it continued, of course, to employ outside auditors.

Some time after McSwiney went to Dayton, George Mead tele-

phoned one of the outside directors and said he was going to introduce him to a young fellow from Brunswick who was "destined to be
president." When word of that call got around in the company, it
didn't endear him to some people, especially those on the white paper side of the business, who regarded all brown paper folks as persons to be wary of.

After their first chance encounter, Mead and McSwiney often met in
the office on Saturday mornings. For several years Mead had tried out
ideas on Lewis, sought his advice, and asked his appraisal of people.
Now the conversations involved the three men—Mead, Lewis, and
Mac—although Mead came more and more to talk with McSwiney
alone. That almost certainly reflected his interest in grooming Mac for
greater responsibilities.

"One of the reasons George Mead paid a lot of attention to me,"
McSwiney said, "was because he had a lot of confidence in Walker
Lewis."

In his late seventies and early eighties, Mead often stayed home
during the week. In the afternoon he would call McSwiney and ask
him to drop by on his way home. "I don't know how many times I'd
stop at his house," Mac said. It was commonplace for Lewis to be
there, too.

One weekend Mead telephoned McSwiney and asked him to come
over to the Mead house for a chat. Mac said he couldn't; he had promised Jewell he would paint their old, dilapidated swimming pool. So
Mead drove over and sat on a three-legged stool on the bottom of the
empty pool, and the two men talked while McSwiney painted.

Sometimes Mead wanted to talk on Sundays. His wife suspected it
was his way of getting out of going to church: "He had to talk to Mac."

More than once, after a long discussion with McSwiney, Mead
would tell his wife, "Mac is one hell of a guy."

He got into the custom of taking McSwiney with him on trips to
Washington and New York to visit people Mead had worked with at the
highest levels of government. Among the people Mac met on those trips
were former President Herbert Hoover; James F. Byrnes, who had been
an associate justice of the U.S. Supreme Court and U.S. Secretary of State;
and Boss Kettering. At such times McSwiney spoke very little; he sensed
that Mead wanted him to "listen and learn."

One of those conversations stuck in his mind. It was in Hoover's suite in the Waldorf Towers in New York. Kettering was there, too, and in the course of the conversation he said, "Give me the 10 percent at the bottom of the class, you take the 10 percent at the top of the class, and I'll beat you."

Mac's interpretation of Kettering's statement was that the bottom 10 percent would listen and work—and help—while the top 10 percent might slow a leader down with too much debate.

There were those who were unhappy about Mac's conversations with Mead, which circumvented the formal system of reporting that George Mead himself had established. One of them was Whitaker, who called McSwiney in one day and said, "You're going to get in trouble, Mac."

"What do you mean?" McSwiney asked.

"You can't say the things you say to Mr. Mead," Whitaker responded. "He doesn't put up with that."

McSwiney tried to explain that he was not "talking back" to Mead or undercutting anyone, but that candor was simply his native style—as he put it in later years, "You ask me something, and I'll tell you what I think about it."

Looking back on the incident many years later Mac said, "I think Mr. Mead found in me somebody that just told him what they thought. And I think he was wise enough and smart enough to understand that I was not doing it for personal gain or to put anybody down."

McSwiney, Tally Mead, and some of the other younger men believed that the company needed to integrate forward into the box and container business through acquisitions because of the vertical integration of rival companies. Both of them used their best powers of persuasion on George Mead. So did R.J. Blum, president of the Mead paperboard sales subsidiary.

Blum suggested the Jackson Corrugated Box Company, headed by William J. Cassaday, Jr. Jackson Box manufactured shipping containers for food, cigarettes, beverages, auto parts, and other products. It had plants in Cincinnati and North Carolina, and interests in other corrugated box companies. While Mead tried to make up its mind, the West Virginia Pulp and Paper Company made an offer to buy Jackson Box in 1954. As soon as George Mead heard about the other offer, he made his own offer to buy 49 percent of Jackson Box. Mead bought the other 51 percent a year later.

"Jackson Box broke the logjam in the finance committee," Tally Mead said later.

It unlocked other deals that were pending, including the acquisition, in 1957, of the Atlanta Paper Company in Georgia. This company was a pioneer in multiple packaging (initially the six-pack), a product requiring a special wet-strength paperboard (which Mead could make readily because of its research and technical expertise), and a full line of packaging and shipping products, as well as corrugated containers. In a matter of three years, Mead bought or merged with 10 corrugated container and packaging companies besides Atlanta Paper and Jackson Box. In addition, Mead acquired three white paper manufacturers, Wrenn, Hurlbut, and Chillicothe Paper Company. Mac and Warren Kampf were responsible for Mead's acquiring the first merchant distributor (Cleveland Paper Company) and many others later. Eventually the Federal Trade Commission and the U.S. Department of Justice compelled Mead to divest itself of some of those acquisitions. McSwiney felt, however, that the acquisitions had a positive effect on Mead's position in the industry. Only a few of the acquisitions, which added significantly to Mead's sales and prevented the erosion of earnings in the paperboard group, would have sailed through the process of board approval without the strong support of Tally Mead, who was chairman of the board's finance committee.

The Atlanta Paper acquisition brought Arthur Harris, Jr., who headed that company. He became a group vice president of Mead and a member of Mead's board of directors. Harris was, in McSwiney's view, "very ingenious—a near genius." And, it was generally agreed, he could be rather difficult. Harris's father once said of him, "He may irritate you but he'll never bore you." To which Mac heartily agreed.

Harris had the initial concept of taking Mead Packaging international. Money was always a problem, but with Harris's persistence and some financial ingenuity on the part of Harris and McSwiney, Mead Packaging operations in France, Holland, and Japan got off the ground. The French venture nearly went under, but operations in those countries survived and grew rapidly. Today Mead Packaging is the leader in this field in both domestic and international markets.

Much of the credit for that state of affairs, McSwiney felt, should go to Harris and to Greene Garner, Robert O'Hara, Marcel Prot, Bob Neff, and Leo Benatar—men whom Harris had recruited and men who were survivors of his intense management style.

Thanks to Harris, Mead also gained a reputation as a serious patron of the arts—a reputation that lasted 10 years but faded after he left the company. Harris had initially linked business and the arts by sending his customers reproductions of commissioned paintings. Then he sponsored juried competitions that made a play on his first name, "Art Across the South." The first year Mead put up $25,000 to purchase paintings based on their competitive ranking. The price paid to each artist was that placed by the artist on his or her work. Soon there was "Art Across the Northeast," and before long the entire country was involved.

"Those were 10 wonderful years," Mac recalled. "With Arthur's inspiration and the funds that I was able to scrounge from the corporate till, we were able to send the works to many universities and museums. The windup at the Louvre in Paris, with spotlights and fanfare, was one that will be long remembered."

Sargent Shriver, brother-in-law of John F. Kennedy and the first head of the Peace Corps, was then in Paris and opened a number of doors for Mead. A host of artists came to the show and McSwiney, along with a few other Mead people, wound up having breakfast just before dawn at Les Halles, which was then Paris's famed produce market.

In 1957 Sydney Ferguson retired as chairman. Whitaker moved up to succeed him as chairman of the board. A chemical engineer, Donald F. Morris, became president and George H. Pringle, a mechanical engineer, was named executive vice president. All three were from the white paper branch of the business, although the brown paper business accounted for more than 60 percent of the company's profits.

At the same time, McSwiney was elected vice president for development. He, Tally Mead, R.J. Blum, and William J. Cassady, Jr., who was by that time vice president for all container operations, were brown paper men. Rodney Boren was elected a vice president, too; he later became president of the Fibre Box Association.

Among the many acquisitions of container companies, Mead acquired the Ottawa River Paper Company. Its controller, William W. Wommack, who helped to negotiate the merger, stayed on with Mead. Thirty-five years old, he was a chemical engineer from North Carolina who had earned an M.B.A. at Harvard.

Wommack was critical of the acquisition program because he thought it lacked focus. Top management, consisting of white paper managers, seemed to think of people on the brown paper side of the business "as shirt sleeve rather than Brooks Brothers," Mac said. There had been an opportunity to pick up an entire chain of converters, but Mead had passed this up because the price was felt to be too high. That meant that individual companies had to be bought, which "increased the management problem," as Wommack pointed out.

"Some of the acquisitions were not the best companies in the world," McSwiney said. "But it is doubtful we would have made it without them." His reasoning was that the company had to move quickly because of the head start of its competitors and because most of the more desirable acquisition candidates were no longer available.

The difference in viewpoint reflected the contrasting temperaments of the two men. Wommack was highly analytical. McSwiney was pragmatic, intuitive, and action-oriented.

Wommack had an experience early on in his service with the company that he never forgot. It involved a powerful executive, Al Mahrt, Mead's top financial officer and the head of its share of the Georgia Kraft joint venture. Mahrt had been with Mead for about 30 years and was nearing retirement. During the wave of mergers he headed a committee that had been set up to coordinate the operations of Mead in its proliferating paperboard business. Wommack served on the committee. "I was told that we did things by vote," he recalled. "I voted against Mahrt once, and he said to me, 'Young man, we weigh votes here, we don't count them.'"

The Georgia Kraft joint venture began in 1956 with its largest customer, Inland Container Company, based in Indianapolis, Indiana, as its partner. Prior to the go-ahead by Mead and Inland, Al Mahrt went to Brunswick and, with the help of McSwiney, devised the financial format for the kraft company. Its main features were patterned after the Brunswick Pulp concept, a pattern McSwiney never forgot and used many times to "bootstrap" Mead into continued growth.

The first plant at Macon, Georgia, overran its estimated cost by some $12 million, an unbelievable amount at the time, but with Mahrt minding the till it became very profitable. The Macon plant was followed by one at Rome, Georgia, named for Herman Krannert, founder of Inland Container. Later there was another plant at Mahrt, Alabama, named for the Mead officer.

By 1984, Georgia Kraft was the largest producer of kraft linerboard and coated kraft board in the world. During the course of these developments, Georgia Kraft acquired some 1,016,000 acres of forest lands and controlled by lease another 238,000 acres. Indeed, Brunswick Pulp and Georgia Kraft, between them, came to own approximately 7.6 percent of the forest lands in the state of Georgia; that totaled about 5 percent of the total land area of the state. Initially, the kraft companies were owned 60 percent by Mead and 40 percent by Inland, but Inland later insisted on a 50–50 arrangement, to which Mead reluctantly agreed. A part of the compensation was provided by Inland in the form of $3 million in cash through a wholly owned subsidiary of Mead. This money later was used by Mead to fund its share of the Mead–Noranda joint venture, Northwood.

After coming to Dayton in 1954, McSwiney began to be involved with the kraft company and in time became its principal advocate and representative, along with Henry Goodrich, who had been brought in to succeed Herman Krannert of Inland. McSwiney and Goodrich became good friends, despite the difference in their temperaments. Goodrich was quiet, extremely well organized, and very talented. The combination of McSwiney and Goodrich, along with their respective organizations, brought about probably the most cost-effective facilities in the southern kraft industry.

The initial general manager provided by Mead was Herbert A. Kidd, a caustic, benevolent autocrat widely known as "Captain Kidd," who brooked little interference from anyone. He was followed by E.V. McSwiney, Mac's brother, who was trained and coached jointly by Mahrt and Kidd.

George Mead was proud as he watched his dream of penetrating the southern kraft industry gradually taking shape.

Leveraged capital and the efficient kraft operations combined to provide Mead with earnings which largely supported the company. Without those earnings Mead would have had difficulty surviving. In McSwiney's opinion, those earnings also paved the way for Mead, in later years, to begin to establish its white paper operations on a sound basis.

Soon after his election to vice president in 1957, McSwiney urged that Mead develop a "sound and aggressive marketing organization" within the corporation. McSwiney and Tally Mead wrote a joint memorandum to Whitaker. In it they said, in part:

> At one of our early policy meetings, Mr. Mead emphasized what he considered to be the order of importance of the various functions of our business, saying that in his opinion Finance came first, Sales second, and Operations third. Your [Whitaker's] reaction was that they were all about equal ingredients, not unlike the chicken and the egg.

The memorandum said Mead now had a "golden opportunity" in marketing, contrasted with the other two areas. It urged that Mead's senior management "formally and systematically focus attention on the marketing area of our business."

The following year McSwiney, in a memorandum to Morris, the president of Mead, warned of the problems the company was running into as it strove for increasingly large volume in its various markets. He wrote, "The tendency, where emphasis is on volume, is to lose perspective as to profits." To guard against this, he urged the installation of sophisticated and systematic financial reports and controls in order for management to keep on top of things:

> Just a few years back, the Mead corporate structure was simple enough (white paper mills, the .009 mills, Georgia Kraft Company — about 10 operating facilities) for a few people like Sydney Ferguson, Al Mahrt, H.E. Whitaker, and yourself to almost literally keep the total business in your mind. Today we have 33 different operating facilities. We can visualize a total of 40 operating facilities in the not too distant future. In addition we have sales offices covering the entire United States.

McSwiney urged on Morris a decentralized approach to management and an organization that focused on profit centers as the basic unit of control:

> The Executive Committee meeting offers the ideal time and place to focus this information. This recommendation is strongly influenced by the success of du Pont in controlling multiple "profit centers" — they are reported to use the Executive Committee as a focal point of ... control data.

Not long afterward, McSwiney was made head of the Paperboard Division. Clearly, the promotion was George Mead's decision. Although he had suffered a series of strokes in 1958, his impact on the company was still pervasive. There seems to be little question George Mead had decided that McSwiney should lead the corporation in the years ahead. The day before he died, he told his brother-in-law, Bill Jones, "I would feel safe turning the company over to Mac. I trust him enough to turn it over to him now."

George Mead died early on the morning of New Year's Day, 1963, at the age of 89, mourned by all who knew him as a warm, generous, tolerant, intelligent man who respected the dignity and rights of all people. He had the common touch, and he never fell into the trap of putting people into categories. He once said to McSwiney, as they flew to New York, that he never wanted to feel he had ever "used" anyone.

Before the year was out, Morris, the president and chief executive officer of Mead, died after battling a malignancy for several months. It was presumed throughout the company that George Pringle, the executive vice president, would now take Morris's place as president. The outsiders on the board of directors felt otherwise.

The eight outsiders were Stanley C. Allyn, of National Cash Register; Clarence Francis, of General Foods; John J. McDonough, of Georgia Power & Light; William L. Dempsey, of the investment banking house of Drexel & Company; Alan H. Temple, of National City Bank of New York; Bill Jones; Dr. John M. Walker, George Mead's son-in-law; and Walker Lewis.

For the first time in the company's history, the outside directors now decided to play a decisive role in affairs. They gathered together and decided that McSwiney must be made president rather than Pringle. Whitaker agreed with them, so the group constituted a majority of the directors. They sent word to McSwiney.

"I don't know," McSwiney responded. "Give me a few minutes or a day or something. Let me come back and talk to you."

McSwiney's reluctance wasn't lack of ambition. Indeed, when he was still executive assistant to Whitaker, he and Walker Lewis were walking along a street in New York one day when McSwiney said, "I want to be CEO—not for power, but because I think I can do something for the company."

"Do it through Bill Jones," Lewis counseled.

So McSwiney wanted to be president. But he knew the time might not be right. Pringle had a very loyal following in the white paper part of the business, and with good reason. McSwiney thought him "thoroughly likable," although he was somewhat puzzled by the intense dislike that Pringle, a Canadian and a graduate of McGill University, harbored for Harvard and the Massachusetts Institute of Technology. McSwiney felt that the people of the white paper branch would do everything they could to undermine him if he became president instead of Pringle.

Of course, within minutes Pringle heard about the board's proposal. He went to Walker Lewis and then before the full board and in a highly emotional state argued that he should be made president. Lewis and Bill Jones conferred and then Lewis went to see McSwiney.

Mac had already decided he shouldn't take the presidency at that time because of Pringle's strong following in the white paper group, so he and Lewis had no trouble agreeing on what should be done.

McSwiney went before the board and urged them to give the presidency to Pringle.

"Make him president and I will work with him," McSwiney told the directors. "I'm not going to be a problem. In a couple of years, you can switch it over to me, if that's what you still want to do, and I think we'll all be better off."

An agreement was reached that McSwiney would serve as executive vice president with the understanding that his *de facto* powers could in a given situation be greater than the title implied.

Years later Dr. Walker said, "Mac could have had the job, but he let Pringle take it. It shows what kind of a man he was."

People do not rise to the top of great corporations unless they have consuming ambition. There are very few instances where individuals have been able to resist the temptation to get to the top the first time the opportunity arose.

Five

Servant Leadership

Coming back from a meeting in New York in the days when George Mead was still active in everyday company activities, he and McSwiney began talking about the company's present and future. McSwiney told the older man that he was concerned about whether the company was doing as well as it should. Mead said he agreed, adding that maybe he was "a bit at fault." McSwiney said he thought the company would have to do a lot of things differently in the future.

"You're right," Mead said. "You're going to have to do things a lot differently."

From the moment he became executive vice president, with the additional power that the mantle of heir apparent gave him, McSwiney began his efforts to move the company in new directions. He deferred to Pringle as the titular leader of the organization—"I never tried to upstage him or undercut him," McSwiney said—but he moved vigorously in the reorganization and integration of the paperboard side of the business.

The white paper business was another matter.

"They wouldn't let me in," he recalled. "You'd go over to Chillicothe with some thought and ideas, and they'd tell you, 'We don't do it that way in the Mead Corporation.' "

He decided to bide his time with the white paper people. As he once remarked, "If I ever had a quality of merit—often misunderstood—it was that I always perceived you could get a lot farther if you could wait—use time—until a person was in a frame of mind to endure whatever he was going to have to put up with. In other words, until whatever was inevitable became more acceptable to him."

It is a cliché that people make an organization. Like most clichés, it has become one because of its essential truth.

McSwiney felt that change within Mead had to come as a result of change within the people of Mead. That was always McSwiney's strength and his weakness. "He thought he could change people," Walker Lewis has said. In some ways he could, and did, change people to some extent. But there were a few times when his belief in the ability of people to improve themselves led him to make optimistic personnel choices that didn't work out.

In the late 1960s, however, McSwiney probably was right in thinking that change was needed with respect to the people of the company. He thought there was a somewhat permissive, easy-going attitude in the company. People were polite and worked as a team, but there was not the zest, the edge, that arises from competitiveness and striving. There was too much of a routine, nine-to-five atmosphere. For a man who had always worked long hours out of sheer enthusiasm, that was hard to understand.

McSwiney proceeded to shake things up, in a continuing effort to revitalize and improve the attitudes—and the performance—of management at all levels.

As the annual report for 1966 said, "From a sharp inquiry into our professional recruiting requirements and methods to a variety of programs to stimulate, interest, and challenge all levels of management through increased involvement in fundamental decision-making, we are carrying on the task of building a corps of quick, skillful, and motivated managers."

At first there was some thought given to establishing within Mead a management school patterned after one maintained by General Electric at Croton-on-Hudson. "But as soon as we looked into it," McSwiney recalled, "we realized that we couldn't afford it. Then we thought, why not set up a program by identifying outstanding scholars and professors and bringing them in to conduct well thought-out, in-house seminars?"

What McSwiney had in mind was saturating management by immersing everyone in the same experience. He decided to send the entire top cadre of Mead—about 300 persons in all—through eight-week seminars on the latest thinking in the art of management. The purpose, in his words: "to take a fresh look at leadership skills, relate the newest ideas and developments by outside experts to practical applications at Mead, discuss new approaches and scientific findings." All of this was to be directed to answering a basic question: What is the work of a professional manager?

Privately it was his feeling that there was "a lot of resistance to change at Mead" and the seminars might bring about a willingness to look at new ideas and accept new patterns of behavior.

The seminars were put together by F.D. Crowther, vice president of corporate planning, who had come to Mead from General Electric; Arthur M. Weimer, who had been dean of Indiana University's Graduate School of Business Administration; and John Mee, professor of management at Indiana University. The format was that of most management programs, a mixture of lectures, case histories, and discussions. The instructors were among the most stimulating social scientists and management theorists in the country. The manager-students went through the course in groups of about 35 each, starting in the latter part of 1967 and continuing through mid-1969. The first seminars were held near the campus of Denison University, in Granville, Ohio, a few miles east of Columbus. Although the location later was shifted to the Bergamo conference center in Dayton, the 18 months of seminars came to be called the "Granville Experience."

It was an intensive intellectual, and sometimes emotional, series. (There was no formal physical education program, but most of those who attended engaged in some sort of exercise or sport, which proved to be an important balance.)

The manager-students heard Frederick Herzberg explain that no matter what management does about motivation by fitting people to jobs and vice versa, the only way to really motivate them is to give them challenging work. (He added that after receiving a financial reward people were always ready for another one.) Initiative has to come from within. David McClellan talked about the "hierarchy of needs."

He said that different people have different needs. It is necessary to find the right ways to reinforce different people according to their varying needs. Rensis Likert discussed his classification of types of organizations, from rigid systems at one pole to open systems at the other. He named the four main types: exploitative-authoritative, benevolent-authoritative, consultative, and participative.

Summing up the Granville Experience, McSwiney said, "The mission of the corporate manager these days has to be that of leadership by the use of wisdom beyond knowledge, of belief beyond fact, and motivation of increasingly educated followers through inspiration and persuasion beyond command authority."

In more prosaic terms, he discussed the practical application of two approaches to management, Theory Y and Theory X. Advocates of Theory Y, he said, suggested that higher order, personal drives (based on ego and needs for self-fulfillment) must be considered, especially in the upper levels of a corporation like Mead. He went on to say:

> While most of us might adopt and believe in Theory Y, our tendency is probably to start with X, or the authoritarian approach. A few years ago the two concepts of what motivated human behavior in an organization were thought to be in direct conflict. We know now, however, that we must synthesize the two. Both are applicable.
>
> For example, it is still necessary to "make" people do what they should (at times). That is, it is necessary to resolve conflicts of interest and specialization (i.e., between sales and production) when the larger interests of the company are involved.
>
> I'm suggesting that the practical manager today recognizes the value of Theory Y as a motivator of men and women, but at the same time knows that some people, sometimes, have to be bossed.

Some Mead managers enjoyed the course and benefited from it; others found it distasteful. It had not been the custom for Mead managers to question—or to have questioned—practices that they took for granted. A few felt their status as leaders threatened by the open exchanges in the classrooms. A number resented being forced to crack the books again. So it happened that the seminars provided a kind of self-selection process for eliminating those people who would not be happy in the kind of company environment McSwiney was trying to create. Men and women who felt that way tended to look for jobs in other companies. But those who found the experience exhilarating remained with the company to help reshape it for the demands of the last quarter of the twentieth century. Among them were Burnell Roberts, who became chairman of the board and chief executive officer in 1982, and Greene Garner, who preceded Roberts as CEO.

As the Granville Experience indicated, management development had become a major concern of McSwiney. To help him sort out his thoughts and suggest new approaches, he turned to a new member of Mead's board of directors, Vernon R. Alden, president of Ohio University at Athens, Ohio. In 1962, at the age of 38, Alden had been named to head that institution, the youngest president of the university since its founding in 1804. Like McSwiney, Alden was intensely interested in leadership and how it could be stimulated and nurtured in people; like McSwiney, he welcomed innovative ideas; like McSwiney, he was willing to cut across organizational lines.

Moreover, as a young university president, Alden was highly knowledgeable about the currents sweeping through American society at the time. It was a period of great unrest. The Vietnam war had triggered protests among the young and among older people too, and dissatisfaction with the social order spread beyond the debate about the war to other issues, many of them unrelated to the war. The college-age dissidents would soon be entering the work force and it could be assumed that they would be among the next generation of young managers. Alden's understanding of the young people was helpful to McSwiney.

It was Alden who introduced Robert K. Greenleaf to McSwiney. Greenleaf had served in management development in the New York offices of the American Telephone and Telegraph Company for 33 years, retiring in 1962 as director of management research. He began teaching at the Harvard Business School and also at the Alfred P. Sloan School of Management at the Massachusetts Institute of Technology.

In his history of AT&T, *Telephone*, John Brooks called Greenleaf "one of the more extraordinary figures in AT&T management." When Cleo F. Craig was president of AT&T he used to call Greenleaf his "kept revolutionary," but others called him "the conscience of AT&T."

An outside consultant who knew Greenleaf during those years has been quoted as saying, "Bob didn't give a damn about status, and he never deferred to anybody. If you asked him a question, he answered without influencing. He tells it like it is."

Greenleaf himself once said, "I was an inside student of things. I had influence but I never had power."

At AT&T, Craig, the president, had "a strong feeling...that [our] people were living far too much within themselves; that top management urgently needed a broader outlook on life and a better understanding of their fellow citizens so that we might properly serve them and avoid unwelcome regulation." So Craig encouraged Greenleaf to develop a humanistic course of studies for managers. Groups of 20 middle managers were sent to college campuses—University of Pennsylvania, Swarthmore, Williams, Dartmouth, Northwestern—for 8-to-14-week courses that emphasized literature, history, and the classics.

"At their peak," wrote John Brooks, "Craig-and-Greenleaf-instituted management training or mind-broadening courses were taking the entire Bell System management cadre off operations an average of one week per person per year, and were costing the company many millions per year." (Of course, that was some time before the courts ordered AT&T to divest itself of the Bell System companies.)

Was the program (which was largely abandoned in favor of more conventional management training courses after Craig left AT&T's presidency) successful?

Brooks, an outsider who was in a peculiarly good position to judge, wrote, "Taken all in all...the programs improved Bell management morale, served to point the company's leadership in a more public-spirited direction that would be a life-saver in the next decade, and provided a classic example of an economic policy responding to good times by assuming a new benignity."

Greenleaf's career had been followed with interest by Alden, and when the older man began teaching at Harvard Business School, where Alden had earned an M.B.A. and served as associate dean, Alden asked Greenleaf to serve as a consultant in developing programs for encouraging young people with leadership potential. It was Alden's feeling that there was an "over-supply of detached observers" on American campuses and an "under-supply of young people who can and will take responsibility—doers, innovators, and risk-takers."

The idea of recruiting Alden for Mead's board of directors had orig-
inated with McSwiney, who was impressed with Alden's thinking on
leadership development. It was natural, therefore, that Alden one day
introduced Greenleaf to McSwiney and suggested that McSwiney engage Greenleaf as a consultant. "Mac seemed to me to be the kind of
person that wanted to have a Bob Greenleaf sitting around and doing
exactly the kind of thing he was doing for me over in Athens," Alden
later remarked.

The two men hit it off from the start. In part, this may have been
because Greenleaf did not, even unconsciously, feel the least bit con-
descending about McSwiney's lack of a formal higher education.
Greenleaf was skeptical about the value of a university education as
an imparter of wisdom. He liked to say that his own epitaph should
read, "Potentially a good plumber, ruined by a sophisticated education." He often said, "The reason McSwiney is different from other
people is that he never went to college."

But Greenleaf also believed that the advanced management program that McSwiney had taken part in at Harvard Business School had
a greater benefit for him than for most participants because it came at
a point in McSwiney's self-education where it could do the most
good.

It is probable that another facet of Greenleaf's personality appealed
to McSwiney, and that was Greenleaf's feeling for people. A Quaker
and a man deeply concerned with ethical matters—he wrote a number of books on the theme of "servant leadership" published by the
Center for Applied Studies and later by the Paulist Press—Greenleaf
took a serious view of corporate America's responsibilities. So did
McSwiney.

"Mac is, at heart, an idealist," said his friend, Walker Lewis. "He's a
do-gooder."

That aspect of McSwiney's personality was often disguised by his
bluntness of manner, but it was apparent now and then in comments
he made about various persons and institutions. Of one institution,
for example, he once said disapprovingly, "It seemed to me at times
that it projected a surface attitude that people were things to be used."

For years Greenleaf worked with McSwiney, shuttling between
Dayton and his "retirement" home in New Hampshire. He was an ex-

cellent listener and a sounding board for ideas. He was a neutral observer who, when asked, could give dispassionate observations. He was a mediator who could convey feelings and views in an objective way. McSwiney gave him carte blanche to move throughout the company, talking with people and listening to their ideas and problems. People trusted Greenleaf and they did confide in him.

"I told him, 'If you hear of any problem that I should know about, tell me,'" McSwiney said. "'Don't tell me who told you about it, or who is to blame—just what the problem is.'

"And he always understood that what I needed from him was information, not solutions to problems. It was my responsibility to come up with solutions to problems."

In some degree Greenleaf and Lewis provided for McSwiney the sounding boards that McSwiney and Lewis had provided for George Mead. Lewis was a discreet insider "who didn't have an ax to grind," as Greenleaf put it; "he was about Mac's age, and he was not a rival."

McSwiney recalled, "Bob Greenleaf and I used to go over to Walker Lewis's house in the afternoon and sit there for hours figuring out where and how we were going to help develop some of the people we had and then where we were going to get some other good people to bring in. It was an obsession of all three of us."

Organizational changes—how the organization related—were McSwiney's ideas. The number, quality, diversity—the talents and kinds of people needed—were the principal subject matter for Lewis and Les Rollins.

Rollins, who had been assistant dean of the Harvard Business School, had a special interest in young people. (He helped a young man named Warren L. Batts to go to the Harvard Business School. Batts later became president and chief executive officer of Mead.) "Rollins was good at getting young people to see and believe in their potential," Mac said. "He had the ability to inspire young people."

Greenleaf's emphasis was on how people should interface.

Most of the dialogue between McSwiney and Greenleaf concerned situations and people, according to Greenleaf. "Most of my talks with Mac have been very brass tacks," he said; "what to do about this or that." Not solutions, but clarification of the problem or issue.

Greenleaf found, as did others, that McSwiney could be a very careful listener, though he often had the disconcerting mannerism of not appearing to take any interest in what was being said. This was deceptive. The idea would emerge at a later time "re-potted," as one consultant put it. "It grows in him and becomes his plant."

"It is clear that Mac has to do a lot of his thinking in conversation," Greenleaf said. "Not that other people have to respond. He needs someone who will listen. My job was providing a focus. Mac just had to say it, get it out. Mac is very articulate. He finds it easier to talk with outsiders than with colleagues—the colleagues are too much a part of the game. Colleagues inevitably have agendas of their own, reflecting their own self-interests. He needs people that he is close to but who are outside the game."

"It's curious," Greenleaf once said, "Mac reads everything I write, and mostly I send it to him in draft form—and he's a good critic and comments on it. But we never sit down and discuss his ideas. We've never had a discussion about them."

When Greenleaf sent McSwiney drafts of books and other materials, McSwiney would make copious notes in the margins.

"It wasn't just reading my thoughts," Greenleaf said, "it was analyzing them, commenting on them, and writing. He has probably done as much with what I've written as anybody."

That's an important point, for Greenleaf wrote some profound works on leadership and the nature of institutions. It is clear that the content of those works reflects, to a significant degree, McSwiney's beliefs, which coincided with Greenleaf's. There is no question that Greenleaf influenced McSwiney's opinions, but it seems equally clear that McSwiney had considerable influence on Greenleaf's ideas, too.

Of Greenleaf's efforts to put his concepts down on paper, McSwiney said:

> I guess Bob had it latent in him all his life. He had not articulated it very well earlier, although he was writing and thinking about it.
>
>   I don't think he had had exposure to many people in positions like mine who were as candid as I was with him. So he found it rewarding and meaningful, I think, to test some of his ideas and thoughts. The other side of the coin was that it was an interesting dialogue for me to reflect upon.
>
>   We both had the feeling that you have to keep dialogue open and

you have to keep it straightforward. In some situations—within a family, for example—it is sometimes just as well to avoid dialogue on some matters, but in a corporation dialogue must be reopened when it closes, and a third party is often the best vehicle for so doing. We both felt that we were in a society moving from autocratic to pluralistic action. That you couldn't dominate people. You had to involve them and give them an opportunity to present their views. And then you had the responsibility of making a decision.

Greenleaf's views were set forth in such works as *Advice to Servants* (1975), *Servant Leadership: A Journey into the Nature of Legitimate Power and Greatness* (1977), *Teacher as Servant: A Parable* (1979), *Servant: Retrospect & Prospect* (1980), *Seminary as Servant* (1980), *Mission in a Seminary* (1981), *The Servant as Religious Leader* (1982), *Life's Choices and Markers* (1986), and *My Debt to E.B. White* (1987). Many of Greenleaf's essays were published under grants from the Lilly Endowment.

At the heart of Greenleaf's writing is the concept of "servant leadership." This seems to echo the Gospel According to Mark, chapter 10, verses 44 and 45: "Whoever wants to be great must be your servant, and whoever wants to be first must be the willing slave of all. For even the Son of Man did not come to be served but to serve, and to give up his life as a ransom for many" (*The New English Bible* translation).

In fact, Greenleaf's work was inspired to a large extent by the writings of the German Nobel laureate, Hermann Hesse (1877–1962). Hesse is best known for his *Siddhartha* and *Steppenwolf*, but it was his 1932 work, *Journey to the East*, that especially influenced Greenleaf.

McSwiney has said, "Greenleaf's servant-as-leader is a very important concept. I don't believe that in the world we live in today you are effectively serving the people that are with you unless they perceive that by being with you they are better off. In essence, you've got to be benefiting them, and it can't be an ego trip in which you are using them to build another pyramid."

Philosophically, servant leadership tries to deal with the reality of power in everyday life—its legitimacy, the ethical restraints upon it, the beneficial results of the appropriate use of power. That makes it different from many other ethical concepts, which tend to view power as bad per se.

In *Teacher as Servant*, a fictional character talks about the president of a large business:

> He comes through as a tough, aggressive, high achiever and a successful person. What makes him effective here is that he really has sorted out the issue of power and he is very realistic about what is required to be a servant in this highly organized and very competitive society. Some people are put off by the word *servant*. It connotes soft do-gooding to many and a lot of people … are turned off by the word. But here, at the head of this large company, is a fellow as hard as nails who has thought it all through and can communicate what he believes a servant has to be if he is to be a constructive influence.

The man in question was almost certainly modeled on McSwiney. In *The Servant as Leader* Greenleaf wrote:

> The leader needs two intellectual abilities that are usually not formally assessed in an academic way: he needs to have *a sense for the unknowable* and be able to *foresee the unforeseeable*. Leaders know some things and foresee some things which those they are presuming to lead do not know or foresee as clearly. This is partly what gives leaders their "lead," what puts them out ahead and qualifies them to show the way.

There is nothing namby-pamby about the servant leadership concept, as more than one passage in *The Servant as Leader* makes clear. Discussing mediocrity, for example, Greenleaf wrote:

> What is mediocrity? Is it not anything that is substantially less in quality than what is reasonable and possible with available resources, human and material? "Mediocrity is the truly diabolical force in the world," said Burckhardt.
>
> In the Western world I believe that this all too common fault, settling for mediocrity, derives from a flaw that is right at the heart of traditional moral law. When Moses came down the mountain carrying the law, chiseled in stone and bearing God's imprimatur, he may have laid the groundwork for our present condition. If we view Moses as a human leader, subject to error like the rest of us … he may have yielded to the temptation, common to this day, to attribute the law to "those higher up" rather than to assume the burden of

justification himself. We do not know his conditions; he may have felt that he could not be sufficiently persuasive as a mere rational man. But how much better it would be for us today, if, as the inspired man he obviously was, he had presented the law as a reasonable codification of experience and wisdom, a summary of those sensible rules to guide individual conduct and as the basis for a good society. This would have opened the way for continued growth of the law with further experience and would have made the rational justification of the law always a contemporary concern. The law, thus derived, would still have been essentially religious in the root meaning of *religio*, to rebind. Human beings are rebound to the cosmos so that, as intellectual individuals, probably estranged by their intellectuality, they can belong in this world and be at home in it.

There may have been two further flaws in the original concept of the law. Most of it was "thou shalt not's" and they are quite categorical. The few affirmations are general, and conformity with them is difficult to establish. This allows the interpretation that if one obeys the prohibitions, one is virtuous.

Then, by stating the law as uniform for all persons, regardless of their capacities, rather than placing a greater obligation on the more able, the better endowed persons are relieved of obligation to measure up to their opportunities and their potentials. This permits many to be seen as law-abiding when, in fact, their performance is far below what it might be.

In the same work, Greenleaf wrote:

While I would like to see more nonservants converted to servanthood, my greater hope is that more of those who are natural servants, who get joy out of serving, will become aggressive builders of serving institutions. Within these institutions the opportunity may seem larger for those in higher status positions, but as more and more people, regardless of their status, are asserting their autonomy and articulating their beliefs, literally everyone who is inside and who has some force as a person can be an institution builder.

Those outside can criticize, flagellate, and disrupt, but only those who are inside can build.

For the servant who has the capacity to be a builder, the greatest joy in this world is in building.

The words were Greenleaf's, but the concept was one that McSwiney had lived by all his life, even in the years before he met

Greenleaf. McSwiney was a builder, and nothing gave him more joy than building. At Mead—with the help of directors like C. William Verity, Jr., Dr. John M. Walker, Paul F. Miller, Vernon R. Alden, Walker Lewis, and, above all, Bill Jones, with whom he was in constant touch in person, on the telephone, or by mail—Mac was working to build a good company into a great corporation.

At the beginning of that effort, he later said, he "never dreamed of the immensity of the task of taking a small company with modest talent and building it into an immense and diversified entity." The key ingredient was people, he realized. Two particular bastions of strength were William W. Wommack and Gerald D. Rapp, "men of greatly different temperaments and skills, with completely different perspectives and behavior." With people like them, and many more, he was sure he would succeed in making Mead the corporation he wanted it to be.

Six

Fostering High Technology

In 1958, not long after he became a vice president, McSwiney had argued for a new emphasis on marketing within Mead. Five years later, after he became executive vice president, he was able to see to it that marketing got the attention it deserved. He called the program "Marketing at Mead"—not the most exciting label in the world, but it got the point across. The annual report for the following year said, "Perhaps the most significant element during the year for the future of the corporation was an increased dedication to marketing as a way of corporate life."

McSwiney was quoted as saying, "We are henceforth organizing this company in support of our marketing aims."

A special section of the annual report described meetings, promotional campaigns, and other activities intended "to insure that all segments of the organization keep their energies directed toward satisfying customer requirements, rather than on production-oriented goals."

An unusual number of people—unusual for Mead, at least—were promoted for the purpose of developing "strong, young, marketing-oriented management for the future." One of those who moved up was William Wommack, who took McSwiney's old job as head of the paperboard group.

In the course of integrating toward markets, Mead moved into the school market — notebooks, pads, and similar school items — in 1966 by acquiring a company called Westab, Inc. The president of Westab, Paul V. Allemang, was a management consultant who had been brought into Westab by an investment group. Allemang and McSwiney were neighbors, and through their friendship Westab became one of Mead's groups of divisions. The other major elements of the company were pulp sales, paper and related products, paperboard and its related products, and paper distributors.

Speaking of this period, McSwiney later said, "In the early days of diversification, our idea was that we had to get mass [i.e., size] to survive. In my mind we were never a conglomerate and never intended to become one."

In 1967 Pringle, the president, put into effect a new organizational arrangement at the top of the company, the President's Office. Its members, besides Pringle himself, were McSwiney; Allemang, who was in charge of administration of the corporation as a whole; and Dr. George H. Sheets, who had many years of experience in research operations and in handling the affiliated companies and Mead's pulp sales throughout the world. This was intended as a transitional device, to smooth the way for McSwiney's assumption of the ultimate responsibility for the company. Seven months later, Whitaker, the chairman, retired, and so did Pringle.

McSwiney became president and chief executive officer. It was 1968 and he was 52 years old.

It was an emotional day. George Sheets was about six months older than McSwiney and widely respected for his intellect, work habits, and experience in the company. There were those who felt that Sheets should have been named president and CEO instead of Mac. But when McSwiney and Sheets discussed the matter, Sheets told him, "The board made the right decision." Mac was ever grateful for Sheets's unstinting support.

During the brief existence of the President's Office, McSwiney had started to expand and diversify the company in keeping with his belief that mass, or size, was vital if the corporation was to be a survivor.

One of his concerns was the cyclical character of the paper industry, or the "forest products industry," as many were now beginning to call it. In a number of speeches, McSwiney drew attention to the "peak and plunge" pattern of the industry caused largely by overexpansion and augmented by normal national recession and growth periods, all of which caused earnings per share to be volatile. This brought into sharp focus the problem that investments in the industry were of a long-term nature—20 to 30 years—whereas the investors' interest was of a short-term nature. This paradox, of course, is common to many other U.S. industries.

"Because of the cyclical nature of the paper industry," he said, "up to now most paper companies have been reluctant to project a rosy future. I think we'd have to admit that we've been one of the herd."

He believed that paper companies had to break out of the trap by increasing sales and earnings faster than the growth in Gross National Product.

During the 1960s, a great part of Mead's expansion had been in the pulp business. One decision was to assume a partial interest in British Columbia Forest Products, a company with saw mills and an outstanding pulp mill on Vancouver Island. Mead purchased pulp from BCFP for use in its white paper mills. Mead Pulp Sales acted as world-wide sales agent for BCFP. Another action was to go into a joint venture with Noranda Mines Limited of Canada to build a pulp mill at Prince George, on the Fraser River in British Columbia, about 450 miles north of the U.S. border.

As an illustration of the principle of leverage, Mead's total investment for those two endeavors was $3 million for its share of Northwood, the company that built the Fraser River mill, and $10 million invested in Brunswick Pulp and Paper. The money invested in Brunswick, along with a contribution of a 29.05 percent interest in BCFP by Scott Paper, enabled the Brunswick operation to carry out a $40 million to $45 million expansion program and to provide a $10 million cash dividend to Scott and an asset dividend to Mead by Brunswick Pulp and Paper of 50 percent of its direct interest in BCFP. As McSwiney said, "Seldom had so much been undertaken with so little."

In these matters a major role was played by George Sheets, a Mead executive vice president. "George was Mead's most gifted pulp and paper manufacturing executive," Mac said. "He was a chemical engineer by training, and among the ablest that one was likely to encounter. It is hard to think of any area of Mead where his talents were not applicable. When he retired in 1980 he had spent his entire business career at Mead."

Sheets and Mac established a warm relationship with Adam Zimmerman and Alf Powis of Noranda Mines, their counterparts in the Northwood project, and Ian Barclay and Ken Benson, their counterparts in BCFP. McSwiney, Zimmerman, and Powis later acquired, for Mead and Noranda, sufficient BCFP shares in the open market so that among them they controlled a majority of shares. This in turn enabled them to consolidate BCFP earnings with their own. Scott Paper, still a large BCFP share owner, "did not applaud this move," according to Mac.

Mead's output of paper throughout the 1960s increased at a steady rate of about 5 percent a year in tonnage, with the edge as usual for the brown paper side of the business. By 1967, brown paper accounted for two-thirds of Mead's total production of 1.5 million tons of paper and virtually all the profits of the company.

Looking back on that period McSwiney said:

> The white paper machines were old and the facilities were run down. Our mill at Escanaba, Michigan, was small and inadequate, and the Chillicothe operation was also in poor shape. But we knew how to make quality paper on this old equipment because Mr. Mead had emphasized the importance of the company's research facilities. Mead's name in the white paper market place was extremely good because we made quality products. But it took an arm and a leg to make those products, which earned a very inadequate return. All the money made in the paperboard group seemed to go into the white paper business, doing little rebuilds of this machine and that facility, and so on. After an in-depth study by James S. Evans, who headed the white paper operation, we came to the conclusion we had to somehow make those facilities cost-effective or get out of the white paper business. I emphasized to the board of directors that we didn't have any choice. Because of our tremendous investment in time and research, and the value of our name in the market place, I strongly favored finding a way to stay in the business.

The first step was to shut down and dispose of seven small, old machines at Chillicothe. It was decided to greatly expand and modernize the small, obsolete ground wood mill at Escanaba on Michigan's upper peninsula. The principal reasons for this decision were the quality, quantity, and cost of wood fiber in the upper peninsula, which had been identified by a study. The construction cost was estimated at $56 million, which would make it the largest single capital expenditure ever made by Mead up to that time. The program called for the construction of a 300-inch-wide machine to produce 100,000 tons a year of coated paper for books and periodicals. This would enable Mead to take advantage of what the annual report called "a continuing shift away from uncoated papers for many books to coated papers with matte surfaces — exactly our specialty."

Funds were provided by a $56,675,000 Cornell Township, Michigan, Industrial Revenue Bond issue, without which the project would not have been possible.

The decision to build the paper machine first was made in order to establish increased market position in the coated field and to capitalize on the cost of market pulp, which was low at the time. Because funds were not available it was decided the pulp mill would have to come later. As it turned out, the pulp market never was in phase with the construction program and there were those who felt Mead was "at sea," as Mac put it.

For the long pull, the mill had to be integrated, so in 1968 the board gave approval for Phase Two, the construction of the pulp mill. The pulp mill was to add 220,000 tons of kraft production to the company's annual output, a portion to integrate the new 300-inch coated paper machine and the balance for sale on the open market. "And now the pulp market was once more in an undersold position," McSwiney recalled ruefully.

Again, money wasn't available within Mead or to Mead. After a great deal of pondering, McSwiney and Al Sealy went to the West Coast to see Harry Gray, then financial vice president of Litton Industries, who later spearheaded the dynamic growth of United Technologies. Gray was a man willing to entertain somewhat unorthodox proposals, and he and McSwiney got together on an arrangement whereby Litton did the engineering and managed construction of the project and took 20 percent of a joint venture at Escanaba, while Mead took 80 percent. On that basis, the venture was able to obtain the necessary long-term financing for the new Escanaba pulp mill. Later, Mead purchased Litton's 20 percent interest. Litton profited and Mead was off to a strong start in modernizing its white paper facilities, with an integrated, high-quality, and very cost-effective facility.

"After some bad days, followed by some good days," Mac recalled, "Phase Three was undertaken—installation of another machine, which brought about total integration of the pulp mill and the paper machine."

In devising the joint venture approach to financing Escanaba, McSwiney displayed again his agility in dealing with financial matters. As Paul Miller, a Philadelphia investment manager who was on Mead's board, said of him, "Mac has a tremendously fast financial mind and understands the dynamics of finance within a corporation in a way that I have never seen before in anyone. He seems to comprehend all the intricacies instantaneously—all the interconnections."

He needed a quick mind for financial matters in those days, for the late 1960s was one of those periods, of which there have been a number since World War II, when "merger mania" rose to fever pitch. Conglomerates were gobbling up companies at a breathless pace. In 1968 alone over 4400 companies worth $43 billion in assets disappeared in mergers, most of them taken over by conglomerates. After Jones & Laughlin, the nation's ninth largest steel producer, was acquired by Ling-Temco-Vought (later known as LTV, which in 1986 became one of the biggest companies ever to seek the protection of Chapter 11 of the Bankruptcy Act), C.W. Verity, Jr., president of Armco Steel Corporation, the nation's fifth largest steel producer, had a talk with McSwiney. Verity was a member of Mead's board of directors (in 1987 Verity was named Secretary of Commerce by President Ronald Reagan).

"Bill said to me," McSwiney recalled, "'Maybe we should consider putting Armco and Mead together so they [the corporate raiders] won't bother us.'"

McSwiney replied, "Well, I don't know whether a paper company and a steel company make any sense, but let's keep in touch with each other. So we have."

A short time later a rumor circulated in Wall Street that the Cities Service Corporation was going to go after Mead. The rumor was well founded. Cities Service was looking for a merger with a company that had a broad resources base, and Mead was one of the possibilities it considered.

"Woodlands were the kind of thing we were looking for," said John L. Burns, Cities Services president, in later years. "They were a renewable resource, and of course we were in the oil business."

Burns knew and liked Tally Mead and other Mead people, so he made a "friendly inquiry," as he put it. He and his colleagues invited McSwiney, Tally Mead, and some of the other Mead board members to a dinner at the Sky Club atop the Pan Am Building in New York City.

"I'll never forget it as long as I live," McSwiney said.

Pringle, who was beginning to display an elderly demeanor, had a tendency to fall asleep after a good dinner, and he did just that on this occasion, snoring gently.

"I think maybe he did us a favor," McSwiney said, "because the Cities Service people probably thought, 'Well, if he can sleep like that through a discussion like this, there can't be anything in Mead that we want.' "

McSwiney himself had "absolutely no appetite" for the deal, and after that evening there was no further discussion of it.

He himself intended to go on the acquisition trail, but not as a raider. "Free associations; no short-term marriages," he told shareholders. He said he didn't want Mead to be a conglomerate but a "coordinate." The growth strategy, he said, "would be directed toward profitable, long-term, multidivisional growth in sectors of the economy where we can achieve strong performance."

In planning for acquisitions, Mead was hindered to some degree by its previous success in expanding its paper business. In 1965 the Federal Trade Commission gave Mead five years in which to divest itself of six of the corrugated box and container plants that it had earlier acquired, and in 1968 the U.S. Department of Justice moved under the Clayton Act to compel Mead to give up some 15 or so of the merchant houses—paper distributing companies—it had absorbed between 1957 and 1967. Eventually, through negotiations, Mead was able to get the government to reduce the number of companies it had to dispose of to nine of the smaller units.

The lawyer responsible for the negotiations was Gerald D. Rapp, working with both Harold F. Baker, Mead's Washington counsel, and Bill Wommack, who provided management commercial strategy. Rapp had grown up in a small town in Nebraska. After graduating from the University of Missouri, he earned a law degree from the University of Michigan in 1958 and went to work for Smith & Schnacke, the law firm that represented Mead. Rapp worked closely with Walker Lewis, handling details of hearings and meetings, working with the government lawyers, and gradually becoming involved as legal counsel in other Mead activities, such as acquisitions, divestitures, financing, and various commercial transactions. Inevitably, he came into close contact with McSwiney, who found him adept at taking charge of special projects covering a wide variety of problems and issues that demanded attention. He was flexible, imaginative, and good at putting many of McSwiney's concepts down on paper in drafts that were then worked over extensively by McSwiney and others.

In 1970 McSwiney asked Rapp to join the Mead staff as assistant general counsel. In later years, Mac often said that he had probably "never known such a unique individual—a mind that never ceased to seek and find answers to problems." Rapp, Mac said, was viewed by some as "a laid-back corporate lawyer"—which some might consider an oxymoron—but McSwiney found him to be a key resource. "What he couldn't think up or solve," Mac observed, "he found someone else who could."

"The merger law was in the process of development at that time," Rapp said. "Nobody really could say this does or doesn't violate the law, or this acquisition will be prosecuted and that one won't."

One thing was apparent as a result of the government court decrees: if Mead were to engage in any more acquisitions, they would have to be outside the paper business, if antitrust problems were to be avoided.

Years later, in retirement, looking back on his career, McSwiney would say of his acquisitions, "If you are in the dog business and you acquire a lot of dogs, some of them aren't going to bark."

Some of Mead's "dogs" didn't bark.

One of McSwiney's admirers and supporters on the Mead board of directors was Dr. John Walker, whose wife, Louise, was a daughter of George Mead. Dr. Walker, who was credited with major contributions to the corporation's progress as a member of its board, said, "McSwiney wasn't perfect by any means. He could make mistakes, and he did. Some of his more controversial acquisitions were the furniture business, for example, and the iron business."

The "iron" business was not Armco, as one might have supposed, but the Woodward Corporation of Birmingham, Alabama, which had iron and coal mines, a limestone quarry, four blast furnaces, a coke and chemical by-products plant, and 50 miles of railroad track, on which were 10 locomotives. Woodward previously had acquired companies that made ductile castings, plastic gaskets, and a number of other products.

Some of the Mead board members were doubtful about getting into a business so different from paper, but McSwiney said, "My primary interest was cash and liquid resources. The Woodward acquisition gave us leverage in making available added capital and some cash. I always perceived the merger as increasing our size. I felt a bigger base was meaningful and critical for the long pull if we were to develop a great company.

"As it turned out, we received several other benefits from the Woodward deal. One was William R. Bond, its CEO, who recommended Bill Spencer [William M. Spencer III] to Mead's board. Spencer proved to be of inestimable value. Bond himself came to Mead with Woodward and became an executive vice president and board member. He was a lesson in persistence, humility, and loyalty."

The Woodward company was indeed strong financially, but it brought with it to Mead a host of other problems. For example, its work force was represented by unions that Mead had not dealt with in the past, and the Woodward employees were used to very different working conditions and bound by different kinds of personnel and security policies than those that governed Mead employees. Another problem for Woodward was competition from high-grade Venezuelan iron ore.

The "furniture business" that Dr. Walker referred to was the Stanley Furniture Company, of Stanleytown, Virginia, which was, in the 1960s, one of the four or five top companies in its market (dining room, bedroom, and youth furniture), with annual volume about $50 million. At the time, furniture companies were a very attractive investment; some were selling at price-earnings ratios in the high 30s. Just before acquiring Stanley Furniture, McSwiney had purchased a Dayton fabric and drapery business, Payne & Company, and envisioned the development of a Mead Interior Furnishings Group with those two companies as a base.

In later years McSwiney was to say that one of the advantages of the acquisition was that it brought into the Mead fold as a strong director and major stockholder Thomas B. Stanley, Jr.

In a period of 18 months, toward the end of the decade of the 1960s, Mead, through Woodward and Stanley, had entered into about a dozen or so markets, including cement, coke and chemical by-products, custom rubber molding for the oil tool industry, ductile iron pressure pipes, gray and ductile iron castings, gray iron low-pressure pipes, limestone, metallurgical coal, molded rubber gaskets for pipe, draperies and decorative fabrics, and furniture for dining rooms, bedrooms, and youth.

There were also two in-house, high-tech developments—ink-jet technology and an interactive, full-text research service for the legal profession, both of which required very sophisticated computer software. (Mead had been thinking about high-tech for some time. Working with IBM, Mead was probably the first paper company to develop a closed loop in the control and operation of one of its paper machines. McSwiney was convinced that "the world was going digital.")

Ink-jet technology was a direct result of an action that McSwiney took in 1967. To maintain quality, Mead research had evolved largely into a support arm for the various production facilities. This work was now assigned to the divisions. Central Research was now encouraged to engage in new areas, either compatible with fiber and coating technology or, it was hoped, on the cutting edge of other technologies.

This new departure caused the lab to hire a research scientist who had been with the National Aeronautical and Space Administration (NASA). He was R. Perry Taylor, a chemist and biologist, who "didn't fit any organizational chart," as one of his colleagues later said.

Taylor's investigations, McSwiney recalled, "started on the basis of examining a process by which one could do noncontact printing. We were looking for a mechanism by which you could make paper less expensively and also make it less prone to break on the web printing presses. Thus it would be a more cost-effective product."

Taylor began to study the possibilities in noncontact printing. Two approaches then being talked about were laser beam and ink jet. Both had the possibility of being linked to the digital computer. Ink jet seemed to offer great flexibility for color images and text.

Taylor decided to concentrate on the ink jet. The principle involved breaking a jet stream of ink into droplets and then deflecting the droplets to a catcher or letting them pass on to the paper by giving them a positive or negative charge. McSwiney proposed that the scientists set their sights on developing a fixed print bar that would be compatible with an $8\frac{1}{2} \times 11$-inch page with jets along the entire width that would be loosed in an "array" simultaneously as the paper passed beneath. To accomplish this would require up to 250 jet apertures an inch and printing speeds of 150,000 characters or more a second.

The computerized legal research service resulted from Mead's acquisition, in 1968, of a small, high-technology company, the Data Corporation, of Dayton. In a talk to a paper industry trade group, McSwiney described Data Corporation as "a young and vigorous company of about 300 people—most of them scientists and technicians—which specialized in [research and development, largely for the military] in such areas as precision measurement of the optical density of photographic images, digital analysis of imagery, information storage and retrieval, and time-shared computer software systems."

The company had been owned by Lysle Cahill, who ran the scientific side of the business, and William Gorog, who headed the business side. Data Corporation had performed substantial work for the Air Force in the field of microelectronic scanning of imagery. Now Mead had access to important scanning techniques developed by Cahill—techniques that could be adapted to the ink-jet technology now called Dijit.

One of the developments that the Data Corporation had been working on was a computer-based legal research system called OBAR (for the Ohio State Bar Association). This was an effort to develop an "on-line, full-text data base" which would make it possible for the legal profession and others to recall a desired subject matter by entering important key words into a computer terminal, thereby causing the computer to find any and all cases containing the important or pertinent words or phrases. This was accomplished typically in less than 60 seconds, even though many skeptics previously had doubts that this could ever be done.

It was from this modest beginning that Mead Data Central, now an important and growing part of the Mead Corporation, developed.

Lexis® was the name given to the legal research service that now provides law decisions of the appeals courts and the supreme courts of all 50 states and the federal government, as well as regulations and rulings involving taxes, securities transactions, trade, patents, labor disputes, bankruptcy, etc.

Next came Nexis®, the principal credit for which must be given to Robert O'Hara, who had come to Mead as a young marketing man through the acquisition of the Atlanta Paper Company and had a large part in the success of Mead Packaging International. Nexis, now the world's largest full-text information, general news, and business information system, provides full-text retrieval from more than 160 publications, including *The New York Times*, the *Washington Post, Business Week, Fortune*, the Associated Press, United Press International, Reuters, *Newsweek, Time, Tass, Xinhua*, the entire *Encyclopaedia Britannica*, and many, many other world-class information sources.

Of Lexis McSwiney liked to say in later years, "Bill Wommack and I agreed in the beginning that we'd authorize half a million dollars for this project for the great state of Ohio. Twenty-seven million dollars and several years later—with many more state and federal laws and regulations—we made our first buck from it."

He was always especially proud of Mead Data Central, which was better known as Lexis/Nexis. He had a terminal in his office long after he had retired, and used it to obtain important information.

Although he was a "hands-off" kind of manager who was not often seen around Mead Data Central, Mac's positive attitude influenced and motivated people throughout the operation. It even permeated down to the operating engineers and their staffs, who felt supported by McSwiney's confidence. Such interest in computers by a CEO was rare in the 1960s.

McSwiney often was pressured by others to sell off Mead Data Central. They saw it as a drain on profits. On the other hand, Mead Data Central employees often heard stories of his going to bat for them. Over the years, from time to time, various proposals were made to sell off those operations. Although he listened to the arguments, he always decided that Lexis and Nexis should remain with Mead.

Once one of his associates argued that by selling Mead Data Central earnings per share could increase about 15 cents. At that time, earnings were about $1 per share, or a little less.

"Why should we sell such a promising venture for just 15 cents?" he replied.

"I had a deep conviction about the ultimate value of these operations," he said simply.

At one time there had been those within Mead who questioned whether the company was not fraternizing with the enemy by getting involved with computerization. In the late 1960s and the 1970s many business publications were full of predictions that computers would ultimately bring about the "paperless office"—and paper, after all, was Mead's business.

Of course, the prophets were wrong, as they often are. Instead of less paper, many offices use more paper as they increase their employment of computers. A Nexis subscriber who orders a print-out of an article from an old issue of the *Washington Post*, for example, is presented with the article on paper.

In 1983, after McSwiney's retirement, but while he was still a member of the company's board of directors, Mead decided it should not continue to sponsor both the ink-jet and the data bank projects, so Dijit was sold to Eastman Kodak and the ink-jet development disbanded.

But Lexis and Nexis enabled Mead Data Central, in 1986, to continue what the corporation's annual report called "its fast growth," ending the year with a 22 percent increase in revenues.

Seven

Strategic Planning

In 1969 Bill Wommack, the head of the paperboard group, joined the President's Office as executive vice president for strategy and planning. For some time McSwiney had been impressed with Wommack's abilities, especially his independent spirit, which had been displayed on more than one occasion—like the time he offered his resignation in protest of an order from his boss that he regarded as wrong. In the paperboard group, Wommack had kept pressing for financial data that would provide better insight into what was happening as a result of operations. The difficulties he encountered made him increasingly critical of corporate strategic planning as it was then being carried out at Mead—and, indeed, at most other major U.S. corporations.

Early on in his new job, Wommack decided that outside assistance was needed if strategic planning was to be successful. "If you put together an internal group to study this," he said, "the first philosophy they will devise is one that fits what they are doing." The organization he selected to assist Mead was the Boston Consulting Group.

The success of the strategic planning process at Mead resulted from a very involved search by McSwiney for someone highly talented in this process. In the course of his search, Mac found two things that stood out: (1) there were very few such persons, and (2) those who were entrusted with such a position were attached generally to a senior executive office and thus had little or no influence on the organization. After trying out a former General Electric employee,

McSwiney also came to the conclusion that no one was likely to succeed in this role unless he had a proven track record within the company. Wommack's record of success in the paperboard area and his intense interest in the subject made him a natural fit.

At a retreat attended by five or six of the top officers of Mead, they examined a format employed at one time by the Koppers Company and later abandoned. McSwiney was impressed with the format's emphasis on capital allocation—a function he felt Mead needed to improve greatly—and he believed the format had probably been abandoned by Koppers for lack of internal acceptance.

Mac left the retreat with the conviction that strategic planning must play a major role in Mead's future and that capital allocation had to be at the heart of any such effort.

One result of this meeting was the beginning of the Mead *matrix concept* (see Appendix A), which has since become well known among management theorists. The development of the matrix was initially carried out by a small strategic office agreed upon by McSwiney and Wommack, which included Bruce Bedford, Wallace Nugent, and a few other Mead people. Later Jerry Tatar replaced a member of the team. Along with Alan Zakon of the Boston Consulting Group, the Mead group began to help Wommack in implementing the program. The matrix was developed from Mead data, experience, and funding.

Wommack once said, "The capital allocation process is really the driving force behind the strategy of any business." As previously noted, McSwiney emphatically agreed. He also worked with Wommack to initiate a *number-oriented profile* (see Appendix B) that would make "plugged" numbers by managers requesting capital stand out.

Mead became one of the first companies to state in writing for its managers the philosophy underlying the matrix while the ideas were in their formative stages. In a talk before the Harvard Business School Club, McSwiney described the matrix as "an interesting way of determining when and how to get into (or out of) any given market"—but he said in later years that it was much easier to decide what to get out of than it was to feel comfortable about those businesses to get into.

He also emphasized that strategic planning must be regarded as a dynamic process.

In the Harvard Business School Club talk, McSwiney said:

> One of the significant facts of business life today is the continuing shift in market share. Activity in the market place has a tendency to shift to the most cost-effective producers within relatively mature markets. This phenomenon generally applies to both industrial and consumer markets. Furthermore, companies with the largest shares of a market generally produce the greatest margins and the highest returns of investment. What the top-knockers have is what I call "market power," a combination of things that permits (1) the establishment and control of price, (2) maintenance or growth in share of market, and (3) by the first two to have good insight into their competitor's share of market and profits.
>
> This sounds formidable, and so it is. If one gets too greedy in pricing, and therefore has excellent margin, the business will become increasingly desirable to others. On the other hand, if one prices too low, there will not be a desirable return. General competitive theory indicates that the total cost of developing, manufacturing, and marketing a product (in terms of constant dollars) tends to decline by a fixed percentage each time the past production experience is doubled.
>
> A corporate management is concerned with developing a balance of good business opportunities—there is a need for high-growth, cash-hungry businesses and mature businesses which tend to generate funds to feed the growth segments. One needs a clear picture of the real growth opportunities: those which can generate cash, and the ones from which the company had best withdraw.

From the beginning, McSwiney and Wommack had felt that it was essential that Mead's management be brought up to speed on the essentials of allocating and managing resources—the factors basic to strategic planning. But it was obvious to them that it was not practical, nor was there enough time, for them to impart the philosophy to the entire organization.

"It also became clear," McSwiney said, "that we were not trained nor of the temperament to fully develop such a program in a time dimension that would be meaningful. Bill [Wommack] and I came to feel that if professionals in the consulting and academic worlds felt our rationale made sense, they were best equipped to convey it in a believable form to the management team. Thus, we began a series of seminars to fulfill this need."

So the company's top managers—numbering 300 or more—were asked to attend a one-week seminar called "Managerial Economics." The program was led by John K. Pfahl, professor of business organization at Ohio State University, who had also taught at the seminars of the Granville Experience. "He was an exciting teacher," said Wommack, who was not given to lavish praise. The seminar introduced Mead managers to the growth matrix and to return on net assets (RONA) as basic management tools. The managers were told that the yardsticks and methodology discussed at the seminar would now be used in evaluating almost all the company's strategic business units.

This led Wommack to ask the manager of one of Mead's divisions to meet with him. During the meeting, Wommack described a hypothetical company and asked the man what he thought should be done with it.

"I'd sell it by morning!" the man exclaimed. Then he found out that the hypothetical company was, in fact, his own division.

The program was also presented to the board of directors in December 1969. During the meeting McSwiney made plain his intention to give the chief planning officer a high level of authority. He was determined that the planning function would not be isolated from the rest of the organization, an error he felt had been committed in too many corporations.

"I agreed to take the job," Wommack said later, "if Mac delegated part of the functions of the executive office to the planning side. I became chief strategic planning officer. As far as we know, Mead was the first company ever to try this kind of division of responsibilities."

That change took place formally in 1971. McSwiney disbanded the President's Office and became chairman of the board—a post that had been vacant for three years—and chief executive officer (CEO). Wommack became vice-chairman of the board and chief strategic officer (CSO). Paul Allemang became president and chief operating officer (COO). This meant that the CSO and the COO were on about the same level under the CEO—hardly the usual arrangement, and one that was recognized as requiring a greater than normal tolerance for ambiguity and uncertainty.

McSwiney and Wommack decided that the CSO, as previously noted, should set up a small but strong organization to study and plan the best strategic course of action, and to monitor its implementation in the divisions. The COO was invited to attend meetings at any time and was privy to all input, but could not implement a capital plan contrary to the CSO's allocation of resources, unless the CEO overruled the CSO. That seldom happened, as it turned out. McSwiney's feeling was that, if both parties disagreed, they should go back to the drawing board, where, in all likelihood, the most rational course would evolve.

"That was the thing about Mac," Wommack commented later. "In a way it seemed he was giving away a lot of power to create the CSO. But this was not a problem for him. Only a relatively secure man could do that.

"Mac saw the need for strategic planning and found in me a person who, he was confident, would set up a good system and be able to run it. Mac has said it was hard for him to say, 'No,' when one of his managers wanted to do something. He knew he needed a safeguard against his desire to build and his belief that his vision could not be rationalized on a daily basis.

"Mac told me, 'I always wanted to be responsive to a person who had a new idea. I just don't understand how you can expect new ideas to surface if they are crushed by a system or some formula. Let the idea flourish and be tested — in the end the system finds a reasonable answer or the CEO has to decide. Our Lexis project would never have survived otherwise.' "

Implicit in that statement is an acknowledgment of the analytical, rather than creative, nature of strategic planning. Wommack himself was aware of this limitation in the process.

"Corporate planners who have made careers of their jobs," he once said, "are some of the most boring people I know. If you are bright and action-oriented, I am not sure you can be a planner for the same organization for more than several years without losing your mind."

On another occasion Wommack said, "New ventures do not fit into a strategy sequence system since a company really has only two alternatives from which to choose: fund the new venture to win, or pull out. Any other choice is a nondecision. The mortality rates of new business ventures is high, and a company does not win by being an also-ran. One cannot systematize a new venture decision; it is a risk decision based on a judgment as to whether the company can attain the leadership position."

Wommack felt that McSwiney had "delegated" some of the powers of the chief executive officer to the CSO, but McSwiney never saw it in those terms. "Never," McSwiney said. "A CEO can only delegate 'authority within limits,' subject to overrule." True, he always liked to operate through others, even in the early stages of his career, but that didn't mean delegating any of his responsibilities to them.

"The CEO must think of, and be responsible for, all facets of the company," McSwiney once said. "The emphasis is on organizing to get the job done well. True, the CEO can't think about either strategy or implementation all the time. Most likely the time he has available for either doesn't, or won't, fit the timeframe needed; hence the need for wide authority on the part of the CSO and the COO."

Having the strategic planning function in capable hands meant that McSwiney could devote more of his time to other parts of the company that needed strengthening. Because the management structure of Mead was still being developed, there was less friction over the creation of the CSO and his staff as a power center than one might have expected. Wommack believed there was another reason for the lack of resistance to his function.

"Mead had a great success story," he pointed out, "but our success came out of recognition that significant changes were in order. Under these conditions, egos settle down and you say, 'Okay, let's get on with it and worry about egos later.' This purpose gave us unity and helped us over some very rough spots."

The "rough spots" included the economic recession of 1970, the longest and most serious recession the nation had experienced since the 1930s.

"Mac never established the position of chief financial officer in his first tenure as CEO, probably for a variety of reasons," Wommack said. "The Finance Committee of the Board of Directors was chaired by Paul Miller, long recognized in the investment community as being very able in the financial field. Mac had a series of excellent controllers [one of whom, Burnell Roberts, later became CEO], and a very creative treasurer in Bruce Bedford. Besides, Mac had wide experience in financial matters himself. Mac had no misgivings about the office, but felt the time to create this position was later, and he did create the post during his second term as CEO."

Mead sales had reached the $1 billion mark for the first time in 1969, but in 1970 the company's earnings were severely depressed. Return on net assets, which had been 6.0 percent in 1968, fell to 3.7 percent in 1970 (in 1974, RONA was up to 10.9 percent). Return on total equity, which had been 8.0 percent in 1968, dropped to 4.5 percent in 1970 (going up to 16.3 percent in 1974). Reduced demand, because of the recession, cut sales in nearly all Mead's product lines at a time when the company was incurring large start-up costs in connection with three capital projects—the Northwood pulp mill in British Columbia, the $40 to $45 million modernization program at Brunswick Pulp, and the new paper machine at Escanaba—three projects whose costs totaled about $175 million.

It was during this period that the company decided to accept a strike at its Escanaba mill, if necessary, in order to achieve the integration of Social Security benefits with the company's pension plan. The strike lasted six months and was difficult for everyone. It was a test of wills in which the company had to prevail, and there was no disagreement on this score within management. There was never an effort to break the union, but as the strike dragged on, management prepared detailed plans to use helicopters to get people in and out of the struck mill in order to reopen it for operation. Fortunately, the strike was settled before matters reached that state. After operations were resumed, a federally sponsored program, Relations By Objectives, was agreed to by both management and the union, and in time it proved very useful in establishing a positive environment.

After his retirement, McSwiney used to point out, with a smile, "The investment community once thought that money had been unwisely devoted to Escanaba, but now it's recognized as being very profitable, as well as tops for quality and cost-effectiveness in its grade structure."

The strike, added to the problems the national economy was undergoing, came at a particularly inauspicious period for McSwiney.

"That was a rough time for Mac," said Tom Stanley, who joined the Mead board in 1970 and became "a great supporter of Mac":

> It was hell. Everything Mac was trying to do almost came apart in this period. He was trying to change the philosophy of the entire company and introduce a whole new orderly procedure and discipline for strategic planning. At the same time, he wanted to do this without stifling creativity. And then came the recession.
>
> Escanaba was just going on stream—a significant investment of capital in a program that was having a hard time moving. Northwood was also a tough one to get going, and Brunswick was being rebuilt. There were cost increases. So damned many things were going on that sorting them out was a terrible job. At the same time there were the divestiture decisions to be made in such areas a coke, pipe, pig iron, the alloy business, and others such as cement, lime, and certain grades and markets in the paper business.
>
> What Mac was determined to achieve today would be called a restructuring of the business. And he pulled it off. He did what he had been trying to do.

Nevertheless, it was a struggle. Austerity programs had to be imposed throughout the corporation. Budgets were cut. With the fall in the company's earnings, Mead lost its A credit rating at Standard & Poor's. "We kept it at Moody," McSwiney said, "because the personnel there understood the company. They understood where we were, where we were going, and where we were coming out." The quarterly dividend was cut from 25 cents to 15 cents.

Wommack and his team now began proposing some divestitures. The Woodward operation was pared. Wommack found that buying pig iron from outside suppliers would be cheaper for Woodward than continuing to operate its own blast furnaces. If Woodward just sold the coal that it mined, it would do as well as it did in the pig iron business. The company's Red Mountain ore mine was closed, and then two of the blast furnaces were shut down. The last furnace was dismantled two years later.

Of the original Woodward properties Mead retained three units. The ductile castings operation at Lynchburg was widely respected as a producer of quality products. It had been expanded and after its acquisition produced good profits. However, a visit to Japan just prior to another proposed major expansion indicated that, although

Lynchburg could still deliver a quality product at the most competitive prices, it would probably not fit the long-term strategy of Mead and the proposed expansion was cancelled. Murray Rubber was the premium rubber compound gasket producer for the then-booming oil and gas exploration industry. It was in the process of expanding when domestic oil exploration collapsed. Mulga Mines was a high grade metallurgical coal mine operation for which a long-term, cost-plus contract had been worked out with a large Japanese trading company.

Between 1972 and 1977 Mead divested itself of 14 operating units as a direct result of its strategic philosophy. A company memorandum to management personnel said:

> Management felt strongly that these businesses were inappropriate under the strategic philosophy adopted and that the liquidation of these units not only generated capital which could be better used elsewhere, but avoids chasing "problem children" with little hope of turnaround.
>
> Improvement in key operating ratios was significant during the 1971–1977 period. Labor productivity, working capital control, and asset turnover were highlighted as operating variables contributing significantly to the turnaround.

As the economy recovered and Mead's strategic planning began to have an impact, sales and earnings rose steadily. The quarterly dividend was raised to 20 cents in 1973 and to 30 cents in 1974. Obviously, Wall Street was pleased by all of this, but some securities analysts were puzzled by the strategic planning concept, which was new to them. One analyst, who had apparently begun to grasp what Mead's strategic planning was about, said, "They have a tool that will keep them from making emotional decisions. I didn't like their getting out of the lime business, for instance. But they pointed out that, though it was profitable, it was taking a disproportionate amount of management's time."

By the mid-1970s Mead had gotten rid of all of its businesses that were not performing satisfactorily when judged by the matrix, except for Stanley Furniture—and in 1979 Stanley, along with Payne Fabrics, was sold.

In 1977 the company made its first acquisition since 1969, when it bought the outstanding shares of Gulf Consolidated Services, a

Houston distributor of industrial materials such as pipe, valves, fittings, electrical supplies, insulation, and tools to the Southwestern chemical and petro-chemical industries. Mead felt that this company's operations were similar to Mead's merchant distribution group.

There was renewed pressure on McSwiney at that time to sell the Lexis-Nexis operation and Dijit, but he resisted stoutly.

"That's why you've got people like me sitting around," he said a couple of years later, "because in the end it is not a committee decision. If some of the members of management had had their way, we wouldn't have Lexis and Dijit today. They'd have been sold.

"That's not saying I know all the answers, but somebody has to sit on top. That's the way our system works—the way the free enterprise system works."

About the time he was ready to retire, the question of Dijit arose again. He wasn't quite as firm in his support of Dijit then as he was of Lexis.

"Dijit may have a great opportunity a decade away if we see it through," he said. "And if we do we may become the graphics company of the world. But if we don't we should be able to sell it."

That was a true reflection of the McSwiney approach to life.

"A system, with all its numbers," he once said, "can't replace the entrepreneurial spirit—that of moving ahead and taking risks. The world is so dynamic that anything that truly helps you evaluate a good strategic course today should be viewed with suspicion tomorrow."

By both temperament and conviction a risk-taker, McSwiney liked to recall, "I took some high risks. We began to build the Northwood pulp mill in Canada—a $50 to $60 million project—when Mead had only $3 million as its share to put into the operation. Later we had to advance another $18 million (where it came from I still can't be sure) in the form of interest-bearing notes, for construction and start-up costs. But in time this was returned, and Mead and Noranda celebrated with a note-burning ceremony. Mead and Noranda were the proud owners of one of the most cost-efficient pulp mills in the world. Moreover, that pulp mill could draw upon tremendous forest reserves that had been granted to Noranda before the initiation of the joint venture."

Eight

Building a Strong, Independent Board

A lot had happened in the business world since the days when Mead's board, in Bill Jones's words, "did what Mr. Mead told [it] to do." A new phrase entered the jargon of business in the late 1960s, "corporate governance," and the function of directors—and their relative effectiveness in filling that function—was widely discussed.

McSwiney had been pondering the structure and role of the board of directors for some time. Although he was not one to participate in company politics in the usual sense, McSwiney had the ability to win support of many people, including the outside directors on the board. One of the outside board members, Dr. John Walker, said, "Mac sells ideas well, to the company and to the board."

McSwiney was developing some fairly dramatic ideas about Mead's board of directors. But before he gave voice to those ideas, he decided he needed to make clear to Mead's management his concept of true corporate teamwork. His thinking was reflected in a document he prepared and first issued to Mead management in 1970, entitled *Philosophy of Organization & Planning*. As revised in 1972, it said in part:

> Mead, like every organization, fits into a hierarchy of interlocking organizations. To grow—or even to survive—it must have the alle-

giance of its members. Yet it must avoid demands that conflict with the priorities of other ranking organizations.

Common needs and common beliefs bind people together. If these needs and beliefs are perceived to be critical and important, then all else will be subordinated. Rank, status, and all activities will be organized around those needs.

The effectiveness of the organization depends on the people who make it up. Increased delegation and decentralization place a great dependence on the managerial abilities of people throughout the company. This is particularly true of division general managers. These men must be truly *general* managers, able to make decisions on a broad basis involving *all* the functional areas of their businesses. They must balance the financial and technical factors, and be sensitive to the human elements involved in employee and community relations. They need the ability to weigh corporate interests against their own division interests and to evaluate human as well as financial factors on a balanced basis. Above all, they need the ability to inspire confidence and obtain the best effort from their people. Long-range profitability of a division depends on the general manager's ability to handle *all* of these factors effectively.

Staff people must accept the full challenge of their assignments. They need to develop technical proficiency in their specialized areas of knowledge. In addition, they must develop a full understanding of their most frequent role of consultant to the line managers. This carries with it the obligation to analyze the problem thoroughly, make definite recommendations, and state them clearly for the benefit of the line manager requesting the advice. It also carries with it the willingness to respect the line manager's prerogative to accept or reject the advice and make a final decision based on the broad interest of the individual profit center.

The capacity to perform successfully in the challenging years ahead depends on the acceptance by Mead people that common beliefs and needs do bind people together—and that implementation is effected by motivated people, that is, people who are still growing as persons.

The statement reflected McSwiney's lifelong belief in encouraging people to grow to the limit of their capabilities. In its argument that people will subordinate parochial interests to the greater needs of the larger organization if they are bound together by common beliefs and needs that are perceived to be critical and important, the statement also demonstrated how McSwiney's ideas were crystallizing into the concept that Robert Greenleaf would refer to as "servant leadership."

Both ideas were highly relevant, for the document also announced a new, decentralized corporate organization, consisting of six major groupings of businesses, plus the new ventures—Mead Data Central and ink-jet—that reported to William Wommack.

At the time, McSwiney was concerned not only with building company-wide team spirit in a heterogeneous management organization, but also with reformation of the board of directors. Gerald Rapp, the lawyer who was now working closely with McSwiney, said in later years, "I associate [the board changes] more with Bob Greenleaf's and Bill Jones's influence than anything else. Mac would take an idea and bounce it around with a guy like Bill Jones, whom he respects, and Bill would probably say, 'Mac, I think you are on the right track.' So that reinforced him. But I think that early on [McSwiney] embraced the Greenleaf thesis: if you want to build a great company, you build a great board. No matter what anyone says, it has ultimate control. If you have a good board and well-functioning, good people, that's the best guarantee that you'll have a good institution. Over time, you'll get your management development, you'll get your finance, you'll get your people. You can't do it unless you have got the board working actively to see that it's done."

McSwiney certainly believed that Mead needed an informed, inquisitive, independent-minded board that took its work seriously. He also felt that board members "should clearly understand and agree on their function, scope, and duties."

Like most other boards, Mead's board had taken shape as a result of past traditions as well as mergers and acquisitions. Its board still reflected, to some degree, George Mead's tendency to look to friends, family, and top managers to serve as directors. In the mid-1960s, half the members of the board were from management and several of the outside directors had close ties to the Mead family and the company. There were also two members of the Mead family on the board, George Mead's sons, H. Talbott and Nelson. Paul Allemang and Arthur Harris had come into the company, and onto the board, as a result of acquisitions. In 1968, the board was enlarged to 23, the new directors representing the Woodward and Stanley interests as well as McSwiney's new management team. Only 10 of the 23 were outside directors.

There were no outside directors on the executive committee, which did, however, include certain top management people who were not on the board itself. McSwiney regarded the executive committee as the equivalent of the latter-day operating committee. "It served as a means of gaining management consensus on issues to be taken to the full board," he said. "The perception was that they could vote at the board meeting whereas, in fact, the inside directors provided only the information asked for by the outside directors, much as is done today by management presentations. It was perceived authority as contrasted with real authority, but the issue had to be addressed since perception is often as good or bad as reality."

McSwiney believed that service on the board by management people helped them to grow and broaden through contact with outstanding people from the outside, and through exposure to new ideas and experiences. In theory it made sense; in practice it sometimes worked, but sometimes didn't. Some insiders simply didn't work out as board members and had to be eased off the board.

Bill Jones said to McSwiney, "Mac, you probably don't have the kind of support you need."

"He didn't mean support in the sense of 'okay' and everything like that," McSwiney said, "but the kind of questioning, the kind of expertise, the kind of public image, and so forth."

Jones and McSwiney were talking about the need for a board that would have more outside members, people with broad experience and greater stature in the outside world, who would act not only as peers in the boardroom but—when they felt it to be in the best interests of the company—as persons with valid authority.

As a first step toward clearing the way for such a board, the executive committee of the board was reconstituted in late 1969. It became a committee of outside directors with the exception of Walker Lewis, the company's legal counsel, who was secretary, and McSwiney, who was chairman.

The old executive committee now became a management committee; McSwiney called it the "inside board." He wanted its members to think and act as though they would be present at the next board meeting with full responsibility for the best interests of the company. "I thought of it as a meaningful exercise to help them carry out their jobs and improve the company," McSwiney said. "If you are going to build people, give them a sense of the whole, then they need some kind of forum in which they aren't limited by their own responsibilities. All I was after was to give them a chance to see what else was going on in the company and express their views. I think it made them better managers by broadening their horizons.

"It's an interesting thing about life—it often isn't what happens at a meeting, it's what the meeting causes the individual to do before he gets there. He's all hot and bothered, and he writes out his speech. Then he looks at it and recognizes broader aspects of the issue."

Other changes were being made at the board level. The audit committee, which had existed at Mead since the late 1950s, became a committee of outside directors, a decade before the New York Stock Exchange required this of listed companies. One of McSwiney's earliest moves was to strengthen the internal audit group by bringing in Paul Glotzbach, a seasoned professional in the audit field who in time became directly responsible to the board, as well as to his immediate internal superiors. Thus, the board became involved with both the corporation's inside and outside auditors.

In July 1971 the Mead board held a three-day retreat at the Red Lion Inn at Stockbridge, in the Berkshire hills of western Massachusetts. The discussion at Stockbridge dealt with the structure of the board, as well as the question of management succession and strategic planning. In a letter to board members after the retreat, McSwiney said some board members felt the board was too large, that there were too many inside directors, and that "a written guideline concerning the duties and responsibilities of the board would be most appropriate." Pointing out that Bill Jones was the oldest board member in point of service, McSwiney went on to say:

> He will also not stand for re-election next March as per our Board regulations. Because of his familiarity, balance, interest, and weight of judgment with respect to the company, I would like to ask him to serve as chairman of a group of outside Directors to:
> 1.   Make recommendations as to the size, composition, retirement age, compensation, and other appropriate matters relating to the Board.
> 2.   Review with me proposed management succession moves.

In later days William Spencer, one of the members of the committee, said McSwiney's "intuitive" decision to make Jones the committee chairman was one of his most inspired ideas. Jones "was part of the Mead family," Spencer said, "but he had only married into it and he didn't live in Dayton. He could pretty much say the things that others might not like to hear, and get away with it. He was loved and respected."

Explaining his decision to appoint the committee, McSwiney later said, "I looked around and listened to what people thought boards were supposed to do. I couldn't find where anyone had a clear agreement or understanding on this subject, other than just the legal definition. So it seemed to me that rather than for a chief executive to tell the board what its responsibilities were, why wasn't it a prudent thing to ask them what they thought their responsibilities were? In that way, we could have dialogue, and in the end we wouldn't have to persuade them to read, comprehend, and respond to a well-intentioned paper."

After a year's study and deliberations, the committee issued what was immediately dubbed the Jones Report, a document that received wide recognition. Jones himself said, "I'm not sure it should have been called the Jones Report—it would have been better if it had been called the McSwiney Report....The so-called Jones Report is more Mac's development than mine. Being in a small business, I had more time to work on it than he did, and I got very interested in it. But it was done under Mac and with his surveillance. It was good evidence of a finding that the board could be helpful in his long-range plan."

The report unquestionably represented the collective thinking of five outside directors, as well as McSwiney's. The lengthy document covered philosophical considerations; the size and operation of the board and selection of directors; the compensation of directors; and the function, scope, duties, and responsibilities of five committees: executive, finance, audit, compensation, and corporate responsibility.

The report recommended a board of between 12 and 15 directors, "with inside directors not to exceed one-third." Of the board's composition, the report said:

Outside directors should be chosen for the breadth of experience and interest, and the balance they can bring to the Board's deliberations. A candidate's characteristics rather than his position should receive the major scrutiny. Among desirable characteristics, we note inquisitiveness, conscientiousness, integrity, good business judgment, wide range in experiences, and an appreciation of the changing environment.

The Jones Report made five specific suggestions about members of the board:

1. One or more directors oriented to minority, ethnic, or other social concerns may contribute to a balanced response to corporate responsibilities.

2. Heads of companies similar to Mead in size who possess the desired characteristics may contribute worthwhile experience.

3. Large owners of stock (not institutional holders) should be represented on the Board. If the director draws compensation from the company (other than director's fees) which entitles him to the normal fringe benefits, he will be considered an "inside" director.

4. Generally the company will best be served by the omission of investment bankers, consultants, and legal counsel who are professionally engaged with the corporation.

5. Honorary or emeritus directors are not deemed to be in the best interests of the company.

The committee also urged that its report be regarded a living document, suggesting that "the function, duties, and scope of the board be reviewed every five years" by a new committee. The committee said its report should be updated annually to reflect current events or other considerations.

Within a year or so, the Mead board shrank from 23 members to 17, mostly by attrition. By 1975 outsiders comprised 60 percent of the board.

The Corporate Responsibility Committee (CRC) proposed by the Jones Report was first suggested by Paul Miller, a member of the board, during the Stockbridge retreat. He envisioned a committee that examined the corporation's relationships with government and with various sectors of the public. McSwiney had no quarrel with this idea—the subject was being widely discussed at that time—but he felt the committee would be most effective if some of its members were rank and file employees.

True, the Jones Report said the CRC was to "examine and report on the attitudes at all levels of management toward social and environmental responsibilities and concerns," make recommendations on issues and their priorities, and suggest what the company ought to be doing and who in the company ought to be doing it. But the membership of the CRC was something new—possibly unique—in American business. "It is believed that a combination of three outside directors and four members of junior management, drawn from within the company at the discretion of the outside Board members, will provide the means for a true internal audit," the report said. "The committee will be chaired by a member of junior management and will from time to time make reports and recommendations to the Chief Executive Officer, who in turn will report to the full Board when he or the Committee deem it desirable."

In practice, the CRC soon was expanded to include factory and office workers as well as members of junior management.

The establishment of the committee was an expression of McSwiney's belief that a great corporation must make "a constant effort to seek ways of being responsive to change."

In his retirement years, looking back on a lifetime of achievement, McSwiney regarded the CRC as one of his most notable accomplishments.

"Basically, what you're doing is listening to people who are far down the line about how they see and perceive things," he said. "A lot of people are afraid to do this because they are afraid these same people will ask them for something they feel they can't or shouldn't do, or at least make it uncomfortable for them. My idea was entirely different. I didn't think people would normally ask for more than one could probably do, because people usually perceive a system better than one is prone to think, and thus they intuitively know what is likely to be acceptable within the system. What most people want is the dignity of being heard and considered, and after that they are usually quite willing to accept the decision that comes forth from the process."

McSwiney appointed Gerald D. Rapp, who was then assistant general counsel and assistant secretary of the corporation, first chairman of the CRC to get it started. Rapp was succeeded as chairman by Vernon R. Alden, a director. One of the original outside board members to serve on the CRC was Ivan Allen, Jr., a former mayor of Atlanta, Georgia, and a member of Mead's board from 1971 to 1978. A successful businessman, Allen was Atlanta's mayor in the 1960s when Martin Luther King, Jr., led the movement that desegregated lunch counters in that city. As one of the key moderates in the white establishment, Allen was one of a number of courageous civic leaders who helped to bring about a new era of race relations in the South. Allen was a strong supporter of the CRC.

Not all of Mead's management felt the same way. There were those who worried that the official channels of communication were being bypassed through the CRC. This could undercut their authority, they argued. In a business world that lived by clear-cut rules, lines of authority, and tables of organization, the CRC posed many questions that in time would need to be resolved.

The CRC was not the only unusual committee to emerge from the Jones Report. Another was the Executive Committee, which was comprised of the chairs of all the other board committees, plus the board chair and CEO. Like most such committees, it was given "all the powers of the Board with the exception of filling vacancies which may arise on the Board." However, the Executive Committee was authorized to take action only in extreme cases. One exception: the committee was to meet with the chief executive officer periodically "to review and discuss" a number of subjects, the principal one being "organizational development, changes, and concepts (including an annual review of succession for officers and key group managers)."

As though to underline this responsibility for overseeing management development, the Jones Report said a couple of paragraphs later: "The Executive Committee, or an appointed committee thereof, may from time to time be given special assignments by the Chief Executive Officer. They may, for example, be asked to review, study, or consult on such a topic as a proposed management change before it is submitted to the full Board."

As board member William Spencer said, "Mac pushed his Executive Committee into being a management succession committee. At most companies, the Executive Committee of the board is the most important one. But at Mead, it was mainly concerned with succession; it never acted as a surrogate to the Board."

Another person—chief executive officer of his own company—who joined the Mead board at a later period said, "The Mead Executive Committee does what our nominating committee does, and what these committees do in most companies."

Although the Executive Committee was composed of outside directors, McSwiney was its chairman so that he could remain involved in the selection of management and the nomination of directors.

Explaining why he wanted an Executive Committee so structured, McSwiney once wrote:

> Probably the most important duty of the executive committee of Mead's board...is to meet at least annually with the CEO [chief executive officer] to discuss organizational development, changes, and new directions, including an annual review of succession for senior corporate officers and for key group managers.
>
> It is appropriate that such discussions should focus on the depth and quality of management talent in the company; on the implementation of organizational concepts; and on the consideration of possible changes or new directions in corporate structure and organizational development.
>
> Discussions should also take into account the professional development and personal growth of all involved—the CEO, his key associates, and the board members themselves. It is reasonable also to assume that desirable growth will most likely be achieved through a continuous learning process.

That growth process was also furthered by the annual board retreats, attended by both board members and spouses, held at Cabin Bluff, a tract of land near Sea Island acquired by Brunswick Pulp and Paper from Bill Jones in 1942.

Located in a 50,000-acre commercial forest, Cabin Bluff is about 35 miles by car from Brunswick, Georgia, or from Jacksonville International Airport in Florida. There are bobcats and deer, quail and wild turkey, raccoons and wild hogs in abundance. There are rustic but comfortable facilities managed by Rudy Woodward for business meetings scheduled by Brunswick Pulp and Paper and its two corporate parents.

A typical schedule for the fall Cabin Bluff board retreat had the Audit Committee meeting from 4:00 p.m. to 5:00 p.m. on the first day, a Wednesday. On each of the next three days, there were other meetings from 8:00 a.m. to 1:00 p.m. When there were no meetings being held, the directors and their spouses often engaged in less formal discussions about corporate affairs.

McSwiney's reason for starting the Cabin Bluff retreats was his desire to deepen the directors' understanding of the company and to establish procedures that would be taken into account in the decision-making process—part of the continuing and successful effort to make the board a well-informed review and advisory group, instead of the rubber-stamp board found in some corporations. This effort also involved the creation of a board manual, entitled "Concept, Role, and Responsibilities of the Board of Directors."

"When this manual was drawn up," Mac said, "one of its provisions was that the agenda for committees and the board as a whole for the following 12 months would be agreed upon in advance, subject to adjustment to accommodate matters that would arise in the course of the coming months. In this way directors could outline what they would like to hear and learn about the company during the following year, and management personnel would be advised early on as to presentations they would be expected to make, thus providing adequate time for preparation."

There are also presentations about new developments in business generally, and many of the directors have said that, in addition to doing Mead's business during the Cabin Bluff retreats, they also take back to their own companies ideas which, adapted to their own corporate conditions, may prove useful.

Cabin Bluff, in fact, has proved to be a solid contribution to that "continuous learning process" in which McSwiney so fervently believed.

Nine

A Balanced Concern
for People

The problem of management succession was very much on McSwiney's mind one day in 1971 when he telephoned Paul F. Miller, Jr., a member of Mead's board of directors and chair of its finance committee. Miller had been recruited for the Mead board by Tally Mead when Miller was still in his late twenties. McSwiney had great respect for his insight not only into financial matters but also into a broad range of other subjects. McSwiney asked Miller to talk with Warren L. Batts, a 37-year-old Harvard MBA whom Robert Greenleaf had recommended for a top job at Mead. Greenleaf said that Batts was one of the most brilliant students he had ever encountered.

"So Warren came to Philadelphia and visited me in my office and talked for a long time with me," Miller recalled. "He wanted reassurance about Mead. Was Mac for real? Was the management serious about what it was doing? Was it dedicated? I said, yes, it was dedicated, but I had to admit that there was some question whether Mac could pull it off—go through a significant divestiture program. It would take a tremendous amount of effort."

At the time, Batts was president and chief executive officer of a $23 million producer of hand tools and tool containers that he helped to found in 1967. Before that, after getting his MBA, he had had three other jobs, the last one as vice president of a New York-based management consulting firm. At the time Greenleaf recommended him to McSwiney, Batts was ready for another change.

"I was incredibly restless and bored," he later said. "Yet I was at the pinnacle for my family and cultural perspectives; I had what every red-blooded American would like—running my own show, reporting essentially to no one. The board of directors was at our beck and call."

He had indeed achieved a great deal, especially in the light of his background. He came from the world of "plain dirt farmers" along the border of Florida and Georgia. His father served in the Navy and Batts recalled with mixed emotions his father's service to his country and consequent absence from home. Batts finished high school at 16 "and charged out into the world to get a job," much like McSwiney himself a quarter century earlier.

To help support his mother and younger sister, Batts took a series of jobs that he later viewed as "great experience because they were so awful." In one job he served as supervisor of a crew that unloaded box cars of potatoes for a potato chip company in Jacksonville. "Inside the box car it would be 104, 110, 120 degrees," he said. "I lost a lot of baby fat." In another job he monitored the sewing of khaki pants for a wholesale dry goods company. When his sister finished school, Batts finally got a chance to go to the Georgia Institute of Technology. He had to work his way through, and it took him five years, washing dishes in the school cafeteria, working in a department store, and so on. One job was with the federal government, in the National Security Agency. "Their psychological testing, for what it proves," he said, "shows that I'm the ideal spy because I'm almost a totally contained person."

During his college years he married, so that when he arrived at the Harvard Business School, at the age of 29, he was somewhat different from the usual student walking through those doors for the first time. Batts was in his second year at the Harvard Business School when Greenleaf met him in one of his seminars. Leslie Rollins, a close associate of Greenleaf, was Batts's faculty advisor.

Batts and McSwiney were a study in contrasts. McSwiney was somehow always larger than life; whenever he was in a room, he dominated it; one felt that he was bigger physically than he was. He had a ready laugh, a direct look, and frequently prefaced a remark by saying this was the way he *felt* about the matter. Batts, on the other hand, was lean and dark, with a reserved air. He smiled easily and spoke with elaborate courtesy, sprinkling frequent "sirs" in his conversation with visitors.

"When someone hits me with bad news," Batts once said, "I'm not easy to read. I'm calm and cool—calculating. I'm figuring, what are my options?"

He once told an interviewer that he experienced a great detachment about his own thoughts and actions, and often felt that he stood at a distance from himself as an observer when he was talking with someone. This was the direct opposite of McSwiney's warm style. As McSwiney once said, "I've always *cared* for things and persons with which I'm involved." And most people who had dealings with him sensed that.

The two men differed enormously in the degree of ambiguity and nonconformity each could tolerate within the organization. "Mac was not thrown by the vagaries of human nature," as Greenleaf saw it. "He accepted that many people were odd, including himself."

McSwiney was interested in "the psychological aberrations of people," Greenleaf said. McSwiney once told him, "I've been practicing psychology without a license for 30 years."

Where McSwiney was greatly attracted by the uncertainties and variables of new situations, Batts was made uneasy by them. "I'm a very explicit sort of person," Batts once said, and then he added, "I've had to learn to be less explicit as I've been here [at Mead]."

Paradoxically, although McSwiney was a dominating—sometimes overwhelming—personality, he allowed a high degree of individuality to flourish among his executives. Batts, despite his soft manner and an expressed preference for "doing things through a group mechanism," was regarded by his colleagues as having "centralist" tendencies—a manager's way of saying that he was somewhat authoritarian and wanted to keep people in line, though he often talked about "consensus."

The two men spent a great deal of time trying to figure each other out, and a certain wariness sometimes crept into their comments about each other. Batts felt he was "more of a fighter, more of a confrontationist" than McSwiney. Batts once said, "The last thing Mac likes is a confrontation. He'll walk around it, and walk around it, and get someone else to do it."

McSwiney rejoined, "Anyone can have a confrontation—the job of a CEO is to get people to resolve issues. Sending them back to the drawing board is a much better alternative than discharging high-potential people before they have a chance to modify their behavior."

Batts apparently misunderstood McSwiney's "servant leadership" philosophy. Batts once said, "McSwiney has a concept that is a throw-back to another century. You have to have explicit, blind faith and trust in him that everything will work out. Don't expect him to make a commitment and just sit back and let it happen. Put your whole soul and trust in his hand. Leave it to him and he'll make it work out."

Then he added, unexpectedly, "In my case, so far, it has."

Others saw a different McSwiney. Board member William Spencer once remarked, "McSwiney knows how to take the best from people. Warren [Batts] is a superb strategist, and Mac used his ability to build the company.

"McSwiney has a way of making people feel important. He won't often take credit for the things that he himself does. In that sense, he has a great deal of modesty. Once I called Mac in Dayton to congrat-ulate him on a piece of business that had gone very well. Mac said, 'Please call Warren and tell him what a good job he has done.'"

Walker Lewis said much the same thing.

"Mac has amazing self-honesty," he commented once. "I don't think anyone has fought pride and ego more than I have—except Mac. Of course, it's a battle you never win."

Those were the qualities in McSwiney that led him to encourage his subordinates to express their opinions freely.

"He didn't expect people to be his slaves," Lewis said. "He didn't object to people disagreeing with him. Instead, he came back with hard arguments."

Lewis was among the many who were deeply impressed by Batts's obvious brilliance.

"It took Mac a year to get Batts to come to work for him," Lewis recalled. "Batts kept playing hard to get."

As the courtship went on, Greenleaf, who had introduced the two men, told McSwiney he had only one reservation about Batts: the man was, he said, "tightly wound."

As time went on—or so Lewis felt—McSwiney developed "a strong father feeling for Warren."

After Batts finally went to work for Mead, McSwiney never missed an opportunity to praise him, sometimes in extravagant terms. He once told a reporter for *The New York Times*, "Warren Batts is the ablest young executive that I know today. I never had any question about his ability to perform. He can manage any company in America. We were lucky as hell to get a man as talented as that when we did."

When Batts was still pondering whether to join Mead, McSwiney told William Wommack, the company's chief strategic officer, that the company probably would be fortunate if Batts stayed five years. He had no qualms about that, he said, because he felt both Batts and the company would benefit from the years Batts spent at Mead.

During Batts's years at Mead, McSwiney told a visitor that Batts could "turn out to be one of the great men in American industry." McSwiney went on:

"Warren is only beginning to evidence his potential, and if there is one thing that I feel great about, it's that I saw this potential early. It takes time and patience for it to develop.

"The inhibiting factor in his case is his desire to do everything he does perfectly. He wants to do everything within himself. It hurts him if somebody thinks of something before he does or has a better solution than he does. It's not that he doesn't welcome help and so forth. He is really a competitor in terms of how you get things done—in organizing to get them done. These characteristics are of unbelievable value in a CEO. I think when he's 50 he'll feel a little more comfortable."

When Batts joined Mead, in 1971, he was named group vice president of white paper operations and the merchants (paper distributors) division, the oldest and most troubled parts of the Mead paper business. A year later, Batts moved to the corporate staff as assistant to Paul Allemang, president and chief operating officer (COO).

Allemang never expected to spend years in the presidency. "I used to describe my job," he once said, "as running the operations of the company and looking for a successor."

A former management consultant, Allemang spent a good deal of his time, just before his retirement, helping in the work of restructuring the board and developing the corporate responsibility committee (CRC).

In 1973, Allemang—who was in his last year before retirement—was named "officer of the board" and Batts became president and COO.

It might have seemed that Batts was sitting on top of the world at that moment, but there were difficulties for him. Power was shared, to a considerable extent, with Wommack, the chief strategic officer (CSO). Moreover, another person, Richard T. Lindgren, was brought in from outside—about the time that Batts joined Mead—to be executive vice president in charge of the corporate staff, including financial operations. Like Batts, Lindgren had been spotted and recruited by Leslie Rollins, the former Harvard Business School dean who had brought Greenleaf and Batts together. A former executive of Ford, Lindgren was charged by McSwiney with special responsibility to "explore ways to create a more open and fruitful climate for all our relationships, one which permits the maximum creative contribution of all our human resources."

Lindgren was, of course, regarded as a potential rival to Batts for the CEO's post.

In order to exercise some control over policy direction, Batts organized the operational policy committee (OPC), a group of about a dozen top executives. Jerry Rapp later said, "The OPC was set up at a time when Dick Lindgren was running the staff. He had his own timetable for getting things done, and sometimes there was a collision course. Warren had the operating people and Dick had the staff people, and Warren felt that by getting Dick into the room with the operating people the 'we/they' kind of thing might be minimized."

Wommack, too, was invited to OPC meetings, but he rarely attended them.

Batts once explained to an interviewer why he organized the OPC.

"The problem," he said, "was that the second- and third-level staff people would call up plant managers and give instructions about what had to be done, summon them to meetings, fire off memos, and so forth. In the fall of 1973, the group vice presidents met and talked with me about the problem. They were frustrated. They said they felt like ants were climbing all over them. I felt we needed to strengthen their position vis-à-vis the staff if decentralization was going to work. I also felt we needed a vehicle for building common beliefs and goals in the company while recognizing the critical differences among individual units and we needed a coherent way to establish corporate policy."

(Of course, the reference to "building common beliefs and goals" echoed McSwiney's paper, *Philosophy of Organization & Planning*, written in 1970, before Batts joined the company.)

In a Harvard Business School case study—one of three the school conducted of aspects of Mead's operations—Batts was quoted as saying, "I wanted to establish a buffer between the staff and the divisions. A basic function of OPC is to review the ideas generated by the staff before they get sent out to the field. Sometimes it takes 15 drafts to get an idea in shape. But by the time OPC signs off, we can be pretty sure the idea won't upset the apple cart out in the plants. And we avoid the kind of uncoordinated false starts and stops that can kill a good staff idea without giving it a real chance." (McSwiney saw this as an illustration of the process of bringing about change. In essence, Mac said, it was the way for operations to accept or reject staff work, as set forth in the 1970 Philosophy of Organization and Planning paper.)

Some thought OPC was a great benefit to the company. Others had mixed feelings. For example, Charles Gebhardt, director of government affairs, was quoted in the Harvard study as saying OPC had "been very useful," but he also complained about one proposal his group submitted to OPC, "It was astounding how much time OPC took to approve our proposal. We went through this agonizing process of group rewrites over and over. From the discussion I think some of the members hadn't even read our drafts until they got to the meeting."

And James Van Vleck, corporate group vice president, told the Harvard researchers, "I think OPC has been very beneficial both in helping us define what we should be doing and in implementing programs that cut across divisional lines. But there have been some significant costs. There's no doubt that it took longer than it should to get some things approved; what you gain in legitimacy you pay for in speed....If [OPC] has outlived its purpose, should it be abolished?...What does having a committee accomplish that a meeting can't?"

By that time, Van Vleck had succeeded Lindgren, who resigned in 1975. Having, it was generally agreed, done a fine job with Mead's corporate staff, Lindgren had accepted the position of president and chief operating officer of the Koehring Company in Milwaukee.

In 1979, OPC was merged with the Executive Council, another committee of high-ranking managers which reported to the CEO.

Although by this time it was clear that Warren Batts was McSwiney's choice for his successor, McSwiney's determination to build leadership in depth at Mead was gradually being realized through other people, too.

One such was C. Greene Garner, who had come into Mead through its acquisition of Atlanta Paper. Like McSwiney and Batts, he came from modest origins. When he finished high school in Atlanta, his parents had separated and there was no money to send him to college. He worked and went to school at night. When World War II came, he went into the Army Air Corps and emerged a pilot. Mustered out in 1945, at the age of 25, he went to the University of Georgia, completing the four-year undergraduate course in three years.

Starting, as McSwiney had, in the accounting side of business, Garner had been recruited from the Coca-Cola Company by Arthur L. Harris for the Atlanta Paper Company, and came to Mead when that company acquired Atlanta Paper. At Mead, Garner gradually rose through the ranks, getting involved in other parts of the business along the way. In 1969 he was asked to go to Dayton to head Mead's paperboard group. At the time it was a difficult move for the company. Garner was doing an outstanding job as the head of Mead Packaging, where marketing was the key to success, but he was needed as the head of Mead's paperboard facilities.

"One of the functions of a group vice president," Batts once said, "is to resolve the internal conflict that is inherent in an integrated system. The master of that is Greene Garner. He can bring four division presidents into a room—and each one is related to the other in some way and each one has a direct and important conflict built in—and he'll listen in his quiet, fatherly way for a while. Then he'll say, 'Fellows, let me say what we're going to do.' And there is no bull. He's spoken. They know it's over and that's what we're going to do.

"There is a certain authoritarian way that a solution has to be found. There has to be willingness to manage confrontation or self-interest in a constructive way. The group vice presidents mostly do it well; Greene does it the best."

Garner shared with McSwiney an intuitive approach to management. He liked to say, "You can tell what's wrong with a manufacturing facility just by walking through it."

He also shared McSwiney's faith in the efficacy of listening.

"When a guy's got a problem," Garner said, "listen to him. You've got to listen to him and tell him why you're not going to take his recommendation and so forth. A lot of supervisors think they don't have the time to listen. That's not just Mead—we're talking about the problem of American industry.

"If you study what the Japanese have done and the Germans have done, and the way they relate to their people, you can understand why we have to spend more time with our people—from first-line supervisor to the top. We have management people who came up through the marketing route, and they are likely to pay more attention to marketing than to developing people.

"I don't care what kind of machine you put out there, you've got to have motivated people. You have to see people as human beings, help them to develop themselves, keep them informed, listen to them."

In that statement one hears an echo of the Granville Experience.

"Garner was an accountant, but he knew there had to be a better way to deal with the people problem," a man on his staff once said. "Garner was one of the few on whom the Granville Experience truly took effect."

"He became a convert," said another person on Garner's staff.

("Garner was an accountant, but—" sounds a little odd in the context of Mead. McSwiney, who was very much a people-oriented executive, came up on the accounting side, and so did Burnell Roberts, who later became CEO of Mead.)

"I believe in trying to get work done through people instead of my trying to do it all myself," Garner once said. "Warren works so damned hard. Trying to be a leader of people, I guess. Of course, some of that you're born with."

Batts did indeed work hard—12-, 14-, even 16-hour days were not unusual. Indeed, the long hours that Batts worked, as well as his intelligence, were key reasons why McSwiney, who was himself a hound for work, admired him so.

But McSwiney also recognized, as did Garner, that worker satisfaction was a far more complicated thing than many professional managers imagined.

One day McSwiney brought together for a meeting Hugh Black, Mead's vice president for personnel, members of his staff, and some line people. According to McSwiney, "Black was a kind person, but it was 'We' or 'Them' with him." Mac's message was simple: "We cannot foster confrontation with the rank and file. They have to be listened to, and we have to develop patterns and operating means whereby they truly have input."

Not long after Granville, Garner had begun gathering around him in Atlanta a staff of young human resources people who were eager to break out of the old, sterile patterns of labor relations. One of them, Jack Murdock, who later played a major role in helping the division to implement changes in managing people, said, "Major changes—and very significant ones—are taking place in the U.S. work force. Workers are younger and less disciplined to do work by the numbers. They represent an entirely different culture from that of the past. More people want to share power and have greater participation in the bottom line. We had to find ways to accommodate this new kind of situation in order to increase productivity and profitability."

Garner and his young aides decided to establish a showcase. They picked four Mead operations. One was an old paper board mill in Otsego, Michigan, that had been recently acquired; its "previous owners had milked it and walked away," as one Mead person put it, and there were many personnel problems, which had led to a wildcat strike. The second plant, a corrugated box plant at Waterloo, Iowa, had also been recently acquired, and the managers there "did everything just as they liked." The third site was a corrugated medium mill in Harriman, Tennessee, where McSwiney had once worked; the plant was old and worker morale was sagging. The fourth location was the former Atlanta Paper operation in Atlanta, now the world headquarters for Mead Packaging. The Packaging operation in Atlanta was the only Mead plant in a large urban center and the only one with a predominantly black work force.

David Bowers of the Institute of Social Research at the University of Michigan was engaged to do attitude studies at all four operations, and a West Coast consulting firm run by Theodore Barry was employed to study the locations from a productivity standpoint. Then a Harvard Business School associate professor was commissioned to prepare case studies on each of the four operations, using actual names of the employees involved and describing the actual situations as they were perceived by the employees, as well as facts presented by the other two consultants for discussion at the seminar.

Most managements—if they had screwed up the courage to authorize such studies—would have kept the results confidential if they were not wholly flattering, and these were not. But McSwiney never was accused of timidity, and so Garner's staff, lead by John Cleveland, was encouraged to develop a conference for Mead management to discuss the findings of the studies.

But the conference, held in St. Petersburg, Florida, was not limited to Mead management. Invitations to participate also went to national officials from the AFL-CIO and the paper workers union; to the Productivity Commission in Washington; to the U.S. Department of Labor; and Louis E. Davis, head of the Center for the Quality of Urban Life at the University of Southern California. Perhaps the most remarkable aspect of the conference was that the press was also invited.

"We sent everyone full information on the four case histories," said one member of Garner's staff, "after we decided not to disguise them but use everything as it was, by name."

That conference was in the spring of 1972. Batts, then head of the white paper group, was to have come with his people, but neither he nor they appeared. Lindgren was there, and so were people from the other divisions.

Of course, McSwiney was there.

"Mac can dominate a meeting," said one of the organizers of the conference, somewhat facetiously, "so we brought in four moderators to control him."

McSwiney later described the conference in a talk to a group of Mead supervisors:

> What resulted was a solid, no-holds-barred dialogue on how well or how poorly we had made it possible to get work done. We saw striking examples of differences in the ways top management perceived situations (including myself), as opposed to the ways first-line supervisors and hourly employees see them. There were examples of breakdowns in understanding between people and what those misunderstandings cost in terms of production, profits, and morale. And there were examples of how well people at all levels can work together, as well.
>
> I came away from the conference with the thought that there was no real argument over productivity and improved earnings, but rather the emphasis was on the humanistic aspect of work. There must be a balanced concern for people.

In a talk to another group, an industry trade association, McSwiney said, "For too long, I think, collective bargaining has been conducted in this country in an atmosphere of hostility with the emphasis on confrontation and the result is a contract that's no bargain to anybody. The existing rules of the game have been more like rules for warfare than for negotiation."

Dissatisfied with the way labor negotiations were handled, McSwiney asked Jerry Rapp to undertake the corporate personnel function and to decentralize the entire labor and personnel relations staff to the plant level. "After about a year," Rapp said, "only six persons remained in the headquarters staff out of about 26 people originally. Some were transferred to operating units; some went out of the company. Warren did not get involved in this process, although he did think clearing out the stable was a good thing."

A great change occurred in the entire human relations effort at Mead.

"A lot of people began to emerge in the company who worried about the human policies," said Sparrow. "Organizational ideas came up from below and went upstairs for a blessing."

Heavy emphasis was placed on job involvement and job satisfaction, and this helped to promote the kind of innovative ideas that Garner's people—and McSwiney—had in mind.

Racial sensitivity also became a high-priority concern of the company's at the same time. A few weeks before the St. Petersburg conference, a wildcat strike had hit Mead's Atlanta packaging and corrugated container operations. A key figure in the Atlanta strike was Hosea Williams, who had been one of the late Martin Luther King's assistants. Fiery and mercurial, Williams was trying to organize a union for black workers throughout the city. More by chance than design, Williams had picked Mead as a primary target. In the course of the strike there were disorders and police had to be called in.

Vernon Alden later described "the black uprising" at Atlanta Packaging as a "milestone in the education of management and the board of directors about some of the company's problems."

Before that incident, Mead had been like other large companies, basically unaware that it might have problems in race relations. Indeed, apart from the more obvious manifestations of outright segregation, most of American society considered itself, with reason, as enlightened, humane, caring, and tolerant during the 1940s, the 1950s, and the early 1960s. Gradually it dawned on more and more white people that they had not been sensitive to a human tragedy they saw every day, but did not recognize—the plight of the black people. As one great black author put it, a black was "the invisible man."

Mead's Atlanta operation, however, demonstrated the stark reality of the problem. There was not a single black supervisor in the entire facility, which employed about 1200 people.

Unlike most companies, Mead did not try to cover up its problems; it was outspoken about them—as one might expect, given McSwiney's temperament. The 1972 annual report said this about the Atlanta episode:

> Several hundred employees of Mead Packaging and Containers plants in Atlanta, in response to a local civil rights group that was attempting to organize a city-wide minority union, staged a 55-day wildcat strike. Though illegal, it did focus attention on some real problems: minority promotional opportunities; a dust condition; blocked communications.
>
> The dust problem was soon dealt with, a representative council was formed to surface employee feelings more directly, and a new pre-supervisory training program for blacks and females instituted.

Immediately after the strike ended, McSwiney supported Gerald Rapp and Paul Allemang when they inaugurated a series of sensitivity sessions about race relations conducted by an eloquent black minister, the Reverend Charles King. McSwiney himself was in the first group to be exposed to King's picture of what it was like to be a black in white America. Later, King went to Atlanta and other Mead locations, putting managers at all levels through the same harrowing process of self-revelation.

It was another stage in the campaign to turn Mead into a great — and considerate — corporation.

Later in the decade Mead took another major step in employee relations in connection with its paperboard mill at Stevenson, Alabama, which began operations on January 31, 1975. The world's largest and most cost-effective .009 corrugating facility, it had a single paper machine that trimmed a sheet 310 inches wide and operated within a speed range of 700 to 1800 feet per minute. The machine design emphasized conservation of labor, water, and energy.

Impressive as the facility was from a manufacturing point of view, it was equally so with respect to employee relations. Drawing on Mead's St. Petersburg experience and concepts in personnel relationships, Greene Garner, working with his staff, drew up plans for participatory management, believed to be the first of its kind for an operation of this type. Several Mead corrugated box plants, both new and old, had successfully employed the concept of participatory management, but they all operated on 8-, 10-, or, at the most, 16-hour days. Thus they could be shut down and started up without serious consequences. In fact, they did just that at the beginning and end of every operating day.

Stevenson, on the other hand, was a nonstop, continuous, around-the-clock operation. If participatory management didn't work in such an operation, the results could be especially unfortunate.

But, thanks to the efforts of many people — particularly John Cleveland, Dr. Charles Spalding, Peter Wrist, and Clyde Maynard — the plan did work. After resolving some difficult start-up problems with a new chemical and heat recovery process, productivity gradually reached a new level for this kind of operation.

As a Mead document put it:

The basic organizational philosophy is to match individual and business unit goals so that through achievement of one, the other is satisfied also. This implies that every individual and the organization pull in the same direction, thus avoiding adversary roles between individual and organization.

The rationale for the "management system" involves the following key points:

1. Managerial and organizational flexibility
2. Lowest level decision making
3. Individual growth in skills and knowledge
4. An atmosphere which allows questions and comment
5. Work that has challenge and variety by its basic design

The objective is to achieve a higher degree of cost and productivity effectiveness through the matching of individual and business unit goals. We are not seeking social reform, but rather human accord which can perhaps be called more "fun" in work while making greater profits for the company and higher monetary reward to the individuals who make up the organization.

Each manufacturing process has all the skills and resources necessary for use within that process: maintenance, operations, direction, testing, and controlling. These skills may be contained in single individuals or groups who may be continually changing their roles as the work situation requires. Individuals can upgrade their skills for the good of the group (or organization) and the greater the individual knowledge and contribution, the greater the financial reward to that individual.

Group demands call up a maximum effort from the individual; in short, he or she gives more. Working groups sometimes will require resources and direction from higher levels of the organization. This is provided through members of the crew called "Process Managers." Their position in the organization might be compared with that of the conventional foreman. Their role is different, however, since each is a crew member as well as a management representative.

The design provides for easier communications, up, down, and across the total organization. Information is shared, not only on a "need to know" basis, but also on the basis of concern. This organization shares information previously considered sacred to many in management.

There are no traditional hourly production and maintenance workers. Everyone is salaried. Employees are paid for what they know, as
well as for what they do.

Hiring, firing, and discipline are shared responsibilities between
management and members of the work group. Several cases of disciplinary action, also a discharge, have been experienced.

For the first time in Mead's existence—and most likely in the paper industry—a production or maintenance worker could also leave
his or her job for an hour or so (the individual's responsibilities being covered by the group) to take care of personal matters. This was
a privilege that salaried workers had long been accustomed to.

In disciplinary matters, workers turned out to be tougher than management at times, because they saw the cost to them of ineffective
peers.

McSwiney's high hopes for the endeavor were realized in the end,
but not without some people problems. Some managers who were
admirably suited for conventional management styles just didn't seem
to be able to adjust to the new participatory management concept.
Communications on all levels had to be patiently and persistently
pursued.

Before long, there was, in McSwiney's words, "a new and successful
relationship between people" at Stevenson. Much of the credit for
that good relationship, he felt, had to go to John Moore, who was in
charge of the plant at the time.

In Mac's view, the Stevenson experience, together with the corrugating operations, demonstrated that participatory management can
work in almost any kind of pulp and paper operation. The success of
participatory management at Stevenson caused the company to foster
the concept elsewhere in the years that followed. However, in operations with long-standing union representation, progress has been
spotty.

"Stevenson was," McSwiney said, "another experience in supporting, learning, and presiding over a high degree of ambiguity and uncertainty—and one in which I took great pride."

Ten

The Corporate Responsibility Committee

Vernon Alden, a Mead board member, had given a lot of thought to corporations and their internal structures. He had been on the faculty and associate dean of the Harvard Business School and, after a number of years as president of Ohio University during a period of great growth and student unrest, he became chairman of The Boston Company and the Boston Safe Deposit and Trust Company. Besides his membership on Mead's board, he served as a director of six other very large corporations, including Digital Equipment Corporation, Colgate-Palmolive, and McGraw-Hill. So it was with considerable insight that he said, a decade after the establishment of Mead's corporate responsibility committee (CRC), "McSwiney was far ahead of his time. CRC is still unique."

No one but McSwiney, Alden believed, "would have dared to get hourly workers, union members, and blacks, all sitting down with board members talking about problems."

"It has been a tremendous education for me," Alden said. "I learned more about Mead on this one committee than on all the other committees I've been on."

The genesis of the committee was rather odd. When Paul Miller, one of the directors, had brought up the suggestion for such a committee during the Stockbridge board retreat, he had in mind the sort of entity quite a few corporations were establishing at the time in response to social issues—a committee of outside directors who would oversee the corporation's relationships with its various publics.

McSwiney didn't think that kind of committee could adequately uncover and cope with the complex problems posed by modern society.

"There is always a tendency to make special committees or departments for reform programs," he said, "but set them apart from the operations of the organization."

He wanted the entire organization involved in the process leading to better approaches to environmental, human, ethical, and other issues. Otherwise, he thought, "corporate responsibility" would become just "a new buzzword."

While McSwiney was mulling over the matter, Paul Allemang and Jerry Rapp attended a 1971 Conference Board session at which John Collins, a visiting professor from Syracuse University, took part in a debate. Impressed by him, they invited him to spend eight weeks at Dayton that summer developing some ideas on how the company might approach social issues.

The result of his efforts was a proposal for the establishment of what he called a "social involvement committee" including board members, junior managers, employees from operating divisions, and representatives of churches and other outside groups. McSwiney didn't go for the idea of including representatives of outside groups.

"Mac, bless his heart," said Allemang, "took his hands off the committee. He only appeared a few times."

McSwiney stayed away not because of being uninterested—he believed in CRC with a passion—but for two well-thought-out reasons: first, he didn't want CRC labeled "an instrument of the company," in the sense of its being an effort by the company to manipulate its employees; and, second, because he realized that the presence of the chief executive officer at CRC meetings would inhibit the free exchange of information, opinions, and ideas.

The second was especially important because McSwiney viewed the CRC as a means by which the board of directors could get first-hand information about what was going on in the company—information not sanitized by passage through the levels of authority within the company.

James W. McSwiney (left) at the age of four or five.

His father, James Speedy McSwiney, when he was in his late twenties.

His mother, Delia Margaret Conroy McSwiney, when she was about 20. She died at the age of 29.

McSwiney as an Army Air Corps aviation cadet in World War II, at the controls of a single-engine trainer.

McSwiney (right) with A.W.
(Bill) Jones, his friend and
mentor for many years.

McSwiney (left) with his brother Eugene.

The plant of the Brunswick Pulp & Paper
Company, at Brunswick, Georgia, as it
looked in the 1950s, when McSwiney
worked there. Brunswick Pulp & Paper was
owned jointly by Scott Paper Company
and Mead.

Sea Island, the Georgia resort developed by Bill Jones. It was McSwiney's winter residence.

The Advanced Management Program "Can Do Group" at the Harvard Business School (left to right): Dayton H. Clewell, Mobil Oil; Larry Kanaga, RCA; Pancho Alvarez, of South America; Charles J. Forbes, U.S. Steel; James Brammell, U.S. government; and McSwiney.

Friends with whom McSwiney had many dealings: Adam H. Zimmerman (right) of Noranda Mines and Henry C. Goodrich (below), of Inland Container…

…Kenneth P. Benson (left), of British Columbia Forest Products, and Paul C. Baldwin (above), of Scott Paper.

Mead's mill at Chillicothe, Ohio, where the Mead Corporation and a predecessor company have been making paper since the middle of the nineteenth century.

The Northwood paper mill. Mead's share to start — a bare $3 million.

Escanaba — the pivotal move in the commitment to, and rebuilding of, Mead's white paper facilities — made possible only by an industrial revenue bond issue.

*Mead's Mahrt, Alabama, plant, a highly
leveraged, fast pay-out partnership.*

Arthur Harris (left), who became one of
the Mead corporate family as a result
of the acquisition of Atlanta Paper
Company, with famed actress Helen
Hayes and McSwiney during the "Art
Across America" program.

Robert K. Greenleaf outside his Pennsylvania retirement residence. Long the director of management research at AT&T and later a teacher at the Harvard and MIT business schools, Greenleaf was an advisor to McSwiney and a key influence as Mac developed his management philosophy and style.

Some of McSwiney's associates at Mead: Nelson S. Mead (above, left), Gerald D. Rapp (above, right), W. Walker Lewis, Jr. (below, left), H. Talbott Mead (below, center), Dr. George H. Sheets (below, right)...

… *William A. Enouen (above, left), Robert M. O'Hara (above, center),*
Constantine B. Simonides (above, right), C. Greene Garner (below, left),
William W. Wommack (below, right).

A strong and independent board: Mead's directors in 1981, when McSwiney retired as chairman of the board. In 1983 McSwiney retired from membership on the board.

Vernon R. Alden

John C. Bogle

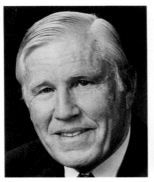

Edward R. Kane

David S. Lewis

H. Talbott Mead

Burnell R. Roberts

William M. Spencer III

Thomas B. Stanley, Jr.

C. Greene Garner

Vincent L. Gregory, Jr.

Barbara C. Jordan

Nelson S. Mead

Charles S. Mechem, Jr.

Paul F. Miller, Jr.

C. William Verity, Jr.

William W. Wommack

Mead's Stevenson, Alabama, plant (above and right) used an innovative team concept of worker participation in decision making. Result: world leadership in productivity and quality.

At groundbreaking for Mead
Data Central's facility outside
Dayton, McSwiney shakes hands
with Ohio Governor James A.
Rhodes as John W. Galbreath
(left) looks on.

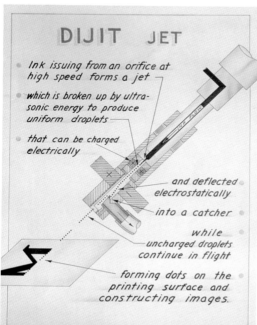

DIJIT JET

- Ink issuing from an orifice at
  high speed forms a jet
- which is broken up by ultra-
  sonic energy to produce
  uniform droplets
- that can be charged
  electrically
- and deflected
  electrostatically
- into a catcher

while
uncharged droplets
continue in flight

forming dots on the
printing surface and
constructing images.

The Dijit jet printing concept (explained above) developed by Mead. David A. Lehman
(right) was manager of project at time of divestiture to Kodak.

Key lawyers in Mead's fight against
Occidental Petroleum's takeover attempt:

(Clockwise, beginning at upper right)

*Joseph H. Flom, senior partner of
Skadden, Arps, Slate, Meagher & Flom,
New York City.*

*Barbara A. Reeves, then of the Antitrust
Division of the U.S. Department of
Justice, later a member of Morrison &
Foerster, Los Angeles.*

*Armistead W. Gilliam, Jr., partner of Smith
& Schnacke, Dayton.*

*David C. Greer, of Bieser, Greer & Landis,
Dayton.*

*Harold F. Baker, senior partner of
Howrey & Simon, Washington, D.C.*

*Peter A. Atkins, partner of Skadden, Arps,
Slate, Meagher & Flom, New York City.*

Major figures in Mead's fight for fairness in the antitrust case:
Samuel J. Ervin, Jr., former U.S. Senator from North Carolina, with William J. Hunter (background), then associate with Howrey & Simon, Washington, D.C., chats with Griffin B. Bell.

Robert H. Bork, former judge, U.S. Court of Appeals, District of Columbia Circuit.

Griffin B. Bell, former Attorney General of the United States, now managing partner, King & Spalding, Atlanta.

Alan M. Wiseman, partner Howrey & Simon, Washington, D.C.

Cabin Bluff, near Brunswick, Georgia, the site of Mead's annual three-day retreat for members of Mead's Board of Directors since 1973. The annual retreat was an innovation introduced by McSwiney to ensure dialogue and learning.

The unveiling.

Dedication of James W. McSwiney Hall, at Sinclair Community College in Dayton, one of the proudest achievements of Mac, a man without a college degree.

McSwiney (right) is congratulated by Burnell R. Roberts (left), his successor as Mead's chief executive officer, and Dr. David H. Ponitz, president of the college.

McSwiney with his grandsons, Richard J. Hutchinson (left) and Douglas Scott Hutchinson.

TOP *McSwiney receives an honorary doctorate from Brother Raymond L. Fitz of the Marianist Order, president of the University of Dayton.*

BOTTOM *McSwiney (left) and Brother Fitz (third from left) with Mac's family (left to right): wife Jewell, daughter Margaret Hutchinson, daughter-in-law Jane, son C. Ronald, mother-in-law Carrie Lee Bellar, and (in front) grandsons Scott and Richard.*

Aerial view of the Miami Valley Research Park and the Miami Valley Research Institute (below), and some of its key figures (left to right): John F. Torley, trustee; Charles E. Giles, administration; Brother Raymond L. Fitz, trustee; J. Michael Herr, legal counsel; McSwiney; Brigadier General Stuart R. Boyd, Air Force Institute of Technology; Barry R. Blacklidge, administration; Peter H. Forster, trustee; Frederick C. Smith, trustee; Thomas E. Heine, Dayton Area Chamber of Commerce; Dr. Paige E. Mulhollan, trustee; Bruce E. Pearson, Dayton Development Council; Dr. Robert J. Kegerreis, trustee. Not present for photo: Donald L. Huber, Dr. David H. Ponitz, and Dr. Arthur E. Thomas, trustees; Major General Elbert E. Harbour, Air Force Aeronautical Systems Division; and Major General Dale W. Thompson, Air Force Logistics Command.

McSwiney with former President Gerald Ford (left), who, as a U.S. Representative from Michigan, was a strong supporter of Mead's plan to initiate its white paper rebuilding program at Escanaba, Michigan.

Despite the frown, probably a squint caused by the bright sun, McSwiney (right), had reason to enjoy this Bogie Busters golf outing. During the day, Ohio Governor James A. Rhodes (second from left) promised state assistance which enabled the Miami Valley Research Park to get off the ground. Mac's neighbor, Cyrus Laughter (center, with grandson David), helped to broach the subject. Entertainer Pat Boone (left) was part of foursome.

McSwiney (center) with Burnell R. Roberts, now chairman and chief executive officer of Mead, and Robert M. O'Hara of Mead at dedication of Mead Data Central facility near Dayton. They are holding a quarter-mile printout from the information banks of Lexis and Nexis.

McSwiney (left) with Boris Z. Milner (right), then the deputy director of Moscow's Institute for Systems Studies, during Milner's first visit to Dayton. Later Mac met with Milner and other U.S.S.R. educational and industry leaders in Novosibirsk, the Soviet science center, and Moscow. With them (background) are Frank Hoernemann (left), former director of the Dayton YMCA, and John C. O'Melia, Jr., executive director of the Center for International Management Studies and director of the International Branch of the U.S. YMCA.

McSwiney (fourth from left) at Mead's affiliate in Lebanon. With him are (left to right) Dr. Joseph Yamine, William Bond, Hussein Badran, Georges Frem, and Abdo Mouaness.

On a McSwiney visit to the People's Republic of China, as guests of the government, Mrs. McSwiney (left) is accompanied by Hiroko Murai, wife of Mead's manager in Japan, Hugh Murai, and Chinese hosts.

*A new generation at the helm of Mead: Burnell R. Roberts (left),
chairman and chief executive officer, and Steven C. Mason,
president and chief operating officer.*

"Naturally, the CRC met with tremendous resistance from line management," Alden recalled. "They felt they were undercut, and to a degree this was correct. They didn't know what the thing was that they confronted."

The Mead annual report for 1972, in a section on the CRC, said, "To help it get up steam, the committee put a task force of gifted students in the field during the summer. They looked into such topics as Mead forest practices and relationships with woods workers; the view of 'advocate' organizations in the consumer and ecological fields; and the views of Mead managers toward their corporate responsibilities."

That was the year of rioting on the campuses against the Cambodian invasion by U.S. forces, the year of the Watergate break-in, and the year of the strike at General Motors' huge Lordstown facility, not to speak of wildcat strikes at two Mead operations. It was a time of protest by blacks, by women, by students, by environmentalists, by any number of other elements of society. Anyone in a position of authority tended to feel besieged, and the feeling that a corporate responsibility committee was looking over one's shoulder did nothing to diminish that feeling. On the other hand, it was precisely because authority, including corporate authority, was under attack throughout the country that the CRC was needed.

"Our goal," McSwiney later said, "was to let people participate in the flow of information. By doing so we'll find out how the organization deals with it. Society was saying: 'We want to be heard.' The board was saying, 'We want to be heard.' People in the organization were saying, 'We want to be heard.' After being heard, most would agree there's a way to find solutions to problems.

"I've always found that as long as you're not perceived as trying to manipulate a situation—as long as you're not trying to accomplish some hidden objective—you don't really have trouble with people. It's only when you have a hidden objective—and it will ultimately come out if you have one—that you lose their confidence and your credibility."

The addition to the CRC, at McSwiney's urging, of two hourly employees in 1973 startled many Mead managers. One of the new members was a union shop steward from Chillicothe; the other was a black railroad conductor on the company railway that carried coal, iron ore, limestone, and slag among the Woodward properties in Alabama.

In the beginning, according to Alden, the CRC operated to some degree as a kind of grievance committee. He cited the time spent by the committee discussing the plight of Mead warehouse employees who worked in all kinds of weather on outdoor loading docks. Although the warehouse employees had complained of working conditions, management had argued that the company couldn't afford to build a roof over the loading docks.

But then management built a tennis court to provide recreation for executives, Alden said. Except for the CRC, the directors wouldn't have heard about that sort of thing. "But we did hear," Alden said, "and there was always the feeling around the company that we might hear."

In 1974, Ivan Allen, who had been a board representative on the committee, retired from the CRC and two board members joined the committee—C. William Verity, Jr., of Armco Steel and George B. Beitzel of International Business Machines. At first Verity and Beitzel thought that the CRC was so much a grievance committee that it ought to be scrapped. The employee representatives also were frustrated because they thought, "What's the good of talking? No one ever does anything about it," in Alden's words.

"There was a meeting in Philadelphia," Alden said, "where the directors kind of exploded and so did the hourly paid workers. They vented their frustrations because, they said, 'We've repeated some of these things a half dozen times and nothing seems to happen.' And the directors complained, 'Well, all you do is talk about nuts-and-bolts things. The line management ought to be worried about these things.'

"That to me was a great meeting simply because there was so much dissension."

But matters couldn't be permitted to remain like that.

"It became apparent that nothing would happen until management became plugged into the CRC," Alden said.

It was a low point for the CRC.

In the hope of broadening the work of the committee, Allemang and Rapp were working toward the close of 1974 on an agenda for the CRC for the following year that would, they hoped, induce it to concern itself with other social problems instead of focusing narrowly on employment conditions.

At that point Warden Seymour, the union shop steward from Chillicothe who had been one of the first two hourly paid members of the CRC, wrote to McSwiney to say he had "become very discouraged with the lack of activity by the committee." He went on to say, "I feel the Chairman of the Board [McSwiney] has a very deep sense of responsibility to all the employees but I feel that people under you are reluctant to accept the changes recommended by this body. I feel the only way the committee can survive is with very strong support from you and Mr. [Warren] Batts [who had become president and chief operating officer in 1973]."

In his reply, McSwiney said he agreed with Seymour's comments about "the reluctance of people to accept recommendations for change from the committee (or anyone else)" and also about "the need for strong support from Mr. Batts and me." He went on to say that the CRC "will find both of us receptive to its recommendations." He also expressed confidence that the committee "reinforced by the board of directors, can be an effective agent for bringing about change within the corporation."

At that point an incident occurred that brought matters to a head.

When Seymour was named to the CRC, he was one of two hourly paid employees on the committee. The other was Quepee Gates, a black railroad conductor. At the December 1974 meeting of the CRC, he announced that Gates had just been fired. The Woodward railroad properties had been sold, and the new owners had no need for his services. Sixty years old and a Woodward employee for 35 years, Gates had been notified that he was without a job at the end of his shift one day, with no prior warning.

"Spike Beitzel and I both sat up in our chairs," Alden later said. "We asked each other, 'How can it be that a guy who's been a loyal worker for so many years can suddenly be thrown out on the street, with no help given to him in finding a job, no warning that he was going to lose his job?' We were both shocked."

At previous meetings the CRC had asked about plant closings and whether there was a consistent corporate policy for dealing with the human problems resulting from them. Some members of the committee had been upset by an inability to get satisfactory answers. As Alden said, "We could hear the complaints and concerns, but there was no way to get them plugged into the line organization."

Now, as a result of the Quepee Gates incident, Alden said, "It was decided that we would insist that the president [Batts] and the vice president for human resources sit in on our meetings. That led to plugging us into the OPC [the operating policy committee]."

Before the December session of the CRC ended, Batts met with the committee.

"Both Spike [Beitzel, of IBM] and I asked Warren, 'What is our policy on plant closures?'" Alden recalled. "We both said we seem to account very carefully for all the machinery and all the building and all the land that gets involved in these things. But we never seem to get a report on the human resources. How many people are going to be out of work? What have we done to help them?

"Warren insisted that there was a policy, and we kept asking him to explain what the policy was.

"There wasn't a uniform overall policy, and it took a solid year for the organization to evolve a policy on plant closures."

In March 1975 Batts came back to the committee with a report. It showed that Mead basically had a patchwork of practices and policies, because many of them were inherited from companies it had acquired. In 1974, because of restructuring and a recession, 1825 people had been laid off, of whom 150 took retirement. Only 500 or so found jobs in other Mead operations and in other companies, leaving 1200 to make do on severance pay and unemployment compensation. Notification given employees ranged from a few hours or days to three weeks. Severance pay, too, varied widely from one operation to the next.

Because of the keen interest of the directors, Batts developed task forces that were dispatched ahead of time to plants scheduled to be closed. There they worked out placement programs to "smooth the transition" to other employment for those being laid off.

"You get to be a real cynic after you've been through this," Batts said later, "because a lot of people would rather take a year of unemployment and stay home and do nothing and then go look for a job. We'll help find them a job, because that's our moral obligation: not to leave the person upon the beach with money that soon goes. We set up employment offices to work with people in dealing with all the agencies."

The involvement of the Operating Policy Committee with the CRC was a turning point. CRC's meetings were increased from four a year to six. The vice president of human resources attended the meetings and the agenda became more systematic. The committee broadened its horizon to include a wider range of corporate concerns.

One of those who was won over to the cause of CRC was C. Greene Garner, who later became chief executive officer of Mead. He had been critical of the committee at first, but after serving on CRC as a representative of the Operating Policy Committee, he "did a 180-degree turn," according to Gerald Rapp. Among other benefits of the CRC, in Garner's opinion, was the "emphasis on safety and employee communications throughout the corporation [that] was attributable to the committee's efforts."

Alden believed that the Quepee Gates incident had persuaded Batts, too, of the value of the CRC, but Alden may have been mistaken.

In 1978 Batts told a visitor in a conversation about the CRC, "You can't have a good manager, a young fellow who's got job offers coming to him, having to put up with being degraded. And these people [some of the managers] thought the CRC was a degrading experience for them.... Here we are, at the bottom of a recession, and we're laying off people. And the question keeps coming up, 'Does the board think we do business in an unethical manner? Is that why they do this?'

"We had a couple of guys who finally left the company. This was not *the* ingredient but was *an* ingredient: the lack of trust in them this implies. It's explicit. That you're going to have hourly employees go around management to come to the top means that you don't trust management. That's the way it's interpreted, even today."

A year or so later, Batts still spoke in essentially the same vein about CRC, whose existence, he indicated, was interpreted by Mead managers as signifying a lack of trust in them.

"It's a continual battle to keep that in perspective," Batts said. "The way I feel is to take everything that happens in the CRC and feed it all back down into the organization so that there's no uncertainty as to what's going on.

"Management has become more and more relaxed now that the CRC is basically an ineffective body. I hate to be cynical, but that's the way it is today. We're slowly building it into something else."

That may have been wishful thinking on Batts's part. More than six years later the CRC was still alive and doing very well.

Indeed, McSwiney would not have let CRC be emasculated during his tenure at the head of the company, and his successors apparently shared his belief in the value of the committee.

This was not the only issue on which McSwiney and Batts did not see eye to eye. Another instance was the publication of a case study of Mead by the Harvard Business School in 1978.

There was nothing remarkable about the findings of the Harvard case study. Batts liked the study and McSwiney didn't. McSwiney wrote a memorandum to Batts about it.

"The basic fault [of the case study]," McSwiney said, "is that it presents the problems and shortcomings that one will find in any corporation—and misses the issue. Is CRC, as it has *evolved* at Mead, a creative tool for management?"

There isn't any point in CRC, he wrote, unless it "enhances Mead's image as a creative and positive leader in the field of management concepts." The case study "does anything but that," he asserted.

McSwiney went on to say, in part:

> There were various levels of management response to CRC: concerned, afraid, complimentary, pride; but in general there was an avoidance of integrating the system in the company. The group vice presidents by natural inclination, and reinforced by a generally negative attitude, directed constant darts at people supportive of the system for two reasons: (1) errors were made; (2) darts at an individual was a subjective way to test to see if CRC could be eliminated....
>
> Later the President [Batts] agreed that the issues being raised were real—that everyone was hearing things faster and more directly than through the usual system. But he recognized that the potential of CRC was not being fully realized because it was outside the "system."...
>
> Batts suggested to the Chairman and CEO the outline now being used to guide CRC. This was the real breakthrough. He did it on his own and things began to take a different turn.

(That had pleased McSwiney mightily. "I knew from the beginning," he said, "that the organization had to accept and adopt the principle of the CRC if it was to work. I could not direct them to do it or it would become no more than many other well-intentioned committees.")

The McSwiney memorandum continued:

> The process of CRC is creative — it is positive — it will always cause tension at many levels in management. But it is not unhealthy tension; any system that knows that its feelings are heard at the highest level will have more time to respond and lead.
>
> The flavor should be that of a company that knew what it was doing — was not spying on its people but was determined to find a way to sharpen the sensitivity of management and was not afraid to let its linen hang out with its Board. In essence, a company determined to have a strong, informed Board, in keeping with the mood of today's society.

The role of the CRC in strengthening the governance of Mead was often overlooked in discussions of the CRC. McSwiney saw the CRC as a key element in ensuring that Mead's board knew what was going on in the company, not just what management — at any level — wanted to report to the board. If the leadership of the company knew what was going on, it could better direct the affairs of the organization. Management, on the other hand, could place faith in the dedication of the company's leadership to the welfare of the entire enterprise, including its lower ranks. This, again, reflected the "servant leadership" philosophy stated by Robert Greenleaf and espoused by McSwiney. Upon reflection, however, McSwiney came to the conclusion that "this was not all that different from the informal council of workers that George Mead set up in 1905 and formalized in 1919, with a committee of 16, 8 chosen by management and 8 elected by employees."

The CRC provided a learning process for the members of the board of directors. As new directors came on the board, they were posted to the CRC to introduce them to the world of Mead. Of course, it took time to cycle all Mead directors through the process, so some veteran

Mead directors, for the first time, were experiencing the cultural shock of this unusual program several years after it was begun.

It was not until 1979 that Paul Miller got his turn on the committee that he himself had first suggested years before. His reactions were mixed, but generally favorable. The first meeting he attended was devoted to ethical questions involving the actions of purchasing agents. Miller was impressed; he thought the discussion had "great value."

But he still felt there were certain questions too sensitive to be discussed with employees. These involved such matters as political relationships and other "external" affairs of the corporation. The discussions of charitable contributions also bothered him a little. These dealt with what kinds of organizations received money, while Miller felt the real problem at Mead was the overall level of giving, which he felt should be higher. (After discussion by the board of directors, Mead increased its level of giving.)

Nevertheless, Miller didn't question the value of the CRC. He just believed there should be a separate committee to handle external affairs. In fact, the CRC did not deal with external matters. From time to time, efforts to involve the committee in external issues were made by some members, but from the beginning, as a result of the influence of employee members, the committee concerned itself primarily with internal matters.

The board members who served on the CRC found the process by which new employee candidates were brought to the committee for evaluation and selection a totally new experience. A new director going through this for the first time said he acquired not only an insight into the company but also an unexpected insight into himself. "You spend a day in the selection of new members," he said. "Each director is teamed with an employee member. You learn about yourself." The man in question was teamed with a young black woman from the hourly work force, and together they had to interview candidates and make up their minds what kind of committee members they would be. "Everyone gets a rating," the director said, "and you try to form impressions about these people." Each member had one vote, whether director or employee. The discussions after the candidates left the room were very revealing, in this director's view: "You learn about your partner, and he or she learns about you."

Executives requested to attend a CRC meeting and give a presentation about their operations sometimes found the experience unlike anything else known in the world of business. Around the table were board members who had wide experience in business and asked tough questions. But questions were also asked by employee members of the CRC, who tended to be skeptical of official company positions and often knew—sometimes from sources in the lower ranks of the company—where the holes were in a presentation.

But in 1988 the board of directors decided, as Burnell Roberts, by then board chairman and CEO of Mead, reported, that "Mead has changed and the business environment has also changed since the CRC was formed." In a statement to employees, he said the employee members of the CRC had done a superb job "of making the company and our directors more sensitive to employee issues," but he expressed the board's concern that "five employees [on the CRC] could not effectively represent the views or the diverse interests of 20,000 employees world-wide."

In order to get a broader understanding of employees' attitudes, the company began a bi-yearly series of surveys of salaried employees, the results of which would be shared with all employees and the CRC.

At the same time the CRC was reorganized to include only board members, who would expand the committee's areas of concern to environmental, governmental, political, community, and other societal issues important to Mead.

Eleven

Separating the CEO's Duties from the Chair's

One of the innovations put in place by McSwiney was the separation of the offices of chief executive officer (CEO) and chair of the board. The concept did not survive after his tenure as chair because a good and strong board decided against it. (This decision was not unexpected. A short time before, the Business Roundtable had expressed disagreement with the concept.) Nevertheless, there are those who believe that the concept—which has been put in place in some other companies—has considerable merit and deserves further trial.

It is clear from close study of McSwiney's statements, as early as the late 1960s, that his mind was working on an idea that ultimately became the separation of offices. But the groundwork was laid for the idea by a review of the Mead board's functions, scope, and procedures that the Jones Committee had urged be done at five-year intervals—a review that never mentioned the possibility of a separation of powers, but examined in detail the entire question of corporate governance.

"We had to be careful as we went down the pike," McSwiney said, "not to perceive the recommended structure of the board as being right, fixed, and nonchangeable. There is always a tendency to say, 'Well, things worked out all right.' But the board will need to be modified as we go along to keep in tune with the dynamics of the situation."

As the end of the first five-year period approached, in the mid-1970s, McSwiney appointed a task force of board members to undertake the review called for by the Jones Committee report. Vernon R. Alden served as chair of the task force. Four of its members had served on the Jones Committee; they were Alden, C. William Verity, Jr., Paul F. Miller, Jr., and William M. Spencer III. There were two other task force members, George Beitzel, an outside board member, and Paul Allemang, an insider whose title was "officer of the board." Gerald D. Rapp, the company's internal legal counsel (and vice president), assisted the task force, and so did Constantine Simonides, a new figure on the scene at Mead.

Simonides was vice president of administration at the Massachusetts Institute of Technology. After World War II he had come to the United States from Greece on an American Field Service scholarship. During the time of student unrest, Simonides, then assistant to the president of MIT, brought in Robert Greenleaf and a Greenleaf associate, Douglas Williams, to prepare a report on campus relations. Later Greenleaf introduced Simonides to McSwiney, who in 1971 offered Simonides a position in the Mead human relations program.

"If the offer had come at a different time," Simonides later said, "he might have recruited me. But it wasn't the moment for me."

Nevertheless, Simonides did serve Mead for several years, engaging in many wide-ranging discussions with McSwiney and Rapp. It was in this manner that he began to work with Rapp, in 1973, to develop a revised agenda for the corporate responsibility committee (CRC). Shortly thereafter he and Rapp went to work assisting the directors' task force, which was now becoming known as the Alden Committee.

The Alden Committee staff work began on July 4, 1974, with a meeting of Allemang, Greenleaf, Rapp, and Simonides in a hotel room in Boston, not far from Greenleaf's retirement home in New Hampshire and along the Charles River near MIT. In the course of the meeting, responsibilities were assigned:

- Douglas Williams was to interview the 18 members of the board of directors, which was comprised of 10 outside members, 7 inside members, and 1, Walker Lewis, who had a foot in both camps, because he was Mead's general counsel but also was a partner in the law firm of Smith & Schnacke, which represented Mead.

- Paul Allemang would similarly solicit the opinions of Mead's top managers.

- Rapp and Simonides had at least two functions—to examine national trends in corporate governance and to bring together all the research of the entire team in the task force's working papers.

The work of the Alden task force took about eight months to complete. McSwiney stayed away from the meetings, just as he had abstained from attending meetings of the corporate responsibility committee. But he knew how things were progressing within the task force.

"I've always been sensitive to things that are going on," he said of that period, "and I have ways of finding out what's going on. But I don't get involved in a lot of things because I don't think the process will work if I do."

Alden described the manner in which the task force worked: "A younger executive sets down the understanding of the meeting in a first draft. At each stage each member must put his seal on the completed draft after it has been talked out and revised. Then the draft would be put together."

After a good many meetings, Beitzel told his colleagues, "Goddamn it, we have to have Mac here. Either it's going to fly or it's not going to fly."

At the next meeting, held in Verity's apartment in the Waldorf-Astoria in New York, McSwiney was present at the request of the group. The others discussed their work and ideas in detail. Then they insisted that McSwiney comment.

"Look," he said, "if this is what you've all come up with, I'll either make it work—accept it and make it work—or you've got the wrong chief executive."

The survey of directors by Williams disclosed, among other things, that management succession was one of their major concerns, as it was for McSwiney. The directors felt, as the top managers who were polled by Allemang did, that the board should be reduced in size, to between 12 and 15 members. (One objective of the Alden Committee was to review the recommendations of the Jones Report in the light of experience, and this had been one of the points in that report.) The directors and most of the people in Mead's senior management believed there should be no more than three insiders on the board, and that new board members should be selected by a committee of outside directors. All but one of the Mead managers thought the mandatory board retirement age should be lowered from 68 to 65.

The Mead directors, in their interviews with Williams, expressed their belief that "directors should be chosen to serve as individuals and not as representatives of any special interest groups." The final report of the Alden group took that position, too, although it conceded the desirability of having board members who were sensitive to "the points of view of women, minorities, youth, educators, and other constituencies."

On the question of outside or insider board members, the Alden Report said:

> A discussion of board composition based upon whether directors come from within the ranks of corporate management (insiders) or elsewhere (outsiders) can be misleading. The issue should be how a member functions on the board rather than where he or she came from....
>
> As a matter of principle, full-time officers and managers should always be at the service of the board. The argument that they should be available at board meetings to give and receive information should not be a reason for them to be members of the board. They should be invited to attend board meetings as frequently as is deemed necessary and useful to the board and to them. We believe the decision of who attends board meetings should be left to the judgment of the chairman of the board. But we do feel it is important that the regular membership of the Mead board should consist primarily of persons with an outside rather than an inside orientation.

In order to improve the quality of information received by the board, and make it easier for the directors to obtain additional information, the Alden Report said, "Presentation by Group and Divisional management should be confined to the day of the board meeting rather than the evening before, and then preferably at the end of the board meeting so that there may be added opportunities for board members to pursue discussions with management personnel in either a formal or informal manner."

The report added, "Care should be exercised to make management reports and other communications the preparation for, and not the goal of, the board agenda. Discussion takes place when informed participants contribute their views and judgment."

Another recommendation was that all committees be chaired by outsiders, with each outside director assigned to two committees. From time to time, the Alden task force said, committee assignments should be rotated. This would "assure an informal network of communications across the board." By 1979, *Business Week* was able to report that Mead's outside directors who chaired committees were spending 25 to 30 working days at their Mead tasks. "I couldn't serve on too many boards like Mead's," William Spencer told the magazine.

Since the chief executive officer (CEO) chaired the executive committee—the only committee still headed by an insider—there had to be provisions for convening that committee if the CEO were unable to do so. To solve that problem, the Alden Report said "there should be appointed a vice chairperson who shall serve in such instances and shall be the director serving as chairperson of the Compensation Committee." When the Alden Report was adopted, McSwiney asked William Verity to be vice chairperson.

In addition to serving as the nominating committee, the executive committee should also "review Mead management succession not less than annually," the report said.

On another subject, the Alden group said, "In essence, the board is concerned with the long-term health of Mead, and it is incumbent that Mead directors assure that corporate objectives are dynamic so that the company may adapt and evolve to meet changing needs and ultimate requirements." For that reason, the task force suggested "the formation of a committee of board members which will meet at least semi-annually to review, query, and examine corporate objectives."

This recommendation had come from McSwiney:

> I went to Beitzel, who had an excellent track record at IBM and I said, "I want to recommend a committee at the board level where we look at the issues of where we are going in this company." That also fits, if you think about it, into the idea of corporate governance in which the board is informed about where you're going.
>
> With Beitzel's background at IBM, I felt he was a hell of a guy to guide a corporate objectives committee, because we would then have a way to discuss periodically at the board level where we were going, where we invested our money, and the rationale for it. It was my way of getting better communications between the directors and officers on the strategic function in the organization.

In 1976, the corporate objectives committee (COC) was established by the board—as the Alden Report had recommended—and Beitzel became its chair. A few years later one of the outside directors, Tom Stanley, said of the committee, "It does not perceive and originate proposals for new investments, but it deliberates them and fleshes out suggestions that are brought before it. It is not a passive group at all—it is very active."

A year later, Beitzel chose to leave the Mead board because of a potential conflict of interest: IBM also was involved in ink-jet technology. Although it was an exception to the principle set forth by the Alden group, that board committees should be chaired by outside directors, the board named William Wommack to head the COC. McSwiney was in favor of Wommack's appointment because he felt it might encourage the board to consider Wommack as a candidate to succeed McSwiney as chairman of the board when McSwiney retired as an officer three years hence. It was McSwiney's thought that Wommack should be chairman, but Batts would be president and CEO. The two men, he thought, had such different talents and personalities that they could complement each other, forming a strong and effective team.

Of course, this was the separation of powers concept—the idea that the role of the chairperson of the board could, and should, be separate and distinct from that of the CEO. Philosophically, it reflected the "servant leadership" desire to substitute for the "hierarchical principle" of most institutions the contrasting principle of the leader who is "first among equals."

In his book, *Servant Leadership*, Robert Greenleaf wrote:

> To be a lone chief atop a pyramid is *abnormal and corrupting*. [His emphasis.] None of us are perfect by ourselves, and all of us need the help and correcting influence of close colleagues. When someone is moved atop a pyramid, that person no longer has colleagues, only subordinates. Even the frankest and bravest of subordinates do not talk with their boss in the same way that they talk with colleagues who are equals, and normal communication patterns become warped....
>
> A self-protective *image of omniscience* often evolves from these warped and filtered communications. This in time defeats any leader by causing a distortion of judgment, for one's judgment is often best sharpened through the interaction with others who are free to challenge and criticize.

In the great majority of American corporations, the chair of the board is also the CEO. But McSwiney was not the only person who saw this arrangement as not necessarily inevitable. In his 1976 book, *Putting the Corporate Board to Work*, Courtney C. Brown, former dean of the Columbia University graduate school of business, wrote:

> In recent years, the practice has grown of electing a single individual to the several posts of chairman of the board, president, and chief executive officer, thus making a single individual the senior officer of the board and of the company. A variation is to elect one person chairman of the board and chief executive officer, and another, president and chief operating officer. In both cases the head man is confronted with the difficulty of separating out his functions and responsibilities as the chairman of the board from those he holds as the chief executive of the company. *The ambiguity of the role of the total board begins right here* [his emphasis].

Brown was one of the people Rapp visited in the course of his research for the Alden task force. Rapp also visited Texas Instruments, a company that was experimenting in various areas of corporate governance, including separating the offices of chair of the board and chief executive officer. This was suggested by Rapp and Simonides as a key issue worthy of consideration by the task force.

In a paper submitted to the task force, Rapp and Simonides wrote:

> The present pattern, in most companies, where the CEO is also Chairman of the Board is the major source of confusion in the distinction of the Board and Management roles and functions. The President should be the CEO because the executive function is accountable to the Board.
> Consider the thesis that the Board, headed by its Chairman ... :
>
>> Is responsible ultimately for company performance;
>> Delegates responsibility to the company executives, headed by the CEO, for the detailed management of the corporation, and holds the executives, via the CEO, accountable for their decisions and performance.

Nevertheless, there was no mention of the separation of powers concept in the final report of the Alden task force—this despite the fact that McSwiney, as he later said, "had felt for a long time that it was an effective way of smoothing the transition of management."

By 1977, Mead's sales stood at $1.8 billion and its net earnings at $98 million. There had been two serious work stoppages, at Chillicothe and Escanaba, but the divestiture program had increased work productivity; in terms of sales per employee, it had risen in seven years from $30,000 to $70,000.

In 1976, McSwiney showed the board an architect's model of a new world headquarters for the company, to be built in the center of downtown Dayton. McSwiney believed the company should be downtown, on what was to be called Courthouse Plaza, to help bolster the city's urban renewal program.

"When a whole city block became available and taxes fixed for a period of time," McSwiney later said, "I came to the conclusion that CEOs had a responsibility to help in urban areas where they could, if the cost to the shareowners was not meaningful. I knew over a long period of time it would be far more economical than continuing to house the corporation in separate parts of our city. And I thought that George Mead would have liked to see the headquarters anchored in his home town and might have looked down with favor."

The Mead World Headquarters building, as it was called, proved to be an impressive addition to Dayton's skyline and a sound investment for the corporation.

The determination to help Dayton's downtown revitalization effort reflected McSwiney's continuing commitment to the solution of community problems, in the tradition of George Mead. Mac was active in many community organizations. In 1980, when the American Jewish Committee held a testimonial dinner in his honor at the Pierre Hotel in New York, the AJC said it was paying tribute to Mac's "efforts in behalf of a host of communal causes." Specifically, said the AJC, the testimonial was being held "in recognition of [McSwiney's] leadership in the effort to overcome prejudice and bigotry, and for [his] devotion to the cause of understanding among all people based on the universal recognition of the rights of the individual and the value of human dignity."

In his acceptance speech, McSwiney spoke of the need to apply the principles of "servant leadership" to the governance of large corporations, and to all other institutions of society, public and private. Those principles, put to work in the real world, he said, could enable modern society to build "organizations which can be models for achievement as well as places where leaders exercise wisdom, patience, stamina—and offer service free of the stifling influence of conforming to a rigid plan, however logically derived."

McSwiney's concern with corporate governance had caused him to ponder for a long time the concept of separating the powers of the chair and the CEO. Robert Greenleaf wrote a paper for a Harvard Business School symposium on corporate governance. In it Greenleaf wrote, in part:

> The recent discussion of the desirability of separating the chairman and CEO roles is made partly to create some space between the CEO and the board. This would also be a step toward providing at least one colleague to the CEO who is well informed, and if a strong person, could deal as an equal with the CEO. Everyone needs at least one colleague who is equally strong and who will "tell it to him straight." But is one such colleague enough?
>
> Beyond the separation of roles, there is considerable advocacy for a strong board, mostly outsiders, with the chairman leading the

board in its policymaking function. This move could add to the iso-
lation of the CEO from a close relationship that usually exists with
outside board members when the chairman is the CEO. What may be
at stake here is the question of power. There may be an uneasiness
with the kind of unchecked power that CEOs, particularly those of
large businesses, seem to have.

Greenleaf saw rule by one person not as a unifying force, but as a
negative factor, potentially damaging to the strength of an organization.

After much deliberation, McSwiney laid the idea before the board's
executive committee, which discussed it for about six months before
recommending to the full board that it be adopted as a modification
to the Alden Report that had been agreed to three years earlier. The
executive committee's proposal, submitted to the full board in April
1978, said that the chair and the CEO, as officers of the board, are
"accountable to the full board for their responsibilities. The
chairman's office does not report to the CEO, nor does the CEO report to the chairman."

The CEO had always been responsible to the board, the report said,
but it added that, "in practice, at times it may seem that the Board is a
mechanism for approving the actions of management." The objective
of the new approach was to establish a board, led by the chair, that "is
involved and understands the affairs of the company"—a board "to
whom the CEO is responsible."

> [This] is consistent with a growing trend of thought among observers
> and critics of the business corporation. Concern is already evidenced
> in some quarters that legislative intervention may be imposed in or-
> der to achieve a degree of public accountability, considered to be
> consistent with the power vested in large enterprises. A move in this
> direction does not restrict the Board in considering other alterna-
> tives, or in adopting long-term structural approaches which may re-
> sult from continuing studies.

The executive committee felt that the arrangements would have to
be worked out in a way that was "compatible with the experience,
talents, and temperaments of the persons who occupy key positions."

One section of the executive committee's report dealt with the general counsel's role, a matter which had not been addressed in the

Alden Report. The committee decreed that the general counsel would report to the CEO. The committee went on to say:

> In carrying out this function, the office of the general counsel will be expected to include a concern for the law as it will be, as well as the law as it is.
>
> Responsive to the American Bar Association Code of Professional Responsibility which requires that corporate counsel have an ultimate professional responsibility to the corporate entity and not to any individual officer, the office of general counsel is directed that, in the event he disagrees with a decision of the CEO to override a professional opinion on a matter where the general counsel considers the impact to be important to the welfare of the organization and one on which the CEO has chosen not to report to the directors that such difference of view exists; or, if the general counsel feels that information which the board should have is being withheld by the CEO, to assume the responsibility of bringing such matters promptly to the attention of the board.
>
> The general counsel, in all events, will first discuss the matter with the CEO to determine if there is simply a misunderstanding. If that is not the case, then the general counsel shall report the matter promptly to the chairman's office and the CEO will have the option of accompanying the general counsel in making his report.
>
> Such procedure is designed to fulfill the general counsel's professional obligation to the corporation and, at the same time, insure that the CEO has the full support of the general counsel in any given important decision unless the general counsel makes it clear to the contrary in a prompt manner.

A few weeks after the board approved the concept of separating the offices of CEO and chair of the board, McSwiney addressed the Conference Board in New York on the changing roles of boards and their chairs. He told the group, "The role of the CEO as both chairman of the board of directors and chief executive manager is, in my view, a working compromise between the historical evolution of boards as advisors to management and the legal definition of directors as having the ultimate responsibility for the actions of management (including the hiring and firing of management and the delegation of executive responsibilities)."

With the adoption of the new arrangement by the board, McSwiney relinquished the title of CEO to Warren Batts—three years before the normal retirement age for that position. However, Mac retained the post of chair of the board because Wommack could not see his way clear to becoming chair of the board without first serving as CEO.

The following year, *Business Week* said Mead had "one of the nation's strongest corporate boards," and noted that many considered it "a prototype of the corporate board of the future." But the magazine thought there was little likelihood that the Mead model would be copied for some time—"at the moment, extremely involved and independent boards are usually possible only when management encourages their development." The magazine quoted the chair of the Securities and Exchange Commission as saying, "If a CEO wants a rubber-stamp board, there is still a damn good chance he'll have it."

McSwiney didn't want a rubber-stamp board, and the efforts he had made to build a strong board now were widely recognized throughout corporate America. Myles Mace, an academic observer who had written one of the key texts on corporate governance, once said in an interview, "Mead is an extraordinary, shining example [of what a board should be]. And when people start saying there's a great reformation [of corporate governance] going on, look at Mead, I reply that Mead is one in a million."

Mace had been following Mead's progress for many years. He had conducted the Administrative Practices class of the Harvard Business School's twenty-fifth Advanced Management Program, which McSwiney had attended, and over the years he and Mac had seen each other from time to time.

But he may not have known McSwiney as well as he might have, for in a *Rutgers Law Review* article in 1979, Mace said, "It is not reasonable to expect CEOs to give up or restrict voluntarily their *de facto* powers of control."

McSwiney, it seemed, was simply the exception that proved the rule.

Twelve

The Largest Contested Takeover Fight

In the early 1970s McSwiney had reason, for a time, to think that an attempt might be made to take over Mead. As he often did, he discussed the matter with one of his board members, C. William Verity, Jr., chair of the board of Armco, Inc.

"I knew Bill had thought a good deal about this," Mac said, "and I also knew that he had taken some steps to react in a proper way, if need be."

"If you want good advice," Verity said, "put Joe Flom on retainer."

Joseph Flom was a partner in the New York law firm of Skadden, Arps, Slate, Meagher & Flom. At the time, the firm was becoming famous as a specialist in acquisition proceedings. Sometimes the partners represented the acquiring company, other times the target company. They also represented the investment banking houses that brokered the mergers.

McSwiney arranged a meeting with Flom, liked him, and put him on retainer. In later years he said Verity's suggestion was one of "the best pieces of advice I ever received."

> Joe Flom is a down-to-earth, nice, warm, decent, intelligent person. He knows the law, he knows the technicalities of these things, and he has the courage to tell you how to proceed. I said, "Joe, come out and tell our directors what we ought to do if we run into a problem."
> He came and laid it out. He said, "Look, if somebody walks in here

and they offer you $100 a share in cash for this company in the morn-
ing, don't call me. Take it."

He told us that if they come in offering something less than the
company's worth, you have two choices. One: if they are a reputable
and good company and come in with a low offer, but raise the bid to
a price that makes sense, a director with a sense of responsibility has
got to consider it seriously. On the other hand: if they come with
something that doesn't make sense, you don't have to sell the company just because somebody comes in and offers more than it is cur-
rently selling for in the market place.

One of the things Flom pointed out to McSwiney was that energetic
efforts to build strong stockholder relations ought to be conducted in
tranquil periods—that it was a mistake to wait until there was a crisis
before trying to give shareholders an understanding of what was happening in their company. With that in mind, McSwiney began a series
of regional stockholder meetings, which were well received by investors. Warren Batts, too, played an important part in financial relations.
Quick, crisp, and in command of the facts, he knew the vocabulary of
Wall Street and pleased the financial analysts with his courtesy and
congeniality.

Early in 1978 Mead's top management reviewed the company's financial position. It was good—almost too good, if such a thing is possible.

The divestment program, together with the improved overall performance and the tighter capital controls, projected a good cash flow.
According to the consolidated five-year plan, about $1 billion would
be available for reinvestment after dividend payments, but only about
$750 million of this would be absorbed by the company's existing
businesses. This was "not an unpleasant problem," as the report said.

However, substantial cash reserves might open the company to attack by corporate raiders—an event all the more likely because the
price-earnings ratio of Mead's common stock was fairly low. If a
raider succeeded in taking over the company, it might expect to recover up to one-third of the purchase price through the company's
own cash and marketable securities.

On the other hand, Mead was in a strong position to defend itself,
if it had to. In McSwiney it had a dynamic, strong-willed leader. It had
an effective management team. Its board was considered one of the

finest in the country. It had been working diligently and successfully for several years to build better shareholder relations. Furthermore, 40 percent of Mead's shares were held by members of management, directors, or the former owners of businesses acquired by Mead.

Toward the end of July 1978, McSwiney and Joseph Baird, the president of Occidental Petroleum Company, met at the Bohemian Grove, an outing of diverse but influential people that was held each summer near San Francisco. Baird told McSwiney that Occidental might be interested in buying Mead's Mulga coal operation in Alabama. McSwiney replied that Mead might sell the property if the price was right.

On August 3, Baird telephoned McSwiney and arranged to meet with him in Dayton on August 10 to discuss a possible Mulga deal.

On August 9, Mead's stock jumped 4⅜—from $23 to $27⅜—on trading of 112,000 shares, almost four times the usual volume of trades in those days. Mead prepared, but did not issue, a statement that it knew of no reason for the activity in its stock. The statement pointed out, however, that a number of analysts had recently recommended Mead to investors.

But it was obvious that "buy" recommendations could not account for what was happening. That evening McSwiney read the statement over the telephone to Baird and asked him if he knew any reason why the prepared statement by Mead might be inaccurate. Baird said he did not, but mentioned that he was bringing Dr. Armand Hammer, Occidental's 80-year-old board chairman, to the meeting in Dayton the next day. McSwiney expressed disbelief that Hammer would be accompanying Baird to Dayton just to talk about the purchase of a small coal mine.

By the time Hammer and Baird arrived at Mead's new headquarters building on Courthouse Plaza in Dayton, the New York Stock Exchange had suspended trading in Mead shares because of unmatched orders to buy 210,000 shares.

Baird almost immediately raised the possibility of a friendly merger of Mead and Occidental. Baird said, "Mead could be the target of an unfriendly takeover." That could explain the heavy activity in Mead's shares over the past two days.

"Fellows," Baird said, "I think it would be to your advantage to consider an offer from us."

To McSwiney and Warren Batts, Occidental emphasized the personal advantages, in the form of options and positions, that could be included in a merger of Occidental and Mead.

Batts told them that the Occidental offer would be studied carefully, but he expressed the belief that the bid—which Occidental valued at $35 per share, largely in preferred securities—was an insult to a company of Mead's stature and performance.

McSwiney said that he and Batts had a fiduciary responsibility to the shareholders and that "personal positions were of little consequence."

Before leaving, Baird brought out a formal letter containing Occidental's proposal, as authorized by Occidental's board. That sort of proposal was known among business people at the time as a "bear hug."

In his autobiography, Hammer said he was startled by McSwiney's hostile reaction, because Baird had given him the impression that Mac would welcome an offer from Occidental. Hammer also was distressed when—according to his version—McSwiney said Occidental would be hearing from Mead's attorney, Joe Flom. "I was surprised," Hammer wrote, "since Joe Flom had already represented us in a proposed acquisition of a Canadian-American company. It is a great comfort to have Joe on your side and a sore distress to have him against you."

As soon as the two men from Occidental left, McSwiney got on the telephone, first to Flom in New York, and then to each of Mead's directors. Simultaneously, Mac mobilized the appropriate Mead managers for immediate action. A statement was prepared for the media. Other lawyers in Dayton, Columbus, Washington, and New York who would play major roles in the fight were contacted as quickly as possible. Something close to frenzy pervaded the ranks of senior management as Mead readied itself for battle.

It is difficult, years later, to conceive of the turmoil that characterized life at Mead during the next few months. Men and women worked almost around the clock. One of the offices at Mead was dubbed "the war room," and with good reason. In that room, and throughout the company—and, indeed, the country—wherever Mead people and their allies were actively engaged in the fight, there were days of utter elation and times of gloom. Usually there was a good reason for whatever mood was felt that day.

"The rumor mill was a source of concern," Jerry Rapp recalled. "Peaks and valleys of optimism and despair could have hinged on the good and bad news rumors from day to day." However, the generals of this war, on Mead's side at least, realized they could not let themselves become preoccupied with rumors. "Consequently," Rapp said, "we decided to pursue and neutralize only those adverse rumors having a major prospect for major morale damage. It was a matter of priorities, and the team morale was a high priority issue to our leadership."

One move that helped morale—and also, coincidentally, internal communications among the various people engaged in the struggle—had to do with eating arrangements. "The community and corporate dining rooms on the top floor of the Mead Tower, filled with art work, a large portrait of George Mead on the wall, memorabilia of George Mead's service to past Presidents of the United States and past accomplishments of other famous Dayton leaders, were converted to a mess hall for the duration of the contest," Rapp said. "All members of the team—whether internal management, financial and stockholders staff, or litigators, paralegals, as well as supervisors and support staff—knew it was possible to satisfy luncheon and dinner needs daily and at the same time accomplish necessary communications with others while picking up the latest information about events on all battlefronts."

He added, "This most ingenious and effective internal communications device proved, incidentally, that when there is full and free access by *all* members to the important current information, there follows an environment for many to seize an opportunity to contribute needed leadership. Certainly this is another mini-sample of the positive results from Bob Greenleaf's conviction that, if permitted, leadership can and will spring from people in the most unexpected places."

A familiar sight was McSwiney, bucking up a weary paralegal in the dining room at the end of a long day, or padding in stockinged feet along the corridor to the "war room," or on the telephone to board members. "Coping with his cascade of ideas and suggestions was a key responsibility of mine," Rapp remarked.

There are endless anecdotes from that time of crisis. One day, for example, a messenger, by mistake, delivered to Mead's lawyers documents from Occidental's files marked "privileged"—meaning that Mead could not have subpoenaed them. As it turned out, most of the information in them consisted of material that did not properly fall within the definition of lawyer–client privilege, but should, in fact, have been subject to subpoena—material that was new and pivotal to Mead's case.

On August 18, Mead sent a letter to stockholders which asserted that the Occidental offer was highly unsatisfactory from the shareholders' point of view. The letter also attacked Occidental's performance. Mead pointed out that Occidental had suffered a $38.9 million loss in the first half of that year, 1978. It pointed out that Occidental's North Sea oil revenues were subject to increased taxation by Great Britain, and that a fifth of Occidental's revenues and earnings came from Libya, "an area of questionable stability." The letter reminded shareholders that Occidental had signed consent decrees with the SEC involving the anti-fraud provisions of federal securities laws. Mead recalled that Occidental had entered into three consent decrees in the previous seven years involving allegations of securities fraud brought by the SEC, and that Hammer himself had pleaded guilty to "federal criminal violations" (illegal personal campaign contributions) two years before.

The Mead letter to shareowners also was published as an ad in *The Wall Street Journal* and *The New York Times*. A member of Mead's public relations staff, reviewing the copy before the letter and ad were published, said he felt some of the bare-knuckled, hard-hitting statements about Occidental seemed disturbingly abrasive.

"Any broken bottle will do in a fight like this," replied attorney Mike Mitchell, of the Skadden, Arps law firm.

Some feeling for the sense of urgency that marked McSwiney's activities on the day he and Batts met with Hammer and Baird can be gained from the recollections of one of the directors, Thomas B. Stanley, Jr.

I was at home and had just had dinner, about 8:30 or so, when I got a call from Evelyn Stemen [McSwiney's administrative assistant]. She said Mac was on the phone and had a number of people to call, and would get to me as soon as he could. Meanwhile, she read a note from Mac that filled me in on what had happened at the meeting with Hammer. She read me the letter from Baird to Mac and the statement about the offer. She wanted to know did I have any questions that I wanted to pass along to Mac.

About an hour later he was on the phone to me and gave me a full report on the meeting. On Monday he and I went to Atlanta and met with Ivan Allen to discuss the board's options. As I recall, there was at least one other board member there, too. We discussed the options open to the board, but in the end we decided to fight as hard as we could on behalf of our shareholders.

(The board continued to be actively involved in the fight. Stanley, for example, made several trips to Dayton to help in the fight, and testified in an administrative hearing in Columbus, Ohio.)

The next day, August 11, Occidental made a public announcement of the offer for Mead's stock. Occidental proposed swapping 0.28 share of a new Occidental $10 preferred stock and 0.007 share of a new $7.50 convertible preference stock for each Mead common share, which had been selling at about $23 per share a few days earlier, before its sudden surge in the market.

Stanley, a large Mead stockholder as well as a director, thought the Occidental offer a "terrible proposition—an insult." He pointed out, "The liquidation value of Mead was more than 50 percent higher than their offer. Then, too, it was deferred cash using a low-grade subordinate deferred."

(*Barron's*, the highly regarded financial weekly, also took a dim view of Occidental's proposal. It pointed out that Occidental's "long-term debt and other liabilities, plus minority interests, totaled $1.7 billion...compared to a now-shrunken $1.3 billion of shareholders' equity." Furthermore, the periodical said, Occidental had recently issued preferreds having mandatory retirement provisions, and it expressed the opinion that such preferreds "were little more than debt and so could scarcely be classified as equity." *Barron's* went on to say, "If we follow that line of reasoning...the company [Occidental] winds

up with only about $1 billion in equity and close to $2 billion in liabilities." Because its offer for Mead consisted of such preferred
shares, the newspaper said, if Occidental succeeded in taking over
Mead, Occidental's "debt-equity ratio then...would be a rather untidy
$2.8 billion to $1.2 billion." In its customarily tart and punning fash-
ion, *Barron's* called the kind of preferred stock that Occidental was
offering to Mead shareholders "less fish than fowl.")

McSwiney believed strongly that the Occidental offer was a decision for a fully informed board of directors, not one for a management that might or might not benefit personally. So he immediately
arranged for meetings with his directors—to Birmingham to see one
group, to Philadelphia for another. The Philadelphia meeting was
held in the offices of Rohm and Haas Company, of which Vincent
Gregory, a Mead director, was president and chief executive officer.
"Mac kept a low profile" during the meeting, Gregory later recalled,
but it was clear to all that McSwiney was still angry about the meeting
with Hammer.

The years of building a strong, independent, and knowledgeable
board now proved their worth. Already deeply committed to the interests of Mead and its shareholders, the directors drew together with
management as a team. The directors knew the intrinsic value of the
company and were of one mind that the Occidental offer should be
rejected as detrimental to the company and its owners.

On August 18, after a two-day meeting, Mead's board of directors
formally rejected the Occidental offer as "inadequate and not in the
best interests of Mead stockholders." The hard-hitting letter to shareholders was mailed and published as an advertisement that day.

The battle was now joined. The U.S. Department of Justice later
called it the largest contested takeover bid in history.

Months later, when the battle was over, the directors remembered
how impressed they had been by McSwiney's involvement of them in
the fight from the very first hours. Vernon Alden contrasted
McSwiney's actions with those of the management of another company with which he was familiar. The other company also had been
the target of a takeover attempt, but there, management made little
effort to involve the board and there was much confusion.

The preceding years of working to improve stockholder relations also paid off for Mead. On September 6, in an article on takeover attempts then being pursued, *The Wall Street Journal* reported, "Over the years Mead has won considerable good will among its shareholders and in the financial community, and in a knockdown battle that could turn into a significant asset."

The *Dayton Journal Herald* had already voiced the hope of people in Mead's hometown that the company, which it lauded for its "active civic role in such projects as the Courthouse Plaza development" and Sinclair Community College, would be able to maintain its independence. The newspaper was referring to Mead's decision to aid Dayton's downtown revitalization efforts by building a new Mead corporate headquarters in the heart of the downtown area.

Occidental tried to reassure the local community that Mead would remain in Dayton even if the takeover attempt succeeded. "I want them all to stay," Hammer said. "I like Jim McSwiney."

It is safe to say that the affection was not mutual.

As the war for Mead's independence—what *Forbes* called "The Fight of the Year"—heated up, it was clearly understood by all that Mac, working closely with his board, was the commander-in-chief. "He has bull-like power," Batts said later. "Coming at the end of his career, this was the last thing he wanted. He said on many occasions that he always wanted a full and well-rounded career but had no desire for the experience involved in a takeover."

In addition to managing the business of the corporation, Batts had the responsibility of identifying a possible "white knight" who might come to Mead's rescue if all else failed. He was given that responsibility because it was felt that, as CEO, he would have to live with the circumstances that would exist if such an eventuality occurred. Batts worked closely with bankers and others in the investment community who might be able to help in the search for a possible "white knight." In the course of his efforts, he did identify two or three possibilities. Mead exchanged information with those companies, but no attempt was made to negotiate a deal. That would not be done unless, and until, it appeared that Occidental was about to win.

The news media kept asking questions of Mead's public relations staff, who had no answers to give. It had been decided at the highest level that Mead could have only one spokesperson, and that one would be McSwiney. Thus the opportunity for misunderstandings, erroneous information, or timing mishaps was reduced substantially.

Thus, the five-month period of the takeover war, one of the most newsworthy periods in the corporation's history, was one of great frustration for Mead's internal public relations staff. They were gagged while outside specialists, sponsored by lawyers, took over their territory. "It was not a fun time for an eager corporate public relations staff," in Rapp's recollection.

Flom had pointed out to senior managers and board members the risks of taking and retaining notes of conversations, logs of telephone conversations, and drafts of statements—all of which might, in the hands of a clever trial lawyer, be introduced in evidence, out of context, to suggest something quite different from what the note-maker intended.

If they do no other good, at least it can be said that takeover battles provide income for a wide variety of professionals, including lawyers, investment bankers, and public relations counselors. In this battle to address the financial community, Mead was represented by Flom; by the investment banking houses of Smith Barney Harris Upham & Co., Inc., which was led by Andy Steffan, and Goldman, Sachs & Co., whose John C. Jamison played a key role; and by Gershon Kekst's New York public relations agency. Mead's controller, William A. Enouen, and its assistant general counsel, George Maly, provided internal support and direction to this aggressive financial community team.

Occidental was represented by a team from the law firm of Fried, Frank, Harris, Shriner & Jacobson, headed by Arthur Fleischer, Jr., with Robert E. Juceam as the key trial lawyer; by the investment banking houses of Kidder Peabody & Blyth Eastman Dillon, and Dean Witter; and, in the initial stages of the fight, by the Hill & Knowlton public relations agency, which later dropped out because of a conflict of interest arising from another takeover battle. In Ohio hearings, Occidental was represented by David S. Cupps, Thomas B. Ridgley, Jr., and John C. Elam, all of the Columbus, Ohio, law firm of Vorys, Sater, Seymour & Pease. Other law firms involved in the fight on Occidental's behalf included O'Melveny & Myers, of Los Angeles, and Wald, Harkrader & Ross, of Washington, D.C.

Mead's board retained separate counsel—Allen C. Holmes, of the

Cleveland firm of Jones, Day, Cockley, Reavis & Pogue. There were times, during the subsequent months of the battle, when the board excluded everyone but Holmes from its deliberations.

Rapp, Mead's general counsel—whose work day, like that of many of the others involved in the fight, usually started at 6:30 a.m. and ended about midnight—coordinated the work of several teams of lawyers. One team, consisting of Joseph Flom and Peter Atkins, both of Skadden, Arps, focused on financial and legal strategy. Others directed by Rapp included a group of litigators. Chief litigation strategist was Harold F. Baker, senior partner of Howrey & Simon, a Washington firm famous for its antitrust litigation practice. He was ably assisted by Alan M. Wiseman, Peter E. Moll, and Scott E. Flick. Also very important to execution of the trial strategy was a Dayton trial team led by Armistead W. (Bill) Gilliam, Jr., of Smith & Schnacke, and David C. Greer of Bieser, Greer & Landis, another Dayton law firm. Peter Work, then of Jones, Day, played a major creative and liaison role with the antitrust division of the U.S. Department of Justice after it joined the litigation. Indeed, numerous lawyers from Skadden, Arps; Howrey & Simon; Smith & Schnacke; and Jones, Day were involved in the trial effort lodged in Judge Rubin's court in Dayton.

Law firms in Louisiana, North Carolina, Florida, Michigan, Missouri, and other states also represented Mead in litigation aimed at Occidental during the takeover fight.

The first legal salvo involved Stuart Shapiro of Flom's firm, who concentrated on proceedings involving the Ohio antitakeover laws and "blue sky" regulations. He was assisted by John J. (Jack) Chester, of Columbus, Ohio, and by Chester's partners, Roderick H. Willcox and William B. Saxbe, a former Attorney General of the United States. At the same time—to slow the pace of Occidental and provide early, precious time for Mead to organize its counteroffensive—Peter Atkins coordinated an assault on the Occidental offer with teams of lawyers at the Securities and Exchange Commission and in numerous states under "blue sky" laws. ("Blue sky" laws are state statutes designed to protect the public from buying fraudulent securities by requiring full disclosure of adverse information.)

The federal government was yet another front where lawyers were active on behalf of Mead. This aspect of the Washington work was covered by Clark M. Clifford, who had been Secretary of Defense in the administration of Lyndon Johnson and an intimate advisor to several Presidents. His special concern was assuring that Occidental received no unfair advantage from the national administration. In McSwiney's view, Clifford did his job well.

Yet another team in Washington led by former U.S. Assistant Attorney General J. Stanley Pottinger of Troy, Malin & Pottinger, undertook the "due diligence" aspect of the case. In effect, this meant scrutinizing Occidental's affairs for information that might be of interest to Mead's shareowners. Pottinger was ably assisted by his Washington associates Randy Mott and Ed Kleppinger and by Joseph Troy, who headed the Troy, Malin, and Pottinger office in Los Angeles. They unveiled and developed information concerning Occidental's environmental problems. They also uncovered leads related to the differential in prices between so-called "old oil" and "new oil."

Of great importance to Mead's defense was information dug up in late November and early December by the Pottinger team about corporate governance allegations, including some of Occidental's accounting practices and questionable practices related to Occidental's board of directors' service. Armed with this information, Hal Baker's litigation team sought depositions from Occidental's outside directors. Before all the directors could be questioned in deposition proceedings, Occidental dropped its tender offer (following the trial on the antitrust issues) and the directors' depositions became moot.

The Mead defense was widely believed to be the most massive effort ever mounted in such a case up to that time. Every day 10 or 12 teams of lawyers were taking depositions somewhere, from someone, on behalf of or against Mead.

For weeks at a time as many as 100 out-of-town lawyers and their assistants stayed in Dayton, taking part in the fight.

"At one time," board member Stanley later recalled, "we had several hundred legal and paralegal people working. There were times when some of them worked three days and nights straight. It was like being at war."

Mead's two corporate jet aircraft put more miles on their logs than any other Falcons in the country that year.

The costs of all of this must have been substantial. Mead was reported to have spent about $10 million that year for legal and public relations expenses. Occidental's costs certainly must have been higher, because that company also had to deal with expensive problems that arose out of disclosures made during the takeover fight. Months later, after Occidental retreated from the fray, Mead tried to recover a portion of its costs from Occidental through a law suit, which later was withdrawn pursuant to an agreement between the parties. (One of the reasons that Mead agreed to the settlement was that Occidental, paradoxically, had become one of Mead's biggest customers through the purchase of corrugated boxes by Occidental's wholly owned subsidiary, Iowa Beef Packers, Inc.)

None of those developments could be foreseen on August 18, when Mead, acting immediately after the negative vote by its board on the Occidental offer, filed a suit against Occidental in the U.S. District Court at Dayton, alleging violations of the federal securities laws. This rapid response set the tone for what followed. By thus seizing the initiative, Mead was able to wage the principal fight in Dayton, its home base.

Three days later, Federal Judge Carl B. Rubin looked down at lawyers for both companies as the opening skirmishes began in the war of suit and countersuit. (During the weeks that followed, the attorneys knew that a second war was being fought: Judge Rubin, whom lawyers for both sides knew, liked, and respected, was in a battle for his life. Stricken with cancer, he was undergoing chemotherapy during the period of litigation. Although he had many bad days, Judge Rubin continued with a very demanding schedule. "A determined professional," Rapp said, "Judge Rubin exhibited much courage and deep concern for the pursuit of a fair judicial result." In the end, Judge Rubin appeared to have won his war. Ten years later he held the position of senior judge for the Southern District of Ohio and was still going strong.)

Mead accused Occidental of violating federal and state laws in making its formal tender offer. Occidental charged that Mead made false and misleading statements about Occidental in its statements and advertisements to shareholders.

Shortly thereafter, Mead asked that the Ohio Division of Securities hold a hearing to determine whether Occidental was violating the state's "blue sky" law by not providing Mead shareholders with enough information about Occidental's business. Subsequently Mead filed similar state securities law actions in half a dozen or so other states.

The vigor of Mead's counteroffensive unquestionably startled Occidental, and probably many other people. Mead had been perceived, rightly, as a gentlemanly organization, not a street fighter, and there were many who did not realize that gentlemen can be tough, too.

In his autobiography, Hammer complained, "The next thing I knew, I was walking into my office and found the corridors almost blocked with packing cases piled almost to the ceiling." Mead had subpoenaed "all of Occidental's corporate records *for years*. A whole warehouse of documents had been emptied" for Mead.

Judge Rubin ruled that such matters were relevant to the controversy, because they obviously bore on information shareholders needed to make an informed decision. The judge said, "It is apparent, even at this early stage of the litigation, that conduct of management of Occidental Petroleum Corporation may be a matter pertinent to decisions by shareholders on the exchange offer."

This ruling gave Mead access to a million or more documents gathered by the U.S. Department of Justice during its investigation of Occidental. The files were available only under restricted conditions, but they provided information and leads that Mead's attorneys were able to utilize.

The Mead investigation focused on three major areas.

The first was the matter of Occidental's questionable foreign payments. What was uncovered in that area was later reported by the *Washington Star*:

> Occidental Petroleum Corporation, under questionable legal circumstances, has dispensed about $30 million since 1969, including secret payments to an Arab prince, a Nigerian diplomat, and unnamed persons who may have been evading taxes and currency exchange laws in foreign countries, according to an internal [Occidental] corporate audit.

The second involved Occidental's environmental problems. One of its subsidiaries, Hooker Chemicals and Plastics Corporation, was then suffering considerable notoriety because of environmental problems at the Love Canal in upstate New York. Mead engaged environmental consultants and visited at least 10 environmental agencies in regions where Hooker had operations.

As a result of that investigation, Mead found that Love Canal was only one of Hooker's environmental problems. In Montague, Michigan, it was found that toxic wastes were leaking from Hooker's property, creating what the *Washington Post* later described as "extremely serious environmental problems."

Cleaning up such "contaminated areas in a manner which satisfies existing standards of environmental protection," Mead contended, "will run into many millions of dollars and Occidental further faces substantial liability to individuals and businesses injured as a result of those practices."

The third issue was corporate governance as practiced at Occidental. As *The National Law Journal* later told its readers, Stanley Pottinger, in one of his many "due diligence" investigations on behalf of Mead, checked out a "rumor that Dr. Hammer had required other directors to submit to him signed, undated letters of resignation as a condition of serving on the board."

> I called Dorman Commons, a former director in San Francisco, told him I represented Mead, and said I understood that he had submitted such a letter. He said he had. I said I'd be on the next plane out. We subpoenaed him and got his statement.
>
> It was like bells going off. We thought it was a major break in the case because it was such a bizarre practice that it would ignite the SEC.

When the issue was raised publicly, Occidental said officially: "Occidental is aware that Dr. Hammer obtained undated resignations from a small number of past management directors."

All in all, the information dug up by Mead and its attorneys was destined to have not only short-term, but also long-term, consequences for Occidental. As *The New York Times* commented, "This illustrates the dangers faced by a corporation that attempts a hostile takeover, because the information in the Mead case threatens to plague Occidental in the future."

Mead's counterattack against Occidental was not only hard-hitting but also innovative. When Mead argued that Occidental had failed to disclose in its SEC filings substantial liabilities affecting the company's financial stability, Mead's action gave impetus to what *Business Week* later called "a U.S. drive to curb double-talk"—that is, the custom of some companies to provide different and conflicting information to different government agencies, such as the Internal Revenue Service and the SEC. Citing Mead's defensive actions, the magazine said, "Challenging companies' statements by comparing filings with regulatory agencies with what the companies tell the SEC and their shareholders was pioneered by a group of Washington attorneys involved in thwarting unfriendly takeover bids."

In October, the hearing examiner for the Ohio Division of Securities, Nodine Miller, having ploughed through 25,000 documents, found 14 instances where Occidental's required disclosures were either inadequate or misleading. These lapses, she said, "reflect its attempt to round off the jagged edges of its capricious actions." Furthermore, she found "Occidental's global operations were riddled with risks," which the company had not told its shareholders. She also ruled that the Occidental takeover bid had received "rubber stamp approval" from Occidental's board. Reporting on her findings, *The New York Times* said that, even though state securities agencies are expected to be protective of companies headquartered in the state, nevertheless Miller's remarks had to be considered "blistering."

Shortly thereafter, Occidental won a round by obtaining the right to make corrections in its prospectus as ordered by Miller.

One of Mead's most effective actions was its attack on Occidental under the federal antitrust laws. While the securities litigation was being pursued, Hal Baker's troops were working day and night putting together the massive antitrust complaint, which was filed on September 18, 1978. At the same time, Hal Baker followed through on his strategy of trying—successfully, as it turned out—to persuade the federal government that it should also file an antitrust complaint. The Justice Department's complaint was filed October 11, 1978. This was considered by many observers to have been critical to Mead's ultimate victory.

As a conglomerate starting with oil and moving into other fields, including coal and chemicals, Occidental was sole supplier of resins used in making carbonless papers—that is, paper that could make copies without the use of carbon paper—to Appleton Paper Company, the largest competitor in the field of carbonless papers. Mead ranked No. 2 in carbonless papers. George Mead and Whitaker had authorized installation of coater equipment on which to produce NCR's patented carbonless paper in 1955, and Mead was for a considerable length of time NCR's sole supplier. As NCR began to expand its own resources, Mead felt threatened. So McSwiney opened negotiations with NCR with the aim of enabling Mead to offer its own product in the market place. The negotiations were successful, and Mead was able to enter the carbonless paper market in 1971. The net effect of an Occidental acquisition of Mead would have been the accomplishment of a monopoly in carbonless paper, resulting from Occidental's control of the resins used by Appleton and Mead's manufacture of carbonless paper.

Occidental, through its subsidiary Island Creek Coal Company, was one of the largest producers of coal in the United States. Mead had moved into the coal market through its acquisition of the Woodward properties and was one of the top producers of metallurgical coal in Alabama. Occidental was a potential entrant into that market.

At the same time, Occidental had become the dominant United States producer of sodium chlorate, an important bleaching agent in the pulp industry. Mead was in the process of expanding its production capacity of sodium chlorate. If Occidental's sodium chlorate capacity were added to Mead's, the concentration of economic power in that specialty chemical would have been even more intense.

But the most striking fact, in terms of antitrust significance, was that the combination of Appleton Paper's dominant share of the U.S. carbonless paper market—55 percent—with Mead's 28 percent, connected by Occidental's supply of chemicals to Appleton, would give the merged Mead–Occidental organization 83 percent of the principal chemicals used for the production of carbonless papers, a highly desirable and growing part of the paper industry.

A federal attorney in Los Angeles, Barbara Reeves, believed that there was a substantial antitrust issue at stake in the case, and she persuaded her superiors in Washington that the Department of Justice should intervene. As a result, the Department of Justice filed suit in early October to enjoin the merger under the Clayton Act. But the Justice lawyers put their emphasis on another product, coated paper. Mead had a substantial share of that market. The government argued that, if the merger went through, Occidental, being much larger than any of the paper companies, would be able to pour money into Mead to increase its production of coated paper, making it the dominant firm in that field, lessening competition, and driving out smaller competitors. The CEOs of five competing paper companies went to Dayton to testify against a Mead–Occidental merger. The government's "deep pockets" theory of antitrust policy was described as "novel" by *Business Week*.

How well was the separation of the offices of chairman and CEO working under the siege conditions in which Mead found itself?

Despite all that was going on, Rapp somehow found the time in late October to deliver a short but thoughtful paper at a Business International Roundtable Seminar on "Issues in Corporate Governance and Disclosure." On a program that included SEC chairman Harold Williams, Rapp wound up his remarks by saying:

> As most of you are aware, our board and senior management in recent months have been operating in a tender offer climate, which produces extraordinary pressure on any corporate structure. So, it goes without saying, our structure has been subject to unusual stress at this point....
>
> Given this context, I will venture the following comments on the growth of corporate structure under unusual conditions of test and tension:
>
> 1. My first point has to do with *integrity*. As the result of the chairman and CEO being separate, but working together and with due regard for the responsibilities of each other, a sense of high integrity pervades the entire organization—I feel that this sense of open, visible, cooperative independence permeates the entire corporate structure. It sends down the line a message of confidence and stability in an otherwise uncertain climate.
>
> 2. Next, I would say there is additional *resilience* which results from the distinction between the top functions: i.e., the chairman leading the board in its important responsibility of interfacing on behalf of the shareholders' interest on major policy

matters, while the president/CEO is running the business and providing service and support to the board. The separation does not serve as a barrier between them—more like a fire door—resulting in a conservation of effort and increased effectiveness, helpful in maintaining a balance in the overall decision-making process.

3.   One final note should be the recognition of the additional burdens involved. There is no doubt that having a CEO who is not a board chairman takes more time, more interactions, careful attention to a myriad of details of communication, probably a need for greater empathy, and surely more expense, as special counsel, advisors, or consultants are engaged at times just to guide the board. There are more meetings and more time commitments, all imposed on short notice.

I believe, on balance, that the additional burden is worth it if we are to get the best possible performance from corporations today on behalf of their shareowners in the complex climate of the need for candor and boldness and open communications in the face of an uncertain, almost mysterious, if not capricious, economic market.

The takeover war, with its many battle fronts, became focused on Judge Rubin's new courtroom in Dayton Federal Courthouse as the trial opened on Mead's request for a preliminary injunction against Occidental's efforts on the ground that the proposed acquisition would violate the antitrust laws. The galleries were packed as the trial team of Gilliam and Greer used the ammunition gathered under the direction of Hal Baker and Alan Wiseman to demonstrate in a six-week hearing that Mead's position carried a substantial likelihood of success. The smooth coordination of Mead's legal effort was a tribute to Gerald Rapp's ability to demonstrate in performance the integrity, resilience, and poise under stress which were the subject of his remarks at the Roundtable Seminar.

About the first of November, Occidental learned that the SEC was launching a formal investigation into the question of directors' tenure at that company, an investigation that was formally announced toward the end of that month.

A few weeks later, Judge Rubin issued a 10-day restraining order while he considered Mead's request for a preliminary injunction on antitrust grounds. In unfriendly takeovers, it is axiomatic that the deed must be done quickly; time tends to be on the side of the target company. The restraining order, and the possibility of a subsequent injunction, did not bode well for Occidental's raid.

On the eve of a final decision by Judge Rubin, which many believed would be favorable to Mead, Occidental on December 20 made a public announcement that it was withdrawing its exchange offer.

"We felt that it was not just the top fellows at Mead," Baird, of Occidental, said, "but all of management was against us. Whether we won or lost, it was the feeling of our board that we would have a hell of a job managing Mead."

So Mead's war for independence, which had taken all the combatants on a series of ups and downs for months, came to an end.

McSwiney, Batts, Wommack, Rapp, and others in senior management at Mead who had been deeply involved in the battle had sensed for several days that victory in the takeover fight was theirs, and that Occidental was going to give up the struggle. They felt a sense of relief that the fight had been won. Later, the leading members of the winning team—lawyers, public relations counsellors, investment bankers, and Mead staff—were invited to celebration dinners.

Middle management at Mead reacted in a much more emotional way. There were impromptu parties, cheers, and T-shirts ("Ferocity Crew") especially printed for the occasion. As Rapp put it, there was "something of a Mardi Gras atmosphere" at Mead.

All of which proved that what Baird said in the end was true: all of management, at every level, had been arrayed against him—a manifestation of the loyalty and affection that McSwiney, as the embodiment of the corporation, was able to evoke from his followers. In the true spirit of servant leadership, they were ready to follow because they believed that he had their best interests at heart in making leadership decisions.

The same was true of Mead's board, which was strong, knowledgeable, and independent—and thus able to be much more effective and supportive during the fight—because McSwiney wanted that kind of a board.

There was an irony in this, for a long-time member of Occidental's board was Neil Jacoby, the widely respected faculty member at the University of Southern California's business school. In his 1973 book,

Corporate Power and Social Responsibility, Jacoby, who died a few months after the Mead battle, wrote:

> The board must become more independent if it is to perform its central function of auditing the performance of the operating management. As [Myles] Mace found, many directors do little more than rubber-stamp management's recommendations. Outside directors generally lack time to master the information necessary for effective supervision. Insider directors have the knowledge, but are reluctant to challenge their superiors in board meetings. *The key to better corporate government is to increase the power, the independence, the range of competence, and the compensation of outside directors in public corporations.* [Original emphasis.]

For Baird, there was a sequel to the whole affair. As Hammer told the story, after it became clear that the Mead takeover attempt was going to fail, Baird wanted to keep after Mead, and Hammer wanted to drop the attempt. Baird said he would oppose Hammer. "Now it had become more than a ghastly messed-up takeover bid," Hammer wrote in his autobiography, "—now it was a fight to see who was CEO of Occidental."

When the issue came before the Occidental board, Baird lost. "That was the end of Joe Baird's presidency," said Hammer, with a certain satisfaction.

Seven years later, when he was in Moscow for a meeting of the U.S.–U.S.S.R. Trade Council, Rapp met Hammer at a reception in the U.S. Embassy.

"How's McSwiney?" Hammer asked.

"Fine," replied Rapp.

"Give him my best," said Hammer.

Thirteen

Antitrust: The Fight for Fairness

The takeover fight against Occidental occurred at a time when Mead was already deeply involved in difficult and complicated antitrust litigation. All the time that Mead's senior managers were struggling to avoid the unwelcome embrace of Occidental, they also had to continue what had become a long-drawn-out series of court cases brought by federal prosecutors—cases that Mead regarded as clearly unfair to a company like theirs, which, they argued, had worked diligently to obey the antitrust statutes.

Throughout the 1970s and into the early 1980s Mead, along with most of the forest products industry, found itself buried in an avalanche of antitrust litigation. Virtually all product lines were involved, including folding cartons, corrugated containers, linerboard and medium and fine papers, and pulp. (Mead was not involved in the investigations of the plywood, lumber, and paper bag industries.)

In order to deal with the various criminal investigations and the criminal and civil litigation that followed, Mead had to make a major commitment of management and corporate resources, as well as an outlay of millions of dollars in fees to outside counsel and economic experts.

How did Mead get embroiled in this quicksand, despite its extensive antitrust compliance program? And how can a company insure that it gets a fair shake when it is unjustly accused?

In 1960 the electrical equipment antitrust cases—both criminal and civil—sent shock waves throughout U.S. industry. For the first time, high-level corporate officials went to jail for price-fixing and bid-rigging. Consequently, alert executives recognized that they had to establish meaningful antitrust compliance programs to avoid a similar fate. Mead was one of those companies.

On February 5, 1962, Mead sent to personnel of all divisions and subsidiaries a standing instruction HO-9 (headquarters order) entitled, "Compliance with the Antitrust Laws." This document described practices forbidden under the antitrust laws—all price-fixing and bid-rigging agreements being per se illegal. HO-9 also instructed Mead employees, when in doubt about conduct, to consult the corporation's general counsel. "There must be no misunderstanding or compromise of the Mead Corporation to comply strictly and completely with the antitrust laws," said the order. "No employee shall enter into any understanding, plan, or scheme, express or implied, formal or informal, with any competitor, regarding price, terms, or conditions of sale, production, distribution, territories, or customers...."

What most Mead employees did not know was that there had been a policy debate within the ranks of senior management about whether to issue HO-9, not because of what it said—everyone was in agreement about the need to obey the law—but because a grand jury investigation was underway, creating a delicate situation. Walker Lewis, then general counsel, along with Stan Freedman and Ford Ekey of Smith & Schnacke discussed with Mead management the extent to which its policy position in a formal statement would be pressed, regardless of how it might be used by critics of the company. Lewis's argument won the day and despite the risks HO-9 was issued without delay. Since that time it has served as Mead's consistent corporate policy.

Donald F. Morris, who was serving his brief term as chief executive officer of Mead, followed up this firm declaration with clinics on the antitrust laws in various locations of the company. Testifying later before the federal court in Houston during the corrugated container criminal case, McSwiney described these sessions and how they came about:

Mr. Morris felt [that], in getting this over to our people, you needed clinics so that you could explain to them *why* we were doing what we were doing so that they could understand it and accept it, and they could try to carry it out.

By way of explanation, the way our company's always been run, we've never felt two or three people at the top could make things work at the bottom unless there were clinics, unless there were seminars and programs where things were explained to people in small groups. We've done that in all the history I've been in the company.

It's just a way of life ... to make sure people understand. We don't take for granted that a memorandum explains something to people, because it's just too complex.

The clinics on antitrust were conducted on a rotating basis throughout the divisions and subsidiaries. To assure corporate antitrust compliance policy within Mead during the 1960s, Smith & Schnacke employed first Jerry Garfinckle and later Jim Timoney — both lawyers who had worked for the Federal Trade Commission — as enforcers of HO-9.

Corporate preoccupation with antitrust matters in the mid-1960s was intensified by the realization that the penalties for inept or careless handling of antitrust considerations were mounting at an alarming rate. Directors, stockholders, and management alike were deeply concerned by the sudden ballooning of treble damage civil lawsuits for price-fixing following the criminal proceedings involving the electrical industry conspiracy.

The whole treble damage process was given further impetus by the revision of court procedures for class actions. In 1966, Rule 23 of the Federal Rules of Civil Procedure was modified. Thereafter, when a class was found to exist, there was no need for class members to opt into the litigation. Rather, they could remain silent and be considered part of the class reaping the benefits of any settlement or judgment. The Judicial Panel on Multidistrict Litigation was created to consolidate cases filed in different federal court districts around the country. As a result, the modern class action suit came into being by 1970 and set the stage for the blockbusting suits to come.

In 1974, President Ford signed into law the Antitrust Procedures and Penalties Act, which made the violation of the antitrust laws a felony. What had hitherto been a misdemeanor with a maximum fine of

$50,000—and, therefore, perhaps not taken all that seriously by corporate America—now was a felony for which individuals could be sent to jail for three years and fined $100,000. Moreover, the felony status meant that any individual convicted lost his or her civil rights, including the right to vote. As for corporations, they could be fined a million dollars now. There is no doubt that this legislation got the attention of CEOs.

In the summer of 1974, when the antitrust legislation was moving through Congress, McSwiney took occasion to bring Warren Batts, then Mead's newly elected chief operating officer, together with the group vice presidents to discuss antitrust issues. McSwiney reiterated that "HO-9 was our gospel, the thing we live by." Jerry Rapp, who had become general counsel, consulted with Hal Baker of Howrey and Simon, a Washington, D.C., law firm noted for its antitrust expertise, for ideas to assure compliance.

Rapp and Baker brought forth an additional idea. They suggested to McSwiney that lawyers follow up the top-level directives with private interviews with Mead personnel involved in sales, which would be protected by the attorney–client privilege. It was believed that such confidential interviews would result in candor and permit management to determine what additional efforts were needed to achieve compliance. McSwiney approved the idea wholeheartedly.

Despite these extensive efforts to achieve antitrust compliance, the Antitrust Division of the U.S. Department of Justice brought indictments in 1976 against 22 companies, including Mead, and 47 individuals, alleging that they had conspired to fix prices of folding cartons during the period prior to December 1974. The case was brought under the old misdemeanor antitrust statute.

Mead was more fortunate than most of the other defendants in that it did not have any senior executives indicted. Only one person at a junior level in the sales organization was indicted from Mead.

Given the penalties under the misdemeanor statute, Mead and others elected not to contest the charges. The fear was that a loss in the misdemeanor case would have broad adverse implications in the related civil cases brought by private plaintiffs. Mead was fined $35,000. Numerous executives of the other defendant companies, including CEOs, received fines and jail sentences for brief terms, as well as sentences to perform community work. Mead's employee was given a nominal $1500 fine.

It seemed that Mead's efforts to achieve antitrust compliance had been largely successful, but the criminal case was not the end of the folding carton litigation. As a result of the various changes in the antitrust class action rules, Mead and others in the industry found themselves swamped with dozens of cases which were consolidated in federal court in Chicago. These private actions were brought by a cadre of experts in the plaintiffs' antitrust bar and were certified to proceed as class actions on behalf of all purchasers of folding cartons throughout the United States.

Mead now found itself confronted with a dilemma. Even though management believed that Mead was innocent of the charges and that its customers were not damaged by any acts of the company, it could not authorize a trial in the civil litigation when the damage exposure would be in the hundreds of millions of dollars.

The problem Mead faced was the common law doctrine of "joint and several liability," which in effect allows the injured party to collect from a single company all the damages accruing from the actions of all alleged co-conspirators. While legislatures and courts had backed away from the full application of this doctrine in securities cases and tort litigation by providing for "the right of contribution," which permits a conspirator to sue other co-conspirators for their proportionate share of the damages, the right of contribution did not exist in antitrust cases. A corporation that went to trial in a civil antitrust price-fixing case, and lost, would potentially be liable for industry-wide damages unrelated to its own market share.

The staggering potentialities of this naturally created a considerable disincentive to go to trial and a very big incentive to settle beforehand for the best deal that could be obtained. Given the stakes at issue, Mead decided to settle the folding carton class action litigation in May 1979 for approximately $13.4 million.

While the folding carton litigation was pending, the Department of Justice had a grand jury in Houston investigating the corrugated container industry and another in Philadelphia investigating linerboard and medium and fine papers.

It is difficult to describe how disruptive antitrust grand jury investigations can be. During the period in question, several investigations were occurring at the same time, all on a nation-wide basis. The disruption could have been overwhelming if not carefully managed. For months at a time Howrey & Simon had teams of paralegals searching files at Mead's Dayton headquarters as well as at plants and sales offices located around the country in order to respond to the extensive subpoenas issued from Houston and Philadelphia. Literally hundreds of thousands of documents were turned over to the Department of Justice. Howrey & Simon established elaborate computerized systems to track down the documents that were given to the government so that witnesses could later be better prepared when they testified. Scores of Mead employees, including executives, testified before both the Philadelphia and the Houston grand juries.

Mead was vindicated in Philadelphia. After a couple of years of extensive scrutiny, the grand jury expired without returning any indictments.

Despite Mead's success in the Philadelphia investigation, however, many private cases were brought alleging that the numerous defendants had engaged in price-fixing in the sale of fine papers, which consisted of a myriad of different products. Some of the cases were brought as class actions. Other cases were brought by state governments, which had been infused with federal money for the purpose of enforcing the antitrust laws. These cases were filed around the country and the Multidistrict Panel consolidated them in Philadelphia.

At the same time, the outcome of the Houston investigation was disappointing to Mead. Massive felony indictments were brought against the corrugated container industry. Fourteen companies were indicted, including Mead. In addition, 26 employees of the defendant companies, including executives, were indicted. Significantly, however, not a single employee of Mead was indicted.

While the Houston investigation was proceeding, and before any indictments had been returned, a considerable number of private antitrust cases were brought against 34 companies. These cases were filed in many different jurisdictions, and the Multidistrict Panel consolidated them in Houston before Judge John V. Singleton, Jr., who also had the criminal case.

The total market represented by the 34 producers of corrugated containers was $8 billion annually. The estimated damages to the plaintiffs, based upon an arbitrary claim of a 5 percent overcharge, came to $400 million, or $1.2 billion after trebling.

All of this antitrust litigation was pending at the time of Occidental's attempted takeover. Just as Mead was determined to remain independent of the clutches of Occidental, so McSwiney was determined not to have Mead labeled as a felon. Because of the importance of the pending litigation to the company, Rapp asked Tony Vradelis, formerly a senior partner of Smith & Schnacke and then Rapp's assistant in the general counsel's office, to be intimately involved in all the tactical decisions. Vradelis spent virtually full time on this litigation, allocating his time between Dayton and Houston. "He provided a unique spirit of optimism, perseverance, and Mead gratitude that complemented the combative and strategic qualities which Hal Baker brought to each battle scene," Rapp believed.

Baker assumed command of the Mead defense trial team in the Houston criminal case within days of Mead's victory over Occidental— a triumph he had helped to bring about. Rapp said, "Baker's transition from one trial to the other on such short notice in such different factual situations and circumstances with characteristic enthusiasm and mental agility required great stamina, a super-human effort."

Mead decided to break with the industry—when virtually all of the indicted companies pleaded *nolo contendere* to the criminal price-fixing charge in the corrugated container case—and elected to go to trial to prove that it had made every reasonable effort to assure compliance with the antitrust laws.

Bob Neff, manager of Mead's Containers Division, became emotionally involved in the Houston trials. He and his wife, Barbara, attended every day of the trials. Neff kept in touch with his office in Cincinnati by telephone.

Sitting in courtrooms, Neff had a lot of time to think about his company, his industry, and the customers they served. He also observed most of his key managers under fire and was impressed with their integrity and strength as individuals. At the conclusion of the trials, Neff returned to his office and executed a management plan that had, as Jerry Rapp later put it, "incubated while he was a hostage of the lawyers in Houston." The new concept, which grew from the ideas developed at the St. Petersburg conference, emphasized the entrepreneurial and independent nature of Neff's managers. Under his plan, each plant manager had more accountability and reward for his own operation, and enjoyed lessened supervision from higher levels of management.

The Houston criminal trial began in January 1979 and lasted for about four months. The Continental Group was the only other corporate defendant to elect to go to trial. In addition, there were several individuals of various companies who also declined to plead *nolo contendere*. Mead's decision to plead innocent and carry this through the full course reflected McSwiney's strong feeling, as he testified at the trial:

Q. Mr. McSwiney, did you have any input into the decision to stand trial in this case?

A. Yes, sir.

Q. Rather than plead guilty or no contest?

A. Yes, I did.

Q. Why did the company decide to defend this case?

A. Well, as I have indicated, we had a tough antitrust compliance program. It was working. Our people in our offices believed in it and it just made sense for me, for us, to stand trial and prove it.

The jury returned a verdict in favor of Mead and the other defendants in April 1979.

There was jubilation in Mead's offices in Dayton over the vindication of Mead's stubborn insistence on going through to the very end. But despite the victory in the criminal case, Mead still faced the massive private antitrust cases that had been certified to proceed as class actions.

Because so many of the defendants in the criminal case pleaded *nolo contendere*, those companies created a stampede to settle the civil litigation.

The plaintiffs' lawyers also were well aware of this. Recognizing the gargantuan potential liability in the civil cases, the plaintiffs' lawyers quickly exacted rapidly escalating prices for settlement. One of the first companies to settle the private civil litigation was one of the larg-est producers of corrugated containers in the United States. By set-tling, however, plaintiffs gained two things: a war chest to finance the litigation against the others and the cooperation of a prominent in-dustry member who had been found guilty of a felony violation. In turn, plaintiffs gave up nothing because of joint and several liability—that is, this large company was able to shift its damage liability to the defendants who chose not to settle. Other companies quickly fol-lowed the path of settlement blazed by the large company.

Mead, which had only 3 percent of the market and had been ac-quitted in the criminal case, intended to persevere rather than capit-ulate to the escalating demands of the plaintiffs. Before the criminal case was tried, Mead's co-defendant Continental had decided to cut its potential liability in the civil litigation and settled for $27 million. By the time of the civil trial, the other defendants had paid over $325 million to settle—the largest settlements in the history of antitrust lit-igation. Eventually, the plaintiffs' war chest was estimated at more than a half billion dollars, including earnings on investments and other income. The legal fees paid to plaintiffs' counsel exceeded $50 mil-lion and the legal fees paid by the defendants must have been staggering.

Determined not to pay what it regarded as ransom and flushed with victory in the criminal case, Mead elected to go to trial in the civil case in May 1980. Westvaco Corporation, which had not been indicted in the criminal case but was named in the civil case, also proceeded to trial with Mead, although it settled during the trial.

Mead recognized that it was charting very uncertain waters. In civil cases, plaintiffs' burden of proof is not as great as in a criminal case. Rules of evidence often are applied differently.

Mead's legal team, led by Baker, included some of his associates, among them Bob Ruyak and Bob Green, as well as other lawyers, paralegals, and secretaries from Howrey & Simon—as many as 30 at a time in Houston. Houston trial lawyer Fletcher Etheridge played a significant role. So too did Peter Max, an extraordinarily articulate and brilliant economist, who could interpret economic data with great clarity.

In the civil case, three members of a Memphis, Tennessee, law firm—Frank Glankler, Jim Raines, and John Irvine (who later left the

Memphis firm and joined Mead)—were part of Baker's defense team. Glankler had represented an Owens-Illinois officer who was a defendant in the criminal trial. In that case, in his closing argument to the jury, Glankler accused the government prosecutor of "trying to sneak the dawn around the rooster." His client was acquitted.

During the course of the Houston grand jury investigation, employees of a number of companies asserted their rights under the Fifth Amendment in order to be granted immunity from prosecution. In the criminal case, the government gave immunity to those people prior to their testimony so that the defendants had an opportunity to cross-examine them. But in the civil case, many of the same people— more than 150 in all—again asserted the Fifth Amendment in the course of depositions. The judge allowed the fact of the assertion of the Fifth Amendment into evidence over the objections of Mead, which argued that the ruling was contrary to established law. There was no way that Mead could cross-examine witnesses who were asserting the Fifth Amendment. In addition, the court—in what Mead's attorneys insisted was an unprecedented ruling—permitted the wholesale reading of transcripts of grand jury testimony of witnesses. Again, Mead was unable to cross-examine that testimony. Mead argued vainly that such evidence was highly prejudicial and denied it due process of law.

Finally, the judge ordered Mead's attorney, Hal Baker, to turn over to the plaintiffs notes he had made of his confidential communications with Mead employees back in 1974 and 1975. Those notes were admitted into evidence, despite the objection of Baker that they were protected by the attorney–client privilege.

The series of adverse rulings by the judge helped Mead in one sense: if the jury ruled against Mead, the rulings would provide the basis for an appeal, and knowledgeable lawyers believed that the appellate court would reverse the lower court on those grounds.

In fact, the jury in the Houston corrugated container case did find against Mead in September 1980. Again the judge surprised experienced lawyers by not requiring the plaintiffs to prove the dollar amount of damages that the class members allegedly sustained. Instead, the judge dismissed the jury and appointed a special master to hold hearings to determine the amount of damages.

As matters turned out, no damage judgment was ever entered in the case, although the plaintiffs estimated that trebled damages would amount to more than $1 billion and that after subtracting the $325 million in settlements that the other defendants had paid, Mead would owe $750 million, or an amount equal to Mead's shareholders' equity at the time.

While the decision naturally cast a cloud of uncertainty over the company's financial affairs, it was obvious that whatever figure eventually was arrived at, Mead could not possibly pay anything near $750 million. If Mead had been liable based on its own market share, it would have owed some $45 million.

The lawyers for the plaintiffs were aware of the high risk that the judgment would be reversed by the Court of Appeals. They also realized that the special master proceedings might go on for years—and that the validity of those proceedings was doubtful.

In the adverse civil verdict situation, Baker was reinforced by Rapp, who for purposes of developing a settlement alternative, engaged Griffin Bell, former Attorney General of the United States; and Herbert (Jack) Miller, of Washington, D.C., who, as Assistant Attorney General in the Kennedy Administration sent Teamsters boss Jimmy Hoffa to jail.

There was an ironic twist to the corrugated container case. There Mead and the other defendants had been accused of trying to keep prices too high. But in another case, Mead and other companies were accused of conspiring to keep prices too low.

That case, too, was a class action, brought by Franklin Container Corporation and Tim-Bar Paper Company on behalf of themselves and other independent companies like them. They were independent converters who purchased containerboard and produced corrugated containers. The Franklin Container case was transferred to Philadelphia and later settled for $200,000 to avoid the cost of litigation.

While the Houston civil litigation involving corrugated containers was in trial, the fine paper civil cases were set for October 1980 trial in Philadelphia. There were two sets of cases pending: one, a class action on behalf of all purchasers of fine paper in the United States; the other, a series of non-class actions brought by a dozen state governments.

The class action cases were scheduled to go to trial first. Mead and others had been vindicated by the federal grand jury in Philadelphia and had decided to fight the civil cases. But when the Houston verdict came in September 1980, management recognized that it could not expose the company to two potentially adverse verdicts at the same time. Obviously, the pressures to settle the class action were enormous. On the eve of trial in early October 1980 the five nonsettling defendants, including Mead, finally agreed to a settlement of approximately $11 million (which was about the estimated cost of the litigation), even though all of them were convinced of their innocence.

The state government cases were still pending. They had a significantly lower damage claim, so Mead and some of the other defendants decided to go forward with the trial of those cases after settling the class action. After a two-month trial, the jury returned a verdict in favor of Mead and the other defendants on December 2, 1980. The defendants won the case even though they did not call a single witness. They decided not to call defense witnesses because they believed—rightly, as it turned out—that the plaintiffs' case was too weak to require a defense. Mead felt that the verdict demonstrated the success of the company's efforts to obtain compliance with the antitrust laws.

That still left the corrugated container verdict hanging over Mead's head.

Mead undertook a new strategy to increase pressure on the plaintiffs to settle. Pending before Congress was a measure to amend the antitrust laws to provide for contribution in antitrust litigation—that is, a company's damage exposure would be limited to its own market share and not the sales of the entire industry. If this rule were to be applied to the corrugated container case, Mead's total liability would amount to $45 million, the figure arrived at by trebling damages based on Mead's market share. However, the measure being considered by Congress did not apply to pending cases such as the corrugated containers litigation. Thus, if Mead were to get any relief, the pending legislation would have to be modified.

The company undertook a massive legislative effort to that end. It was not alone. Georgia-Pacific, Weyerhaeuser, and Willamette were in a similar position because of a plywood case, and they joined forces with Mead to have pending cases included in the proposed legislation. So did Milliken & Company, Du Pont, Martin Marietta, Westvaco, and a number of others—some out of self-interest, others because they felt that the law, as it stood, was unfair.

In opposition to the "pending cases group" were the companies that had settled the corrugated container case, as well as companies that were involved in other litigation.

Initially, influential business organizations such as the Business Roundtable, the U.S. Chamber of Commerce, and the National Association of Manufacturers were lined up solidly against the "pending cases group." As the legislative debate intensified, however, those groups eventually changed their stance, either supporting extension of the legislation to pending cases or taking no position on the issue.

The whole affair rapidly grew into one of the most celebrated lobbying battles ever waged in Washington. In the early fall of 1981, syndicated columnists Roland Evans and Robert Novak wrote, "There are two kinds of Washington lawyers today: those getting rich on this legislation and those who wish they were."

For the better part of two years (1981–1982) Rapp spent much of his time in Washington, synchronizing the settlement negotiations with the lobbying effort. The more it appeared that the lobbying might succeed, the more likelihood that the plaintiffs would settle on reasonable terms.

Of course, McSwiney made frequent trips to Washington to talk with lawmakers, their aides, and anyone else who might help in the fight. Others from Mead—people like Greene Garner and Sid Hawkes—played important roles in the fight.

There were a number of people outside Mead's management who were important to the campaign.

Griffin Bell was a key figure in the lobbying effort, as he also was in the settlement negotiations with Judge Singleton. He was one of the members of the Carter Administration from Georgia who had earned a favorable reputation in Washington. Senators and representatives of both parties liked and respected him for his integrity and his forthright, honest manner of dealing with others.

Charls E. Walker, a Republican who had established a lobbying firm bearing his name, was active in Mead's behalf, along with one of Walker's associates, James C. Free, who had Democratic connections.

In the hearings before the Senate Judiciary Committee, a former federal judge and Deputy Attorney General of the United States, Charles Renfrew, of San Francisco, proved to be one of Mead's most articulate spokespersons. Renfrew had presided over one of the earliest paper industry cases which had not involved Mead.

Another notable asset to the Mead team was Robert H. Bork, a former Solicitor General of the United States then in private practice in Washington, who later became a federal judge and, in 1987, was unsuccessfully nominated to the U.S. Supreme Court by President Reagan. In Mead's lobbying effort, Bork prepared and explained a white paper he had drafted in support of the constitutionality of the legislation Mead advocated.

Another well known name was that of Sam Ervin, the former Democratic senator from North Carolina who had chaired the committee that investigated the Watergate affair in the 1970s, resulting in the resignation of President Nixon. When Ervin, who had been practicing law in his home town of Morgantown, North Carolina, since retiring from the Senate, returned to Washington to testify for Mead before the Senate Judiciary Committee, it was the first time he had returned to Washington since his retirement. He was warmly greeted by a packed hearing room of his old friends.

In the fall of 1981, the Mead group could find little, if any, support for the proposed amendment among the members of the Senate Judiciary Committee. Mead launched a grassroots campaign on the issue, aimed at reaching constituents of every senator and representative involved. Sidney Hawkes, Mead's vice president for government affairs, and Alan Wiseman of Howrey & Simon, working with Bill Hunter of that firm, coordinated the overall effort. A massive list of constituents of various senators was computerized so that constituent support could be developed. Packets of information were distributed to newspapers throughout the country. Position papers were drawn up and compromise language was drafted for the proposed amendment. Slowly, step by step, led by Senators Paul Laxalt (Republican of Nevada), Orrin G. Hatch (Republican of Utah), and Howell T. Heflin (Democrat of Alabama), Judiciary Committee members moved Mead's way.

At the end of March 1982, by a vote of 11 to 7, the bill finally was voted out of the committee carrying the highly controversial clause applying the legislation to pending litigation. The language suited no one fully, because it left the whole matter up to the discretion of the courts. From the point of view of the "pending cases group," it was the best that could be hoped for under the circumstances. Nevertheless, it was of prime importance to Mead's settlement efforts, because it clearly implied that among the nation's lawmakers there was considerable sympathy for Mead's predicament. Thus, an additional source of uncertainty had been created that raised questions about just how firm the prospects were that the plaintiffs — Mead's opponents in the litigation — would ultimately prevail.

While the legislation was pending, settlement discussions were going on between Mead and the plaintiffs in the corrugated containers case. On September 7, 1982, Mead's board of directors approved a tentative settlement of the case. It provided for payments totalling $45 million. The payments were to be spread over seven years, beginning with $1 million the first year, $2 million the second, $5 million each of the following four years, and $22 million in 1988, plus interest of 9 percent on the unpaid balance.

The $45 million was just what Mead could have been liable for under the principles of contribution sought in the legislative effort. It was a far cry from the $750 million that the plaintiffs had originally talked about.

Considering the time span covered by the payment plan, the value of money, and interest costs, Mead's settlement was no more expensive than a $14 million cash settlement would have cost it in a lump sum settlement in 1978, in part because Mead, having been acquitted in the criminal case, was able to deduct the settlement for federal income tax purposes. A number of companies paid substantially more in real dollars than Mead did. Indeed, compared with most of the other defendants, Mead's settlement was among the lowest.

From Mead's perspective, the fight was for fairness. In much the same manner as they had in the Occidental takeover attempt, the company's board of directors rose to the occasion. The board was kept fully informed and involved throughout the long process. Board members joined with management in calling on friends to contact legislators on behalf of the "pending cases" legislation and supported the management team's efforts.

Once again, the value of a strong and independent board had been demonstrated.

And once again, strength of leadership—true "servant leadership"—had brought the company through a perilous passage.

Fourteen

To Move the Corporation Up a Notch

A few months after Occidental's unsuccessful takeover attempt, Mead held its annual shareholders meeting in Dayton. McSwiney, presiding at the meeting as chairman of the board of directors, made no reference to the battle. Warren Batts, reporting on the affairs of the company as chief executive officer, devoted just two words to the affair when he told the stockholders, "Despite Occidental, we've had the best year in our history."

Batts said that productivity was improving. Moreover, "We have $500 million to spend during the next five years *over* the $1 billion investment already planned. We're looking at new industries."

The annual report for 1978 was full of facts and figures to warm the heart of any Mead shareholder. Net earnings had increased 23 percent, to $120.9 million, and Mead was now No. 1 in a number of measures of performance in the forest products industry. On two occasions during the year the directors had increased the dividend on common stock. Pulp inventories were low and demand was rising. The industrial and foundry products were doing very well. The company's $200 million planned investment in 1979 would be "the greatest one-year capital program in our history."

The opening section of the annual report, signed by both McSwiney and Batts, said, "Last April, the responsibility of chief executive officer passed from one of us to the other as part of an ongoing plan to provide continuity of management. That test was passed smoothly."

The joint message ended, "Truly, Mead's long-term prospects have never been brighter."

That optimism was justified. But the assumption that the "test" of gradual change in leadership had been "passed smoothly"—indeed, even the idea that the "test" was now behind Mead—had to be regarded as a triumph of hope over realism.

At the time those words were written, McSwiney was 63, two years away from retirement as an officer and two years ahead of the time he might be expected to pass on the CEO's role. Mac passed on the title of CEO to Batts on his own initiative, with the aim of accelerating Batts's stewardship of the company. Batts, the man he had brought in from the outside and then groomed carefully to be his successor, had seized the reins in a way that was reassuringly forceful, despite Batts's soft manner of speech. Batts had merged some management committees and had worked out an accommodation with the corporate responsibility committee.

Government relations on the Washington level was an area that McSwiney enjoyed and engaged in effectively, having been part of the American Paper Institute's first coordinated government relations committee. With the advice and help of Charles Gebhardt, Mac had greatly strengthened Mead's Washington office. In the McSwiney era, government affairs became an integral part of Mead and were no longer regarded, in his words, as "a little brother." When Batts became CEO, he became involved in that area of the company's operations, saying, "I have to be suited up to take over the area when Mac withdraws from it." A colleague later said Batts "did well" in government relations, "like the good soldier who knows what his duty is and does it."

There were differences between William Wommack and Batts over corporate strategy and how it should be arrived at. Now vice chairman of the board, Wommack was also head of the board's corporate objectives committee. Batts, as CEO, had asked Michael Allik, whom he had brought in from Allis-Chalmers a few years earlier, to serve in the role of the company's strategic officer. A major difference between Wommack and Batts was over the concept of consensus in strategy decisions.

"If strategic change is desired," Wommack wrote in a *Harvard Business Review* article that year, "organizational consensus will never bring it about."

McSwiney thought that to be an extreme statement.

"'Never' was too harsh," McSwiney said. "I believe Bill had no real problem with consensus, but if it took too long to achieve, someone had to make a decision."

Batts wanted to move toward a more consensual type of arrangement between staff and divisions with regard to strategic planning. He also wanted to shift the emphasis in strategic planning, "going beyond the garrisons of the individual divisions and [looking] at entire business areas," raising questions like "what areas can we enter and do well at?"

Batts also differed philosophically with McSwiney on some matters, including diversification.

"In my heart of hearts," Batts once said, "I just don't believe that conglomerates will ever be a major factor in American society. I think the homogeneous company has got to be better than diversified companies." Of Mead, he said, "Basically, if we could, the company should become a one-industry company, with a common technology and common thread through it. What we do has to be concentric so that we can explain it to a financial analyst."

McSwiney's rejoinder was that, "if Mead had done this in the '60s and '70s, the company would not have survived." He believed many major companies, apparently based on a single industry, would upon careful examination be found to closely approximate conglomerates.

Before relinquishing his CEO role to Batts, McSwiney asked Batts for one of his top operating group vice presidents. Mac felt the time had come to transfer Lexis and Nexis to an operational mode as contrasted with the developmental mode which had been under the guidance of Wommack. Batts and McSwiney agreed on Robert O'Hara, then group vice president in charge of white paper operations. (O'Hara was succeeded as head of white paper operations by Burnell Roberts, later chairman and CEO of Mead. Roberts was in charge of white paper operations from late in 1971 through May 1974—a period when, for the first time, white paper earnings, largely because of

Escanaba, exceeded those of Mead's paperboard operations, elating both McSwiney and Roberts.)

Earlier Batts had sided with Wommack in wanting to get rid of Lexis and Nexis, but now he recognized their potential and wanted to keep them.

Indeed, Batts wanted to add to the high-technology side of Mead's business. In 1978 he found an opportunity for Mead to acquire a company which had long been experimenting with, and marketing, some products of ink-jet technology. Because Mead still owned Dijit, a patented ink-jet process, Batts believed that the acquisition would fit very well into an expanding future for Mead in that field. He entered into negotiations with the company and then brought the proposal to the Mead board for approval.

McSwiney was on a trip to the Soviet Union with a group of U.S. business managers while the issue was being debated, but he talked with Batts by telephone from Russia. McSwiney was supportive of Batts but he felt that the matter should be fully discussed with the board. As it turned out, a majority of the members of the board felt the company in question was not the most desirable candidate for acquisition, and a number of board members were concerned about getting into a field where Mead would be competing with such giants as Xerox and IBM. McSwiney cut his trip short and returned to Dayton to take part in the discussions. During the board meeting Mac concluded that the directors were not comfortable with the proposed acquisition and he suggested that the matter be tabled for further study, and that is what was done.

Batts was troubled by the rejection of his proposal. A Mead outside director, himself a CEO, said he thought Batts's reaction reflected his newness to the job of CEO. "At the time," the director said, "Warren was just assuming control and he questioned whether [the board's action] was a reflection on management. My board overrules me all the time. It was just a board doing its job."

It was a board, moreover, that looked favorably on Batts. One of the new board members, David S. Lewis, Jr., chairman and CEO of General Dynamics Corporation, had been an acquaintance of Batts, who had first proposed Lewis as a board member. Moreover, Batts had established good relationships with a number of directors who admired his style and ability. Almost all the directors regarded him as an extremely hard worker, an excellent organizer and planner.

Nevertheless, there were aspects of the situation at Mead with which Batts was uncomfortable. The division of responsibilities between the chair and the CEO was one such area. In the summer of 1979 he told a visitor, "The role of the CEO is working with the board of directors. Mac is still doing most of that; I do very little."

About the same time McSwiney said in a private conversation, "Warren and I have a difference in view about corporate governance, but I'm convinced that in time he will see its value."

He added, "You can perceive that Warren's not the kind of person that you can best relate to by telling him what to do. He's the kind of person to whom you should give wide latitude and responsibility."

For several years McSwiney had been thinking about the kind of person a CEO should be. While he was in Colorado, at the Aspen Institute, in the summer of 1979—a year away from his retirement—he began setting down some of his thoughts on paper. As usual, drafts were circulated among a number of people, including Robert Greenleaf, Constantine Simonides, and Gerald Rapp, but the final product was vintage McSwiney. On November 2 of that year he placed the seventh draft of his paper before the board. It ran 14 typed pages, single-spaced, and carried a 22-word title: "Guidelines for Discussion Between CEO and Key Associates and Between the CEO and the Nominating Committee Relative to Organization and Management Development"—hardly a snappy title. But it was an extraordinary document, a statement of belief in the strength of corporate teamwork when carried out in accordance with the principles of servant leadership.

On the title page McSwiney wrote, "The objectives are to ensure (1) there is a constant learning process at work, (2) that it is appropriate for this institution, and (3) there is reason to believe that progress can be identified and measured." Just as he had been when working at the mill level so many years ago in Georgia, McSwiney was still determined to do what he could to make work in the company a learning experience. Like many other self-taught persons, he knew that education is a never-ending process.

To set his discussion in the context of the times, McSwiney offered a number of observations:

> It is generally understood that the United States operates under a pluralistic system of values and modes of behavior based on these values. Yet, quite often, vested and single interest groups are taken to task for optimizing their benefits under the rules of the game. A high percentage of our population does not realize that to do otherwise would be a contradiction to the underlying principles of the pluralism which is synonymous with our notion of a free society.
>
> There is also a perplexity in understanding why, with vested and single interest groups optimizing their benefits under the rules of the game, the results do not seem to reflect what is in the best total interest of society. On the other hand, it does not seem hard to rationalize that, with the dramatic and dynamic changes brought about in society, "traditional" or "accepted" procedures are not likely to produce desirable results, and that a change in the rules of the game should be considered. The query, then, is — in what direction do you begin to query, explore, and move?
>
> As recently as a decade ago, almost all of the major segments of our pluralistic society operated in a manner which appeared to be more orderly, and in many cases could be characterized as autocratic.
>
> For example, corporations were headed by strong presidents who brooked little interference from the public or, indeed, from their own board.
>
> In government, seniority of committees of Congress governed and few brooked interference with the objectives and priorities set by the powerful committee heads.
>
> In labor, union leaders governed with an iron hand.
>
> Even in universities, academic department heads and deans, and certainly presidents, operated more autonomously, not only from their own constituencies, but also from public (or government) scrutiny.
>
> These conditions have changed dramatically in the past decade. Whether one uses critical terms such as "regulation" or "interference," or less critical—but no less loaded—terms such as "openness" and "interdependence," the fact is that almost everything that institutional leaders do today is visible and subject to concerns, criticism, and public scrutiny.
>
> In general, autocratic behavior in the U.S. society has been gradually eroded. We now have pluralistic systems operating in every

phase of our national and even our private lives. In this context, *to be "open" has come to be perceived as being "credible."* [Emphasis added.] And, at this point in time, people somehow seem to feel that being open is synonymous with more acceptable results. Such perceptions ignore that changes in society require change in the rules of the game if the results are to be changed. To put it another way, a system that has become increasingly pluralistic must recognize that vested or single interest groups must be expected to optimize their interests — or else we do not have a free society.

Next, McSwiney took up the mission of the CEO:

> No two chief executive officers could probably be found who would agree that their corporate missions were identical. Most of them would, however, agree that *the central mission of the CEO is to move the corporation "up a notch" and to recruit and develop an organization which, in turn, can move the corporation up "another notch."* [Emphasis added.]

Some of McSwiney's observations stated the obvious, but there were others that would bear pondering by any senior manager. For example, he wrote, "*The chief executive officer should seek people who are better than he.* [Emphasis added.] Once they are members of the top team, they should have the opportunity to lead the team when the need arises. This is what social scientists call knowledge-based authority (as opposed to power based on political or social status)."

Depth of management ranked as a major concern. "Individuals have personal reasons which may compel them to leave the company at a given time, even if their talents are fully appreciated and rewarded," he wrote. "Such departures from the team must not be permitted to disrupt or destroy its effectiveness. In other words, the management team must have some safeguards against the vulnerability created by a thin layer of talent."

Then McSwiney wrote:

> Having built a management team, the chief executive officer must be able to lead both by stepping into things and by "letting go." There is a very subtle but crucial difference between getting things done and what we may call "letting go"; i.e., permitting and encouraging others to exercise creativity and initiative. The chief executive officer must

know that he cannot always have his way on every issue. He must practice, therefore, letting down his personal control guards in order to encourage growth in others that comes from exercising initiative and in order to become comfortable himself with "letting go." This is one of the toughest challenges for an ambitious and powerful personality, and most chief executive officers have that kind of personality almost as a requirement for arriving at their position. Knowing when or how to let go is the key to the dynamics of the chief executive officer's job because it is the only thing—other than the accumulation of wealth—that will assure success of the company after the incumbent has left the CEO post.

This led McSwiney to discuss "the problem of the wise use of power"—a favorite theme in the servant leadership philosophy.

The chief executive officer does, indeed, have the ultimate power, at least in principle. What are the effects of the power on him or her?...

First, power may lead to the delusion, or dilution of clear sight, that comes from what the CEO does *not* learn from subordinates, because of their fear that telling unwelcome news to the boss will hurt them.

Second, the sense of power may lead the chief executive officer to believe that other people will go along with his ideas, even if they do not agree. Such a belief will quickly stifle a pluralistic environment where individuals are encouraged to optimize their views. Ours is a society where pluralism—the opportunity to pursue one's own ideas and views—is the cardinal value in that it permits all other personal and group values to flourish. In his effort to be strong and persuasive about his own ideas, the chief executive officer must be careful not to trample over other people's freedom to pursue and optimize their own thinking. People make their best contributions, and work the hardest, when they act on their own beliefs and in what they believe to be their own interest.

Accepting this as a working principle for the chief executive officer does not make his task easy. But it does assure a dynamic contribution that will go beyond his own reign, because it motivates other people to lead.

The third concern about power relates to the need for the chief executive officer *to exercise his ultimate power in favor of taking risks* rather than playing it safe. [Emphasis in original.] Perhaps the greatest pitfall of powerful leaders is their preoccupation with preserving their power and control and, therefore, their aversion to risk. No plan or system, no matter how well designed, will provide the imaginative force necessary to take risks. At its best, a well-working organization—a business system—will tell you what the dangers are of taking certain actions. It will tell one what *not* to do. Every once in a while the chief executive officer must listen carefully to the signals of the system but then set them aside in order to optimize a longer term variable of growth through adventure rather than by preserving the safety of the status quo.

McSwiney felt that the CEO should place certain limits on his tenure:

Ten years may be a good span of time to preside as CEO of a major corporation. If so, it seems reasonable to assume that the CEO will not, in a sense, be in full control for, say, the first two years. During this period of time, he will be "assessing the rules of the game" (trusting some of the activities that won't impact the "signature" that he is expected to put on the company) and the environment which he inherited, in order to plot his course of moving the corporation "up a notch."

During the last two years in office, the CEO should be working with his associates and the board to effect an orderly transition to a new CEO who has been prepared to understand and carry out a program of moving the corporation up "another notch."

When one thinks about this, it is clear that the CEO is in *maximum* control for four to six years, if his tenure is 10 years.

McSwiney's view of "the sacredness of the hierarchical system," as he put it, was made clear in the next section, where he recommended the use of an outsider—as Greenleaf had been for him—to keep a critical eye on the overall structure.

The use of independent parties by the CEO who have the authority to observe what is going on in the system, but no authority to recommend solutions, has much merit. From these observations he will learn much that could be perceived as threatening in that he will learn of dissatisfaction, tasks improperly carried out, all the things that can go wrong or are just done halfway.

From this kind of knowledge, he will learn to take security, the security coming from the fact that, with the possession of such knowledge, he can better guide the threshold of pain, the tolerance for ambiguity and uncertainty that members of management can stand.

Vehicles such as the CRC [corporate responsibility committee] as developed in Mead also offer experience in dealing with openness, i.e., credibility, that the erosion of autocratic action has brought about.

Next McSwiney was concerned about the CEO's tolerance for ambiguity and uncertainty.

> [The CEO's] special competence ... probably lies in the ability to administer a system that gets optimum performance by operating at a level of threshold of pain and tolerance for ambiguity and uncertainty that will not tip the scales into an unhealthy mental state.
>
> In essence, the foregoing translates into the CEO's ability to perceive the amount of ambiguity and uncertainty that key members of his team can tolerate, but probably more important, the amount over which he can preside. His level of accomplishment will most likely be determined by the perception of the organization as to whether he cares primarily about the system or the organization, or himself. It is unlikely that many people will willingly follow a leader who is not perceived as one who cares. Caring for institutions is analogous to caring for people. But because institutions are made up of many people, the caring is more complex.

McSwiney then raised the question of consensus versus the CEO's ultimate responsibility.

> The CEO should learn to become comfortable and reassured in normally seeking consensus, but should realize that operating by consensus alone is, in effect, allowing the bureaucratic system to take over, thereby abdicating the responsibility which is peculiarly his. The complex machinery of the institution must be understood and supported, but should not take over. The CEO must be the ultimate arbiter with responsibility, and he must exercise it so as to improve the system. Otherwise, the organization will become chaotic or, worse yet, mechanized and impervious to human judgment and intervention.

The "emerging relationships" between the CEO, on the one hand, and his associates and the board, on the other, had to involve "integrating into the system a procedure that will sensitize the CEO as to both what is being thought about and what is going on."

> In some way the "filtering" process of the hierarchical system [that is, the process by which information tends to be kept from the CEO]

must be bypassed so that unwanted and surprising information is al-most instantly available at the top. This is first perceived as (and is) threatening to the various levels in a hierarchical system, but it is amazing how the system can adapt to such a procedure and how much managers, in turn, intuitively increase their hurdle rate for per-formance. The CEO must have courage to keep such a system intact, keep the board apprised, and have the support of the board. In a sense, it is another test of the threshold of pain and tolerance for am-biguity and uncertainty.

Generally, this means an open-base system with tension, and one with an actual and perceived integrity to both its internal and exter-nal environment.

The conclusion of McSwiney's remarkable document consisted of two paragraphs:

The implication or logic of these proposed beginning guidelines is that to deal effectively with the dynamic process at hand, some nontraditional approaches must be considered if we are able to pro-vide a learning experience that will modify behavior in a desirable way.

So, in many ways, an important part of the education of the CEO (before and after appointment to his office) revolves around a pro-cess that encourages and supports him in seeking answers to the con-tinuing expectations of society. The result can and should be that of modifying the CEO's behavior.

Of course, McSwiney, a traditionalist in some respects, had no dif-ficulty being nontraditional when he felt it was warranted. One exam-ple was a new member proposed for the board by the nominating committee in 1979—Barbara C. Jordan, the distinguished former Congresswoman from Texas (one of the first black members of Con-gress from that state since Reconstruction) and later Lyndon B. Johnson Public Service Professor at the LBJ School of Public Affairs, the University of Texas at Austin, and one of the most respected lead-ers in America. After she accepted election to Mead's board, she told McSwiney that an important factor in her decision was that "I didn't ask her if she'd act in what might be called a suitable way—I simply said we would be honored to have her join the Mead board."

Fifteen
Learning from Travel

In his paper on the education of a CEO, McSwiney had argued for extensive travel—not "vacation travel," he emphasized—because through travel to every part of the world the CEO "will begin to understand that the U.S. culture is not appreciated or wanted in many sectors of the world." He said that travel would help the CEO "understand the provincialism of various segments of the corporation and the community in which he operates and lives."

When McSwiney talked of the value of travel in the education of a CEO, he was speaking, as he usually did, from experience. Over the years he visited pulp and paper facilities in Japan, China, Sweden, Norway, Finland, and Canada. He made trips to help locate, finance, and observe the establishment of Mead Packaging in France, Germany, and The Netherlands. In Belgium, there were two operations that required his attention. There were partnerships in a number of companies, including Spain, Austria, and Lebanon. There was a Mead Packaging organization in Japan. He travelled around South America, through Africa, and even to China, where he negotiated with government officials on a business arrangement.

In addition, Mac and Jewell found time to make several other trips that he found enlightening. In 1969, they spent 19 days on an around-the-world trip with about 40 other business leaders. The trip covered France, Germany, Finland, the Soviet Union, India, Nepal, Thailand, Taiwan, and Hong Kong, with a final stop in Alaska. He said later:

One might wonder how much of value could be observed in such a short period of time. But each stop featured a prearranged luncheon, a visit to the U.S. Embassy (almost always including a meeting with the ambassador), and an evening cocktail party. I learned something I always remembered on that trip: that a cocktail party at a good hotel sponsored by American business people will bring out almost anyone of note anywhere — and that includes the Soviet Union.

It is amazing what one can absorb in a short time — differences in culture, attitudes toward the United States, and the prevalence of Soviet representatives, for instance.

Probably the most memorable lunch of Mac's life was served on an Aeroflot plane between Leningrad and Moscow. It consisted of a sandwich bulging with the finest caviar, a small apple, and a small bottle of ice-cold vodka, all in a little brown bag.

In 1967 Jewell and Mac took another business group tour around South America, counterclockwise, starting on the west coast of Panama. From there they went to Colombia, Ecuador, Peru, and Chile. Crossing into Argentina at its southern tip, they attended a cookout and visit with local leaders. There McSwiney saw a painting of an old hobo with a knapsack over his shoulder. "His eyes seemed to say, 'Don't tell me about it — I've already experienced it,'" Mac explained. It struck a chord in Mac, but not in Jewell. Although Mac managed to talk his way onto airliners with the 24×36 inch framed portrait through the rest of Argentina, Paraguay, Brazil, and the United States, the best spot he was able to display it was in an upstairs room in their house that was seldom visited or used.

One benefit of the trip was that Mac came home certain that South America was not a place for Mead. Inflation and unstable governments, he felt, posed a challenge for which Mead was unready.

In 1978 the Center for International Management Studies, affiliated with the International Young Men's Christian Association sponsored a trip for 21 U.S. business leaders and educators to the Soviet Union. The McSwineys took part in the visit. Gerald Rapp, Mead's general counsel, and Constantine Simonides, of the Massachusetts Institute of Technology, who had worked with Mead on various matters, were also among those in the group. Mac was chosen as spokesperson for the group.

"The Russians were fascinated by Mac," Simonides said. "He is very,

very American. He is both diffident and warm. There is a grandeur about him, too. He is a proud man. All those qualities seemed to make Mac the epitome of the American leader in the eyes of the Russians we met."

Besides attending a performance of the Bolshoi Ballet, visiting the Kremlin, and going to museums, the group went to factories and took part in seminars on management skills as practiced in the United States and the Soviet Union.

A highlight of the trip was an overnight flight to Novosibirsk, the Soviet science center. At that time few Americans had had the privilege of visiting that center of more than 1 million in the heart of western Siberia. The group's host there was Abel Aganbegyan, the head of the science center—a man who later became the chief economic advisor to General Secretary Mikhail Gorbachev, according to press reports.

One of the things that particularly impressed Mac was the dedication of the young educators and scientists in Novosibirsk.

"They displayed little desire to travel to the West, or even to Moscow," he said. "They felt they could best serve their motherland where they were. Much of this is probably quite contrary to what Americans are prone to think.

"High school students questioned Jewell about the relative pros and cons of the U.S. and the U.S.S.R. systems. They were polite, but quite sure theirs was the better system."

Before leaving the Soviet Union, the American group met for a last time with some senior Soviet officials. The Russians wanted to hear what the Americans thought about the things they had observed.

"As spokesman," Mac said, "I commented favorably on many of the things we had seen. I concluded with the recommendation that—although I didn't think it would meet with their way of thinking—it might be well for them to consider decentralizing, because it seemed to me that down-the-line decisions might prove to be quite productive."

The Soviet officials made it clear that they thought he was wrong.

There were other trips on which Jewell, for one reason or another, was unable to accompany him. In the mid-1960s, Mac traveled around Africa, beginning at Senegal and working his way down the west coast to South Africa, where he descended more than half a mile into the earth in diamond and gold mines. Then he went on to Zaire in central Africa before continuing to Tanzania and Kenya.

In the 1970s, when the Shah was still in power in Iran, McSwiney and William W. Wommack of Mead traveled to the Middle East, visiting Egypt, Saudi Arabia, Kuwait, Iran, and Lebanon with Mead's partner in Lebanon, George Frem (who later said that "McSwiney is one of the loyalest friends I have ever had"). McSwiney was amused by the attitude of U.S. State Department officials with whom they met. "I don't think they could quite figure out who we were or what kind of a mission we were on. Intrigue is great in that part of the world."

In Iran, Ambassador Richard Helms, former head of the U.S. Central Intelligence Agency, refused to see McSwiney and Wommack. But Mac was able to meet with an American professor who had been one of the faculty members for the Advanced Management Program in which Mac had participated at the Harvard Business School in 1954. The professor was conducting for the Iranian government a modified version of the AMP for Iranian managers.

One day in 1978 Mac learned that the Tokyo office of Mead Packaging was talking with officials of the Peoples Republic of China about an operation that would enable their export beer to move more easily through the U.S. distribution system. It seemed to Mac a good reason to observe first-hand what was happening in China. Through Leo Benatar, president of Mead Packaging, Hugh Murai, Mead's manager for the Far East, and a couple of young Americans living in Beijing, arrangements were made to visit the country as guests of the Chinese government.

Jewell joined Mac on the trip. So did Wommack's wife, Jean, and Murai's wife, Hiroko. They visited a number of inland cities besides Beijing. The trip also included communes, ancient sites, shrines, and the Great Wall. Shanghai was the last stop on the tour.

During the business discussions, the Chinese indicated they would like the most modern equipment available in the United States. Mac said he thought that would be "too much" and that the Chinese would be unhappy with it. He also believed they were mistaken in thinking that they would not need help or instructors from the United States.

Mead offered to sell the Chinese up to 10,000 tons of premium bleached pulp at a set price, but the Chinese thought the price too high. Mac told them that the world pulp market was becoming stronger, and if the Chinese could buy at Mead's price or lower they should do so promptly. But when the Americans left China, they assumed the Chinese had rejected the Mead offer.

Later the Chinese approached Mead again and wanted the company to fill the order at the previous price quotation. Mead explained that the Chinese had rejected the offer. No, said the Chinese; in China an offer is good for 90 days.

"In the end," said Mac, "we scrounged up some tonnage as sort of a good faith investment in potential future dealings."

As a result, Tsingtao® and other Chinese beers came into the United States in Mead packaging.

In late 1979, Jewell and Mac traveled through the South Pacific, from Tahiti and the other Society Islands to the North and South Islands of New Zealand, then on to Australia, the Fiji Islands, and back home by way of Hawaii. One of the things that impressed McSwiney in both New Zealand and Australia was the "unbelievable strength and influence" of their labor unions. "I came away very much appreciative of the ability in the U.S. to resolve labor-management issues, as contrasted with those nations," he said.

For a CEO, he ruminated, looking back over his travels, there are a number of lessons to be learned from journeys to other lands: How easy it is to mix with people everywhere. How truly different are the cultures of different nationalities. How people everywhere truly want to have peace, "but are completely unable to understand why peace cannot be achieved on their terms (and this obviously includes the United States)." Lastly, how great and "heart-rending" is the gap between the haves and the have-nots of the world.

"I had read about all these things, as most people have," McSwiney said, "but until we lived, smelled, and experienced the other societies of the world, it never became real. Only travel lets you truly learn something about the love, faith, greed, and hopelessness of much of humankind."

Sixteen

A Departure
and Promotions

The corporation's annual report for 1979 was able to announce:

> Mead continued to advance in sales, earnings per share, return on
> equity, return on net assets, and dividends. A 17 percent increase in
> net earnings to $141 million took us to a record 18.1 percent return
> on shareowners' equity.
>
> Fully diluted earnings per share reached $5.19. The climb from
> $2.72 in 1974 to 1979's record figure—a compound growth rate of
> 14 percent—is one of the most impressive in the forest products in-
> dustry.
>
> The economy was certainly a firm partner in Mead's 1979 success.
> Demand was strong and rewarding in most of the markets we serve.
> And Mead was ready.

In March of 1979 *The New York Times*, in an article headlined
"Born-Again Mead Paper Leads Revival," said:

> The improvement in Mead's fortunes of late has been shared, to
> some degree, by the industry, which is a good mirror of the econ-
> omy. In boom times, when other industries are producing more, the
> demand for packaging rises proportionately; thus demand has been
> up since 1975. And, as [Mead president and CEO Warren] Batts ex-
> plained, the major expansions begun in the late 1960s, which put the
> company in a bind in the early 1970s, have enabled Mead to capital-
> ize on the recent high demand for most paper products.

It was a good year for Mead, and for McSwiney. After all the energies expended in the battle to fight off an unwelcome takeover, after all the years of building a great corporation, after putting in place the separation of chair and CEO, McSwiney could feel that things were going very well indeed.

Then came a surprise development.

On January 15, 1980, a news release was issued in Dayton. This is the full text of the release:

> Mead Corporation announced today that its Board of Directors has accepted with regret the resignation of Warren L. Batts as the President and Chief Executive Officer of the company. Mr. Batts had advised the Board that his resignation was submitted for personal reasons. Mr. Batts had agreed to be on call to provide future services to the company.
>
> C.W. Verity, Jr., Vice Chairman of the Executive Committee of Mead's Board, the Committee responsible for management succession, stated that Mead's Board of Directors had requested James W. McSwiney to resume the responsibilities of Chief Executive Officer which he had held for 10 years prior to April, 1978, when Mr. Batts was elected to that position. Mr. McSwiney will continue as Chairman of the Board.
>
> The Board also elected C. Greene Garner as President and Chief Operating Officer of the company. Mr. Garner, 59, has been Chief Operating Officer of Mead's Paper and Paperboard Groups since 1978. He began his career with Mead in 1949, and served in a number of executive positions before being elected a Senior Group Vice President. Mr. Garner is a native of Atlanta, Georgia, and was graduated from the University of Georgia with a degree in Business Administration.
>
> Mr. McSwiney emphasized that during Mr. Batts's years with Mead, including his tenure since 1978 as Chief Executive Officer, he made many important contributions which helped the management of the company achieve record performance. He noted particularly that Mr. Batts had played a significant role in structuring Mead's current management team, which will continue to be responsible for Mead's operations.
>
> Mr. Batts stated that his service at Mead has been personally and professionally satisfying and that he shares the Board's confidence in the company's future. He said he was particularly proud to have helped create Mead's strong management team, and of the performance the company had achieved since 1971.

And that was that. Neither Batts nor Mead officials would say anything further, on the record, about his reasons for resigning.

Batts's departure was a painful blow for McSwiney, who had been introduced to Batts by Robert Greenleaf, a man he greatly admired. Greenleaf regarded Batts as probably the most brilliant man he had ever met at the Harvard Business School. McSwiney, too, had been enormously impressed by Batts. He had chosen Batts as his successor and regarded him almost as a son.

Once again the full burden of leadership fell on McSwiney. He agreed to the board's request that he resume the CEO post only on the condition that the job be filled as promptly as possible—within two years at the outside—by a younger person.

Interviewed by a journalist, McSwiney said at the time, "I don't know what my retirement plans are, but I know I won't be here when I'm 70 [he was then 64].

"I didn't expect to be in a position of power again, and I didn't covet it, but I don't consider it an imposition. It was the board's decision.

"It's like the responsibility of life—if you have children, you have the responsibility to raise them."

The new president and COO, Greene Garner, who was 59 years old, had already made it clear that he wanted to take early retirement, so there was no question that his was an interim appointment. It would not be he who succeeded McSwiney. Of course, the succession was a matter for the Executive (Nominating) Committee.

Thomas Stanley, a board member who served on both the executive and the compensation committees during that period, in a private conversation outlined the board's thinking.

"What we tried to do," he said, "was determine the ultimate position we needed to fill. That is, of course, to find a person to succeed Mac as CEO. We needed to leave ourselves a sufficient number of options. If, for example, we wanted to bring in a person as president and chief operating officer, we could do that without causing grief to Greene, even though it accelerated his retirement slightly."

In the circumstances then prevailing there was an unspoken agreement that the separation of the powers of chair and CEO was out—at least, for the foreseeable future. McSwiney's successor would be both chair and CEO.

Even though Garner would not be his successor, McSwiney made a point of exercising as little of the CEO's authority as he could, putting as much of it as possible in the hands of Garner. That included announcing organizational changes to the managers affected by them. As McSwiney said, "The more people relate to him instead of me, the easier it will be to take the next step."

Of course, the business of the company went forward without an instant's pause or hesitation, as it would in any large organization. Events that occur on the highest executive level usually take quite a while before they are felt on the lower levels—if, indeed, they are ever perceptible there. Even at the level of top management, despite some momentary excitement, work resumed under the new conditions very quickly, as McSwiney and Garner picked up the reins that had been held by Batts. They made the decisions that had to be made and took the actions, based on prior decisions, that had to be taken. Some management moves were announced that were being planned before Batts resigned.

In terms of long-range significance, it was probably more important that the team of McSwiney and Garner made it known they intended to get "some of the younger people in key operating spots."

In January 1981, the directors elected Garner CEO—McSwiney was still chairman—and appointed Steven C. Mason, then 46 years old, senior vice president of operations.

Garner felt he didn't know enough about the high-technology side of the business, so he arranged for a number of meetings and presentations on that subject. But he thought the growth strategies were pretty well set for forest products.

Inevitably, people inside and outside the company began a guessing game about who would be chosen as the next chair and CEO. The name that cropped up most often was Burnell R. Roberts.

Roberts, then 53 years old, had been put in charge of Mead's pulp and forest products affiliates when George Sheets retired. He now became executive vice president with the added responsibility of finance. A 1967 alumnus of the Granville Experiment, Roberts had shared in the development of the Mead corporate culture as it was shaped in the late 1960s. A graduate of the University of Wisconsin, Roberts earned an M.B.A. at the Harvard Business

School and then went to work for General Tire & Rubber Company. In 1966 McSwiney recruited him for Mead with a promise that he would soon become controller of the company. Roberts's first post at Mead was executive assistant to McSwiney; as promised, he soon became controller.

Two years later McSwiney told Roberts he'd like the younger man to head the Merchant Distribution Group.

"I've never had an operating job," Roberts said. "You are taking a risk."

"I know that," said confirmed risk-taker McSwiney, "but I want you to do it."

Roberts did well in that position and in later assignments. During the difficult strike at Escanaba, Roberts was head of the white paper group. About the same time, his group started up a new paper machine—always a stressful period for a paper company. Roberts saw it through, and brought white paper earnings up to a point where they topped the earnings of any other segment in the corporation's history.

Roberts's work with McSwiney had given him an understanding of the chair that undoubtedly was helpful.

"Mac does go a lot by gut feeling," Roberts once said, "but he is also very studied in many of his statements and actions.

"Mac doesn't find it easy to criticize. He wraps it up in a story and leaves it up to you to figure it out."

When Roberts took on a new assignment, he made whatever changes he thought were necessary, and McSwiney never questioned his actions.

"When Mac found you could carry the load," Roberts said, "he let go the reins. I never had to worry about what's Mac going to think."

Roberts had also had the opportunity to comprehend McSwiney's sense of relative values.

"There was a time," Roberts recalled, "when Mac was asked to approve a commission system for sales representatives that would result in one Mead sales representative making more money than Mac himself. 'That doesn't matter to me,' Mac said. 'What I want to know is, is he worth it?' Then he approved the commission scale."

Another person who was being viewed with considerable interest was Mason, the newly promoted senior vice president, operations.

Mason was following a family tradition—his father and grandfather had both been Mead executive vice presidents. At the age of 20, straight out of the Massachusetts Institute of Technology, Mason had joined Mead, serving initially in engineering and operating jobs in Kingsport, Tennessee, and Chillicothe, Ohio. Then he had been transferred to upper New York State as general manager of a technical papers joint venture with a German company. When Mead first became interested in ink-jet technology, Mason worked at the central research laboratories in Chillicothe. In 1975 Garner brought Mason into the paperboard group as executive vice president.

"I'm very proud of Steve," Garner said. "He's come a long way. He's got a shot at going a long way in this company."

Obviously, McSwiney and Garner looked outside the company, too, for possible successors, but after considerable deliberation they concluded that the next chair and CEO was within Mead and was a person of "15 years of successful and challenging experience." Of course, they kept the Executive Committee fully informed about their thinking and the progress they were making. McSwiney was outspoken about his intention "to move out no later than 1981." That meant a decision on the succession had to be made quickly.

In fact, McSwiney and Garner, after thorough search and evaluation, had concluded without reservation that Roberts and Mason should become CEO and COO, respectively. However, it was Mac's view that, solely because of Garner's unselfish contribution after Batts's departure, Garner should serve as chair and CEO for the ensuing year only.

McSwiney presented his views at the November 1981 directors' meeting, but after considerable in-depth discussion, it became apparent that the board felt strongly that Roberts and Mason should be moved directly and as promptly as possible into the role of chair of the board/CEO and president/COO, respectively.

After a brief adjournment of the board, the meeting was resumed and in short order a motion was made, seconded, and unanimously adopted, the essence of which was that Roberts and Mason would be elected to their new posts at the annual meeting to be held April 22, 1982, and that an announcement to that effect would be released the day after the board meeting.

McSwiney later said, "With a strong board, you win some, you lose some."

"Mead Establishes Official Hierarchy," reported *The New York Times*.

In April 1982, at the Mead shareholders' annual meeting in Dayton, the new team of Roberts and Mason was officially confirmed.

The Mead annual report for 1981, the last year of McSwiney's 13-year tenure as either CEO or chair, is an interesting document in many ways. For example, the Corporate Responsibility Committee by then had achieved such recognition that its employee members were listed on the same page as the members of the Board of Directors.

Comparing the statistics of the 1968 report with those of the 1981 report shows a growth in net sales from $897,591,000 to $2,899,700,000 — a three-fold increase in 13 years.

Net earnings rose from $31,571,000 to $106,900,000.

Mead was No. 1 in school supplies. More than 150 merchant firms across the country carried the Mead franchise. Mead sold more than 800,000 tons of pulp in the United States and abroad, making it one of the largest pulp marketing organizations in the world. Mead was the leader in multiple packaging in North America, Japan, and Europe. Lexis, Mead Data Central's computerized legal research service, was being used by lawyers all across the nation—and in England and France—making it the world's most-used electronic legal research system. Nexis, a sister system for news research, was being used at a rapidly increasing rate by businesses, government agencies, and news media. And there were a number of other, relatively small segments of Mead, some of which would be sold off as Mead's new leadership adapted the company to the economic conditions of the 1980s.

Clearly, McSwiney had lived up to his ideal of "moving the company up a notch."

At his sixty-fifth birthday party, in 1980, McSwiney had said, "From the time I was 35 or 40 years old I told Jewell [his wife] I didn't expect to make it to 65. I don't know why. It wasn't a morbid thought; I just didn't think that I'd be around then. She would get aggravated with me and say, 'That doesn't make any sense.' So this morning she said to me, 'You made it.' "

He told his friends and associates at the birthday party, "One of the goals I had, when I became chief executive, was to take a good company and make it into a great company. And another goal was to leave one of the best organizations in American industry. Well, we haven't made it all the way, but I don't feel it's immodest to say we have come a long way toward both of those goals—thanks to you, because you're the ones who did it.

"Thank you."

Seventeen

The Builder
Goes On Building

On November 13, 1983, McSwiney turned 68. Under the company rules that he had helped to promulgate, he had reached the mandatory retirement age for directors, so he left the board of directors at the time of the following annual meeting, in April 1984. After so many years, he no longer had any direct involvement with Mead.

"I think Mead, to him, is really his child," said Burnell Roberts, his successor. "He just loves this company."

To be wholly separated from his beloved Mead was unthinkable, so Mead continued to provide him with an office on the twenty-fifth floor of its headquarters building.

He spent more time with Jewell, his wife of more than 40 years, at his second home on Sea Island, off the Georgia coast near Brunswick, the city where his spectacular career had really gotten under way.

He lavished attention on his two grandsons—Richard J. Hutchinson and Douglas Scott Hutchinson—by his daughter, Margaret Hutchinson, who was doing well as a senior representative in the Lexis–Nexis office in Washington, D.C., handling government accounts including the White House staff, the Internal Revenue Service, and the U.S. Department of Energy.

He took great pride in the achievements of his son, Ronald, who had risen to the role of president in the law firm of Smith & Schnacke, and Ronald's wife, Jane, who was the daughter of longtime friends of Mac and Jewell.

Recreation, as most people understand the term, had little interest for him. He played a bit of golf, but no game or sport could really offer an adequate outlet for his energy, which was, despite his years, still impressive.

That energy found expression in community service. As the *Dayton Daily News* commented, "Widely credited with transforming the Mead Corporation from a second-tier paper company into a leader in the forest products industry that has moved into information systems, McSwiney also is responsible for significant changes in the Dayton community.

"He shuns the notion that he wields great personal influence, yet he has been a prime mover behind projects and issues ranging from health care to higher education."

From his window he could look to the southwest section of the downtown area and see Sinclair Community College, of which he became chair of the board of trustees in 1974. Sinclair went from 200 students to some 18,000 in 10 years.

When a list of the five best candidates in the United States for the presidency of Sinclair was drawn—so good that some board members said none of the five would be interested in heading the college—McSwiney decided that one of the five, David Ponitz, then president of Washtenaw Community College in Ann Arbor, Michigan, was the best of the lot. Along with Harold Boda and Dean Graney, of the University of Dayton, McSwiney successfully recruited him. Afterward, McSwiney was wont to say that the recruitment of Ponitz was one of his best days of work.

McSwiney also helped in persuading the board to engage the architect chosen by him and Vincent P. Blair to prepare a master plan and serve as principal architect for its first phase. When Blair, a close friend, retired as chair of Sinclair's board for health reasons, McSwiney succeeded him and served as chair until early 1985. Mac was also proud of having taken the lead in naming Sinclair's theater in honor of Blair.

McSwiney regarded Sinclair as one of his major achievements, and many people in Dayton agreed with him. Of Sinclair, McSwiney said,

"There are so many people that are so much better off because of that facility."

McSwiney had always been involved in issues involving the well-being of the community—and for him the word "community" embraced just about everything. For example, as a leader in the national business community, he had been a member of the Committee for Economic Development since 1975. His contributions to the paper industry were innumerable. One of the most significant, perhaps, was the Institute of Paper Chemistry; for 13 years McSwiney was a trustee—and, for two years, chair—of the IPC, a graduate school granting masters' degrees and doctorates, that had a curriculum developed around the needs of the forest products industry. His interest in education of one kind or another was never-ending.

In his later years, Mac maintained a continuing interest in efforts to revitalize downtown Dayton. That campaign would have had much gloomier prospects if it had not been for McSwiney's decision, in 1973, to build Mead's new world headquarters in the heart of the downtown area. The 27-story Mead Building became the anchor of Courthouse Square, and a symbol of hope for those engaged in the city's economic development program.

Years after his retirement, he was still deeply involved in plans for a high-technology research and development facility east of the city— the Miami Valley Research Park and Miami Valley Research Institute.

It was Albert Sealy, a partner in the law firm of Smith & Schnacke, who first raised the matter with McSwiney. Chair of the board of trustees of Wright State University, Sealy talked about the possibility of that institution, the University of Dayton, and Sinclair Community College joining together to help develop and guide a high-technology research facility. At the time, there was concern in Dayton about jobs because General Motors had disposed of Frigidaire, one of the nation's largest home appliance companies and a major employer. GM later converted the Frigidaire plant to the production of diesel engines and pickup trucks, but there was still a net loss of hundreds of jobs.

McSwiney asked the board chairs and the presidents of the three educational institutions to get together in the Mead dining room on a monthly basis to try to determine whether such a research park was feasible. McSwiney was elected chairman of the group, and Sealy, secretary.

The first step was to obtain the cooperation of the faculties of the three institutions. The chair—John Torley, of the University of Dayton; Sealy, of Wright State; and McSwiney, of Sinclair—asked the presidents of the institutions to put together a paper outlining their strengths and the areas in which they could be of greatest support—with least conflict—to potential occupants of a research park. (The cooperation of the University of Dayton was especially notable, for it had its own research institute, which had been in the business of contracting for such work for a number of years, and its revenues from contract research ran into the millions.)

The group also realized the need and the value of having the Air Force Institute of Technology, located at Wright Patterson Air Force Base, involved. At the request of the Dayton group, the Air Force authorized the commandant and a designated representative to attend meetings, advise the group, and consult, but not to be involved in any financial or administrative way. The Air Force representatives proved most valuable in the work of the group.

The next step was to visit and size up other such endeavors, notably Triangle Park in North Carolina. General Gerald Cooke, a retired commandant of the Air Force Institute of Technology; Robert J. Kegerreis, president of Wright State University; and David H. Ponitz, president of Sinclair, undertook that task, and enabled the group to pinpoint important priorities in planning a research park. The funds to underwrite this came from a small nest egg that Kegerreis and McSwiney had husbanded for several years from another civic project.

McSwiney took the position early on that "we must own and control a mass of land over which we had full control, if we were eventually to succeed." It was also agreed that a master plan had to be drawn up, specifying who might occupy space in the park, the quality and architecture of the buildings that would be erected, the density and the amount of open space, and the infrastructure.

The group was successful in getting the internationally known architectural firm of Edward Durrell Stone and the local architectural firm of Lorenz and Williams to join together to develop the master plan.

For advice about where to locate the park the group turned to a number of persons, including Nora Lake, of the Miami Regional Planning Commission; Donald Huber, a developer; and George Shaw, the head of a local civil engineering firm. The group homed in on an area about 15 miles east of Dayton, about half way between the Wright Patterson Air Force Base and downtown Dayton.

One day McSwiney was playing in a celebrity golfing event called "Bogey Busters." In his foursome were a neighbor, Cy Laughter, who had developed the tournament, and the then governor of Ohio, James Rhodes. The thought occurred to McSwiney "how provident it would be if we could obtain some 675 acres" of a former state farm that had long lain unused. The acreage in question was located on the western edge of the area that the group had been considering. When McSwiney and Laughter broached the matter to the governor, Rhodes pledged his full support. Local legislators also heartily endorsed the idea, and in due course the land was transferred to the Miami Valley Research Foundation.

At about the same time, Central State University expressed an interest in the project and accepted an invitation to become a member of the research park group.

A short time later, Governor Rhodes suggested that state funds would be needed to help get the research park started. With the support of legislators and office-holders of both parties, the state appropriated $10 million for the park. A large part of the funds was used to acquire adjacent property, bringing the total amount of land to more than 1200 acres. Approximately $2.5 million of the funds were used to join Wright State in providing a facility for its National Center for Rehabilitation Engineering.

Later Rhodes's successor as governor, Richard Celeste, endorsed the allocation through Sinclair Community College of $10 million earmarked for the research park. He was also instrumental in providing matching funds for a federal grant for the initial and substantial infrastructure.

As it turned out, the first occupant of the park was a wholly owned subsidiary of Eastman Kodak. The subsidiary, Diconix, Inc., was furthering the research and development of the ink-jet technology that Eastman Kodak had bought from Mead.

"On the basis of a density factor of .25 and an assumption of 300 square feet per employee," McSwiney said, "the park over a long period of time could support some 30,000 to 45,000 employees. That may sound like a fairy tale—but who knows?"

McSwiney regarded the research park as one of the finest examples of partnership involving the private sector, government, and educational institutions.

Sinclair Community College, the downtown revitalization, the R&D park—all spoke to his lifelong interest in learning and in building. It was clear that to the end of his days McSwiney would be learning, trying to satisfy his appetite for knowledge and understanding.

Epilogue

Over the years, even after his retirement from active participation in the management and direction of the Mead Corporation, McSwiney kept trying to distill what he had come to understand over the years into concise statements that might be helpful to other, younger men and women.

In one such paper he wrote that to make the "obvious" happen "requires individualism and persistence."

"Conformism won't do it," he insisted; "confrontation won't do it; but being willing to be one's self because of internal confidence will."

Nobody would ever have accused McSwiney of lacking "internal confidence." The wonder was how this man of humble origins, essentially self-educated, had managed to acquire such self-confidence, drive, knowledge, and determination.

Leaders magazine, in 1984, published an article by McSwiney entitled "Leaders as Learners." In it he expressed the opinion that the "business of leadership is especially complex in the United States" because of our individualistic and independent heritage. "These very characteristics, though a rich asset," he wrote, "have a tendency to conflict with the styles and goals of most organizations. Historically such individualism has found its most productive expression in the lives of great innovators such as those in politics, government, and the arts, as well as in science."

But business must learn to cultivate and nurture such people, he said.

"Few things are without peaks and valleys, or joy and disappointment," he wrote in 1987. "In 1982, the year after my retirement, Mead lost $86 million. But it earned $43 million in 1983, and returned to a more normal and expected earnings level in 1984. The period of loss was affected by interest rates, a recession, and an accompanying deflationary program, as well as the timing of investments based on an earlier optimistic cash flow. But a person of my nature finds it hard to avoid the feeling that somehow, to some degree, I may have been responsible. Fortunately, today, that is not a matter to dwell upon. As I've often said, everything will in time be judged in retrospect."

The company that McSwiney had built into a vast corporation was continuing to thrive under the new leadership of Burnell R. Roberts, chair and CEO, and Steven C. Mason, president and COO. They supervised the divestiture of assets in a number of businesses, representing about 20 percent of 1982 sales, in order to focus on its core business, forest products, and its high-technology success, the electronic storage and retrieval business.

Under Mead's new leadership, the company still did the unexpected when circumstances warranted. For example, in its "1985 Financial Fact Book" the company went in for a candor—even a wry humor—that is not usually encountered in official company publications.

"Many people have made a lot of money in the white paper business over the years," the booklet said. "Unfortunately, Mead has not been one of them."

Then the booklet went on to say, "That situation is no longer true. In 1983, Mead's white paper group set an earnings record of $110 million, a big improvement over our $8 million earnings in 1982, and an even more significant improvement over our prior earnings record of $80 million set in 1979. 1984 earnings from this group shot to $185 million."

For James Wilmer McSwiney, product of McEwen, Tennessee, risk-taker who had usually figured the odds correctly, builder whose structures endured, there was considerable satisfaction in the continuing greatness of his beloved Mead Corporation.

"I tried to do what I believe in," he said. "I tried to move the company up a notch. I believe I did, and there is every evidence that Burnell Roberts is on track to move it up another notch."

Appendix A
Growth/Share Matrix

Real Market Growth	High / 10% / Low	Savings Accounts	Sweepstakes
		Bonds	Mortgages

2×   1×   .5×
Relative Market Share

This relatively simple chart was used as the basis for categorizing businesses and defining appropriate capital funding levels for each of those businesses.

Although conceptually straightforward, the foundation of the growth/share matrix was rich with strategic insight. This foundation consisted of four strategic tenets:

1. *Experience curve.* In any business, a strong correlation exists between accumulated experience and the cost of production. As a business increases experience, costs decline. Therefore, the leader in a particular market will have the most experience, and, if managed correctly, this business should enjoy a cost advantage over its competitors.

2. *Relative market share as a surrogate for experience.* Of course, it would be difficult to measure the accumulated experience of all

the businesses in an industry. Instead, a business's relative market share (i.e., its absolute share versus the absolute share of its largest competitor) should serve as a good measure of relative cost position. If the experience curve is valid and the business is well managed, the dominant player in the market will have the lowest cost position in that market.

3. *In low-growth markets, it's difficult (but not impossible) to change strategic relative share positions.* An obvious outgrowth of experience curve theory is the strategic desire to assume the dominant position in a market. By definition, it should generate the highest profit level in that market. However, if the market is slow growth, it is difficult to wrest a dominant position away from an entrenched leader. It's not impossible, but the costs of the battle and the risk of failure would certainly be increased by the low-growth characteristic of the market.

4. *In a high-growth situation, a dominant position should be defended at all costs and a strategic decision to develop a dominant position should be made early in the life cycle of a business.* Empirical evidence would suggest that in any corporation, businesses that truly dominate a market are treasures; they are rare and valuable. Therefore, the resources of a corporation should be made available to the few high-growth opportunities where a final dominant position is likely. On the other hand, the decision deserves the broadest commitment of management, since the cost of developing that dominant position will surely be high.

With this conceptual approach, it was possible for a corporation to strategically manage a diversified portfolio of businesses. The first step was to segment the corporation's business activity into the appropriate product/market segments. These segments might be operating divisions, but could be product/market entities within a division. Then, for each entity, the analysis would need to be done to position it on the growth/share matrix. This analysis was crucial to the eventual success of the portfolio approach.

Once the positioning was complete, the basic strategic messages were as follows:

1. *Sweepstakes (cash user).* Businesses in that quadrant had potential, but a major strategic decision was necessary: either "get out" or invest to increase share rapidly and develop the lost cost position.

2. *Savings accounts (cash user or cash self-sufficient).* A dominant position was already in place. The strategy key was to make capital available to this unit in order to maintain dominance throughout the high-growth period and to defend the unit from competitive erosion; i.e., invest heavily to maintain competitive advantage.

3. *Bonds (cash generator).* The dominant position needs to be defended. However, at least in theory, the high average earnings of such a business should more than offset the investment requirement.

4. *Mortgages (manage for cash and avoid the strategic mistake of a cash trap).* Two possible management techniques exist: immediate liquidation or slow/measured liquidation. Occasionally a "technology" or "marketing" play could be defined which could reverse the fortunes of a mortgage business. Often, major strategic studies were undertaken to define the potential for such strategies.

Of course, this growth/share concept needs to be tempered with the introduction of other factors that define the success of a business. However, it served as a logical basis for a strategic planning system and the allocation of capital, which was the resource most critical to strategy implementation at the Mead Corporation.

Appendix B
Profile System

Mead's Profile System was developed as part of the strategic measurement system enabling corporate managers to view each of the businesses on a common basis. Its primary purpose was to highlight the general levels of performance and strategic direction of the company's business units in terms of returns, cash generation, and asset growth. The system provided the major subcomponents of these measures to indicate the factors contributing to specific performance.

The Profile System was used extensively during goal setting and the development of business plans. Divisions would make an assessment of the business climate and competitive situation, review their operations, and identify problems and opportunities. From this appraisal, a business plan would be prepared detailing the strategies to be pursued, specific action plans, and the financial impact of these actions on the unit. This became the basis by which strategic performance was monitored.

The Profile System encompassed two principal documents that served as the vehicles for reporting projected division performance. Each contained 11 years of data: 5 years of history, the current year, and 5 years of projected information. Data for the 5 future years would reflect the most probable financial results of the business plan.

IFPS PROFILE SYSTEM

BACKGROUND DATA

DATE 09/01/82 TIME 10:33

DATA FILE: ZSXX CODE: XX PLAN ID: P01 UNIT NAME: NEW PRODUCTS DIV X
PLAN TITLE: 1982 PLAN

	"BUSINESS UNIT" UNIT VOLUME	NET SALES	VARIABLE COST LABOR	RAW MAT	OTHER	TOTAL	MARGIN	FIXED COST S&W	DEPR	ALLOCN	OTHER	TOTAL	OTHER INCOME (EXP)	TIMBER CAPITAL GAINS	BT EARNGS (BEFORE	AT EARNGS INT)
1977	80370	34396	10635	12243	3535	26413	7983	3743	564	42	1711	6060	18	300	2241	1211
1978	83396	39900	11716	13193	5661	30570	9330	3643	590	44	2535	6812	-20	325	2815	1520
1979	84638	43380	11937	13952	7239	33128	10252	3983	628	53	2664	7328	38	350	3312	1809
1980	83686	49444	11532	16606	7278	35416	14028	4321	622	67	3504	8514	100	380	5994	3190
1981	85570	57790	13246	20229	9461	42956	14834	4638	652	79	4039	9408	58	410	5894	3152
1982	87704	68526	14636	25003	11305	50944	17582	4739	672	85	3860	9356	92	445	8763	4639
5 YR	224994	259040	63067	88983	40964	193014	66026	21324	3164	328	16602	41418	260	1910	26778	14310
1983	49210	65258	14797	24417	10634	49848	15410	4854	542	94	4206	9696	60	481	6255	3481
1984	48360	73188	16226	27634	12358	56218	16970	5347	603	103	4453	10506	40	519	7023	4022
1985	49812	81474	19018	30696	12874	62588	18886	5638	903	114	4991	11646	40	561	7841	4527
1986	50682	91410	20424	35889	13953	70266	21152	5934	935	123	5640	12632	40	605	9165	5565
1987	51140	97706	22065	37343	15486	74894	22892	6347	1340	135	6204	14026	40	654	9560	5385
5 YR	249204	409124	92530	155979	65305	313814	95310	28120	4323	569	25494	58506	220	2819	39843	22979

	CASH GENERATED AT EARNGS	DEPR	DEPL	DEFER TAX	TR.OUT & RETR	TOTAL	CASH USED WC CHANGE	CAP EXPEND	TIMBER EXPEND	TRANS IN	OTHER A.CHG	TOTAL	CASH FROM OPER.	SUPPRT CAP. COST	CHG IN RETAIN EARNGS	NEW BORROW	CASH FOR RE DEPLOY
1977	1211	564	94	70	0	1939	422	472	0	0	20	914	1025	905	306	165	285
1978	1520	590	100	82	709	3001	622	504	0	75	40	1241	1760	910	610	329	1179
1979	1809	628	104	85	0	2626	691	328	0	0	0	1019	1607	943	866	468	1132
1980	3190	622	110	69	0	3991	760	1663	1030	0	36	3489	502	1181	2009	1085	406
1981	3152	652	120	64	0	3988	801	676	0	960	-26	2411	1577	1717	1435	775	635
1982	4639	672	122	133	0	5566	905	1047	130	536	66	2684	2882	1942	2697	1456	2396
5 YR	14310	3164	556	433	709	19172	3779	4218	1160	1571	116	10844	8328	6693	7617	4113	5748
1983	3481	542	128	159	0	4310	-739	2020	0	0	14	1295	3015	1989	1492	805	1831
1984	4022	603	132	474	394	5625	1278	3555	0	0	82	4915	710	2371	1651	892	-769
1985	4527	903	142	709	0	6281	1330	4260	0	0	0	5590	691	2805	1722	930	-1184
1986	5565	935	154	1233	0	7887	1626	7845	1500	0	72	11043	-3156	3801	1764	953	-6004
1987	5385	1340	160	1484	0	8369	971	3970	0	0	84	5025	3344	4116	1269	685	-87
5 YR	22979	4323	716	4059	394	32471	4466	21650	1500	0	252	27868	4603	15082	7897	4265	-6214

DATA FILE: ZXXX   CODE: EX   PLAN ID: P01   UNIT NAME: NEW PRODUCTS DIV X
PLAN TITLE: 1982 PLAN

1. *The Background Data Report was used to reflect selected marketing and financial aspects of the Plan* It was essentially an income statement indicating volume, sales, costs, and earnings combined with a cash flow analysis.

2. *The Profile Summary, with the same time parameters, was a numerical evaluation tool.* It was recognized that a good measurement system should reveal changes, trends, and relationships that are relevant to unit performance. A number of important ratios were developed to allow trend analysis and unit-to-unit comparisons.

Under the special section labeled Measurement Per $ Sales, various balance sheet and cost items (PP&E, margin, labor) were expressed in dollar terms as a ratio to net sales. This facilitated the identification of specific productivity and investment intensity trends. In addition, the summary not only showed the distribution of assets, fixed and current, but other key evaluators captured the unit's growth rate, returns, and cash contributions. The significance of the data on the background report was therefore greatly enhanced.

With these and other portions of the Profile System, there were a number of applications at both the Corporate and Division level:

1. *Corporate.* Profile data flowed from the general strategy and action programs embodied in the Business Plan so its consistency with the Plan could be verified: "the words should match the music." Using the sample profile shown here, this business would be characterized by higher growth, lower returns, and using cash over the next five years. Moreover, one would expect the plan to address an unfavorable price environment, eroding margins, and describe programs that result in improvement on certain cost components. Mead also used the Profiles in evaluating Capital Project Requests (CPR). By examining the per dollar sales ratios, it was possible to determine the validity of the assumptions and financial results projected in the proposed project. Again using the sample profile, if the justification for a CPR was based on increasing margins as a result of either price

increases and/or decreasing raw material costs, this change would need to be discussed in greater detail.

2. *Division.* By performing "what-if" and "goal-seeking" analysis, the units could play out the various alternative strategies considered in their long-range planning. Questions could be answered such as: If sales or costs were too optimistic, what would be the impact on earnings and returns? In order to achieve a certain return or cash goal, how fast could we grow and what level of earnings would be required? (Software programs were developed so that the "what-ifs" were not in themselves laborious tasks.)

The Profile System reflected the objectives and strategy of a business unit, its strategic direction. It provided a means of projecting the impact of a division's level of activity and long-term commitments on profit, cash flow, and returns in a format useful for evaluation. Ratios of key financial measures helped management assess unit performance and specific project investment opportunities.

Index